ALLAMAH SAYYID MUHAMMAD HUSAYN TABATABA'I

Spirituality of the Shi'ism and Other Discourses

First published by al-Burāq 2020

Copyright © 2020 by Allamah Sayyid Muhammad Husayn Tabataba'i

All rights reserved. No part of this publication may be reproduced, stored or transmitted in any form or by any means, electronic, mechanical, photocopying, recording, scanning, or otherwise without written permission from the publisher. It is illegal to copy this book, post it to a website, or distribute it by any other means without permission.

First edition

Translation by Abuzar Ahmadi

Contents

Foreword	1
Introduction	4
Discourse One: The Spirituality of the Shi'ism	27
Discourse Two: Trusteeship and Leadership	79
Discourse Three: The Motive behind Creation	107
Discourse Four: The Role of the Supernatural in Society	115
Discourse Five: Is Islam Still Practicable Today?	133
Discourse Six: The Social Status of Women	141
Discourse Seven: Why Did the Prophet Marry So Much?	163
Discourse Eight: Short Term Marriage	171
Discourse Nine: The General Framework of Ownership	190
Discourse Ten: Alcoholic Beverages, Cause of Humanity's...	199
Discourse Eleven: Why Must the Hand of a Thief be Severed?!	206
Discourse Twelve: Muhammad (S) in the Mirror of Islam	213
Discourse Thirteen: About the Knowledge of Imams	249
Discourse Fourteen: The Purpose of Covenants	265
Discourse Fifteen: Ijtihad and Taqlid According to the...	269
Discourse Sixteen: A Short Study of Christ and the Gospel	278
Discourse Seventeen: Adherence to Superstitions	284
Discourse Eighteen: Are Dreams True?	291
Discourse Nineteen: Miracles	296
Discourse Twenty: The Account of Shaqq Al-Qamar and the...	303
Discourse Twenty-One: Clarity, Ambiguity, and Interpretation...	307

Epilogue: A Message to the Conference Held in
Honor of... 323

Foreword

In the Name of Allah, the All-beneficent, the All-merciful

The invaluable legacy of the Household [Ahl al-Bayt] of the Prophet (may peace be upon them all), as preserved by their followers, is a comprehensive school of thought that embraces all branches of Islamic knowledge. This school has produced many brilliant scholars who have drawn inspiration from this rich and pure resource.

It has given many scholars to the Muslim ummah who, following in the footsteps of Imāms of the Prophet's Household ('a), have done their best to clear up the doubts raised by various creeds and currents within and without Muslim society and to answer their questions. Throughout the past centuries, they have given well-reasoned answers and clarifications concerning these questions and doubts.

To meet the responsibilities assigned to it, the Ahl al-Bayt World Assembly (ABWA) has embarked on a defense of the sanctity of the Islamic message and its verities, often obscured by the partisans of various sects and creeds as well as by currents hostile to Islam.

The Assembly follows in the footsteps of the Ahl al-Bayt ('a) and the disciples of their school of thought in its readiness to confront these challenges and tries to be on the frontline in consonance with the demands of every age.

The arguments contained in the works of the scholars belonging to the School of the Ahl al-Bayt ('a) are of unique significance. That is because they are based on genuine scholarship and appeal to reason, and avoid prejudice and bias. These arguments address scholars and thinkers in a manner that appeals to healthy minds and wholesome human nature.

To assist the seekers of truth, the Ahl al-Bayt World Assembly has endeavored to present a new phase of these arguments contained in the studies and translations of the works of contemporary Shī'ah writers and those who have embraced this sublime school of thought through divine blessing.

The Assembly is also engaged in edition and publication of the valuable works of leading Shī'ah scholars of earlier ages to assist the seekers of the truth in discovering the truths which the School of the Prophet's Household ('a) has offered to the entire world.

The Ahl al-Bayt World Assembly looks forward to benefit from the opinions of the readers and their suggestions and constructive criticism in this area.

We also invite scholars, translators and other institutions to assist us in propagating the genuine Islamic teachings as preached by the Prophet Muhammad (S).

We beseech God, the Most High, to accept our humble efforts and to enable us to enhance them under the auspices of Imām al-Mahdī, His vicegerent on the earth (may Allah expedite his advent).

We express our gratitude to 'Allāmah Sayyid Muhammad Husayn Tabātabā'ī (may Allah's mercy be upon him), the author of the present book, and Mr. Abū Dharr Ahmadī, its translator. We also thank our colleagues who have participated in producing this work, especially the staff of the Translation Office.

Cultural Affairs Department
The Ahl al-Bayt ('a) World Assembly

Introduction

In the Name of Allah, the All-compassionate, the All-merciful Read in the name of thy Lord who created; created humankind of congealed blood. Read and thy Lord is the Most Magnanimous, who taught with the pen; taught humans that which they knew not.[1]

...and We Gave Him Wisdom [Hikmah] and Resolving Speech [Fasl Al-Khitab]

I start with the gift of salutations and peace [salām] from Hasan Hasan-zādeh Āmolī, a humble gleaner of the brilliance of the great.

I was asked to write up a biography of the glory-suffused life of the great exegete, divine philosopher, godly mystic, holy jurist, pride of

---

[1] Sūrat al-'Alaq 96:1-5.

Islam, exemplary lecturer, Āyatullāh al-'Uzmā[2] 'Allāmah[3] Hāj[4] Mīrzā[5] Sayyid[6] Muhammad Husayn Tabātabā'ī.

Deserving accomplishment of such a serious matter is beyond the ability of my humble person, who neither knows eloquent Farsi nor coherent Arabic. What can a lowly person with a broken pen write of the eloquence of the Glorious?!

This being said, I did not deem it humane to decline, and thus with my poor resources I shall offer a slight notion of what is recorded in the oeuvre of my memories of the many years I spent in the heavenly presence of this holy saint and under the tuition of this godly instructor. Thus, without formal and intricate penmanship I shall leave the stylus to its simple comportment and proceed as the pen wills.

I need a mouth as great as the firmament, to illustrate the details of this enviable king.

And, if I find such a mouth or even comportment greater, it would fall short in illustrating this virtuous one.

O chronicle! If I say not this much,

the glass of my heart will break of fragility.

When speaking of great personages such as this, who exceed time and space and are eternal prodigies, we can delineate several features. The briefest of these is outlining the time, place, and method of their livelihood, whereas talking of such mundane matters is far from the dignity of these empyrean souls.

---

[2] A title reserved for exceptional religious savants. [trans.]

[3] A designation accorded to a person with great and extensive knowledge. [trans.]

[4] A title used for those who have made the pilgrimage to Mecca. [trans.]

[5] An appellation used for a person whose mother is a direct patrilineal descendant of Alī ibn Abī Tālib ('a).

[6] A denomination used for direct paternal descendants of Alī ibn Abī Tālib ('a).

Thus, in this area we shall suffice with this elocution by sweet-tongued Hāfiz:

To ignorant people the cosmos gives reign to desire.
You are a person of learning and grace; this is your only vice.

When I was afflicted with insufferable travails on occasion of my education, an erudite friend, with whom I had the previous privilege of being roommates, visited me—God bless him—or rather heartened and healed me, and he gave me good tidings that, "O friend! May you savor these tribulations for, to the affidavit of biographies, receptive souls have become illustrious personages and paragons of the age by tolerance of suchlike hours of woe." Indeed neither is the soma of a flower completed in the bud, nor does the visage of a meddler manifest in a shrub. Of the travails of fate comes cultivation of souls, as of the blows of the hammer, sharpness of blade.

The works of every person are manifestations of his wealth

The best depicters of this master are his mysticism, his scientific works, and his lectures. The notables of the theological schools of Qum who lecture in Shī'ah Islamic principles were his students. The glorious "Tafsīr al-Mīzān", pride of the world of knowledge, is one of his fine works and the masterpiece among his entire oeuvre.

In describing the Qur'an, the great Imām, Amīr al-Mu'minīn 'Alī ('a)[7] declared:

---

[7] The abbreviation, "'a" stands for the Arabic invocative phrase, 'alayhi's-salām, 'alayhim'us-salām, or 'alayhā's-salām [may peace be upon him/them/her], which is mentioned after the names of the prophets, angels, Imāms from the Prophet's progeny, and saints ('a). [Trans.]

> *"Parts of the Book of Allah explain other parts and some parts substantiate other parts."* [8]

Also, the Glorious Qur'an describes itself thus:

> *"And We have sent down upon you the Book explaining all things..."* [9]

> *"Allah has revealed the finest account, a book whose verses are similar to each other and repeated..."* [10]

> *"And certainly we have given you the seven oft-repeated verses[11] and the grand Qur'an."* [12]

The meaning of mathānī (which is used in two of the preceding verses) is that which Amīr al-Mu'minīn ('a) referred to when he stated, "Parts of the Book of Allah explain other parts and some parts substantiate other parts."

Mathānī is plural of mathniyyah, which is the participial adjective object form of thiny which means doubling over; like a river that turns and folds back on itself. Such places are called mathānī and due to such folding the part of the river before the turn and the part after the turn become parallel and 'witness' each other.

Qur'anic verses are also such; they bear witness to each other, i.e.

---

[8] Nahj al-Balāghah, sermon [khutbah] 131.

[9] Sūrat al-Nahl 16:89.

[10] Sūrat al-Zumar 39:23.

[11] According to exegeses this refers to Sūrat al-Fātihah which is recited in prayer at least seventeen times a day. [trans.]

[12] Sūrat al-Hijr 15:87

they explain and elucidate one another. In the "Muntahā al-Arb" dictionary it defines thiny as the bend in a river, valley, or mountain pass.

This is a summary of the fine research of this master in "Tafsīr al-Mīzān" regarding mathānī. Accordingly, he has interpreted the Glorious Qur'an using the Glorious Qur'an itself. At the beginning of his exegesis he indicated this important point; summing-up he stated: it could not be possible that the Qur'an be the light and illuminator of all things but not illuminator of itself.

This exegesis is a utopian city of wisdom in which the best and greatest human and religious discourses, in the areas of intellect, tradition, mysticism, philosophy, divine wisdom, morality, society, economy, etc., are discussed.

Think not that this utterance of mine is in conflict with what this master stated in his prologue:

"Verily I refrained from basing the rationales of this book upon philosophical and scientific theories or mystical revelation."

We both spoke true, just as the luminary himself declared at the close of his prologue. Ponder upon it:

"I shall, however, make use of various philosophical, scientific, historical, social, ethical… discussions."

From the blessed tongue of the master himself

On a Tuesday morning, Sha'bān 25, 1387 AH (November 28, 1967), I came into the presence of Master 'Allāmah Tabātabā'ī. Discussion led to the days of the 'Allāmah's education and scientific research. He said, "I was looking forward to spring and summer because in these two seasons the nights are short and I would study and write at night and sleep in the day time."

Then, about his exegesis he stated, "First, I performed much research and enquiry regarding the hadīths in "Bihār al-Anwār", so I could have a publication regarding hadīth. Later, I endeavored much to synthesize Qur'anic verses with hadīth until I concluded that I should write an exegesis.

However, I thought because the Qur'an is an unending sea, if I attempted to address the entirety I might not be successful. Therefore, I picked out all the divine names and attributes and Qur'anic verses regarding eschatology and similar issues and wrote seven independent books on seven subjects.

Later I became occupied in interpreting the Qur'an and now fourteen volumes of the exegesis have been completed and published."

This is what the master said on that day, and later, praise be to Allah, the Exalted, he was successful in completing "Tafsīr al-Mīzān" in twenty volumes in the span of twenty years. At the end of his exegesis, he recorded the completion date in the following utterance:

Completion date of "Tafsīr al-Mīzān" and recommendation to theology students [tullāb]

"The book has been completed and praise be to Allah for I was successful in finishing this composition on the blessed Night of al-Qadr, the twenty-third night of the month of Ramadān, of the year 1392 of the hijrah and continuous praise and peace be upon our liege Muhammad and his family."

Our dear theology students [tullāb] must follow this example, that 'Allāmah Tabātabā'ī took vigil on the Night of al-Qadr [laylat al-qadr][13]by researching Qur'anic verses and thus his exegesis was concluded on this felicitous night. Indeed, one must work in this

---

[13] This is the night in which the Holy Qur'an was first revealed unto the Prophet (S).

way. According to the expressive and eloquent poem of Shams al-Dīn Muhammad ibn Mahmūd Āmolī, the author of "Nafā'is al-Funūn":

It won't be rectified with caprice, nor with desire. For, on this path much dolor must be endured.

At the end of the book "Diyāt", Shaykh al-Mashāyikh, the celebrated author of "Jawāhir al-Kalām" wrote: "The book of "Jawāhir al-Kalām", a commentary of "Sharāyi' al-Islām fī Masā'il al-Halāl wa al-Harām" (The Laws of Islam Regarding Lawful and Unlawful Issues) was finished in the 23rd night of the month of blessed Ramadān, the Night of al-Qadr which was ordained by the Almighty Allah. In this night I was blessed with finishing this book, 1254 years after the hijrah of the Prophet."

In "Mafātīh" of Muhaddith Qummī, regarding nightly vigil on the 21st and 23rd of the blessed month of Ramadān which are considered to be the most probable nights of al-Qadr, Sadūq ibn Bābawayh (may God be pleased with him) was quoted as saying:

"Our master Sadūq said in the book Amālī that if there are two groups in a single gathering of vigil in the two nights of Al-Qadr, one of which are having scientific discussions, the other praying. Attending the former has preference."

In other words, the best of deeds when taking vigil during these Al-Qadr nights is acquiring knowledge.

Introduction

A great master of 'Allāmah Tabātabā'ī: Sayyid Husayn Bādkūbeh'ī

During a lesson, I asked the 'Allāmah regarding trusteeship [wilāyah] and Imamate and talk led to the following holy verse:

> *"And (remember) when his Lord tested Abraham with certain words and he fulfilled them. He said, 'Verily, I shall make you an imām of the people.' He replied, 'And of my offspring?' He said, 'My covenant shall not include the evildoers.'"*[14]

In the exegesis of this verse[15], he had referred to a statement from one of his masters and I asked him who it was. He replied, "The late Sayyid Husayn Bādkūbeh'ī."

Master Tabātabā'ī's education in mathematics

After a class session, on the 3rd of November 1977, on the way home talk of mathematics came up. He said, "In Najaf, our master, Sayyid Husayn Bādkūbeh'ī instructed us to study "Tahrīr-e Uqlīdus".

Therefore, we studied the "Tahrīr-e Uqlīdus" and mathematics for over two years under the instruction of Sayyid Abū al-Qāsim Khwānsārī." Then, he said, "The late Sayyid Abū al-Qāsim Khwānsārī was very skilled in mathematics. They would send him questions from universities. He was a most skilled person in algebra. Recently, he died in India."

---

[14] Sūrat al-Baqarah 2:124.

[15] Al-Mīzān, vol. 1, p. 277.

One day, Master 'Allāmah Tabātabā'ī said to me, "At first, when I came to Qum from Tabrīz, I taught "Sharh-e Chaghmaynī"."

"Sharh-e Chaghmaynī" (Commentaries on the Book of Chaghmaynī) is a book on astronomy authored by Mahmūd ibn Muhammad ibn 'Umar Chaghmaynī who also wrote "Qānūncheh" which is a book on medicine. The commentary on the book was written by Qādīzādeh Rūmī. The commentator was an astrologer in the Samarqand Observatory and also had a great part in compiling "zīj" (Astronomy) by Ulugh Baykī.

When I first went to Qum, students of the Qum Hujjatiyyah School told me that 'Allāmah Tabātabā'ī had installed a type of sundial for determining the direction of the Qiblah and the exact time of noon in Qum for each day. Unfortunately, however, it was not maintained properly and this great scientific work was ruined.

A Turk from Tabrīz, living in Qum, Istikhārah with the Qur'an

After his preliminary and conventional [sutūh] theological education in Tabrīz, Master 'Allāmah Tabātabā'ī relocated to Holy Najaf and studied under great masters such as Hāj Sayyid 'Alī Qādī Tabātabā'ī, Sayyid Husayn Bādkūbeh'ī, Sayyid Abū al-Hasan Isfahānī, Muhammad Husayn Kompānī, Mīrzā Husayn Nā'īnī, and Sayyid Abū al-Qāsim Khwānsārī.

Under the tutelage of these great masters he rose to exceptional heights of theoretical and practical knowledge. After ten years in Najaf, he returned to Tabrīz in 1935. There, he occupied himself with lecturing, writing, and research. In 1946 he left Tabrīz and took up residence in Qum where he instituted exegesis of the Holy Qur'an and education of theoretical sciences and divine principles. Until today, June 28, 1981, his blessed assemblies have been the seat of intellectuals and the school of theology.

Even though many of the people of the theological seminaries of Qum enjoyed his luminous presence, not many were blessed by meeting him. Some of these were allotted with learning mere terminology, some rose to lofty scientific levels, fewer still inclined toward practical mysticism, and hardly any attained the arts of both knowledge and action.

It is in fact as the divine sage Mīrzā Abū al-Hasan Jelveh (hallowed be his grave) wrote in his memoirs, "Currently, most theology students from various cities that desire knowledge have gathered around me. Each for a reason: some just to learn the terminology, others to learn to beautify gatherings, a meager few for their honesty, simplicity, and belief in the spiritual realm. These last few have been described thus:

> *"A great many of the first (peoples), and few from the last (peoples)."*[16]

Anyway, each person became my friend for their own presumption. And he did not seek out the secrets I have within me."

One day, Master 'Allāmah Tabātabā'ī remarked, "When I decided to resettle in Qum, I performed istikhārah with the Glorious Qur'an. This holy verse came up:

> *"There, support and protection belong solely to Allah, the True; He is the best to reward and the best to accord favorable outcome."*[17]

---

[16] Sūrat al-Wāqi'ah 56:13-14.

[17] Sūrat al-Kahf 18:44.

'Allāmah's Great Master: Hāj Mīrzā Sayyid 'Alī Qādī Tabātabā'ī

One of the great masters of 'Allāmah Tabātabā'ī in Najaf was the elevated mystic, lofty jurist, possessor of virtues and gnosis, the late lamented Āyatullāh al-'Uzmā Hāj Sayyid Mīrzā 'Alī Qādī Tabrīzī. This man was a timeless prodigy.

'Allāmah Shaykh Āqā Bozorg Tihrānī wrote about him thus, "He is Sayyid 'Alī, son of Mīrzā Husayn, son of Mīrzā Ahmad, son of Mīrzā Rahīm Tabātabā'ī Tabrīzī Qādī, a God-conscious scholar and self-disciplined erudite moralist. For tens of years there was friendship and association between us.

During this time I found him to be unfaltering upon his path, stalwart and humane in character, great in essence… He wrote an exegesis of the Qur'an from the beginning up to this verse:

> *"…Say, 'Allah (has sent it down).' Then leave them to amuse themselves in their wrongful devotion."*[18]

His father also wrote an exegesis of the Qur'an. From long ago, their house was a place of knowledge, virtue, and piety."[19]

One of his pleasant utterances was that if a person devotes half their life to achieving perfection the time would not be wasted. What 'Allāmah Shaykh Āqā Bozorg Tihrānī said about him, "… I found him to be unfaltering upon his path…" is a valuable attribute because the most important thing in advancement toward Allah is perseverance, the shower of divine blessings and favors are due to perseverance.

---

[18] Sūrat al-An'ām 6:91.

[19] Tabaqāt A'lām al-Shī'ah by 'Allāmah Shaykh Āqā Bozorg Tihrānī, p. 1565, fourth section of the first chapter on the notables of the fourteenth century anno hegirae.

"Verily those who say, 'Our Lord is Allah' and then are steadfast, the angels descend upon them (saying) that 'Fear not nor sorrow rather receive good tidings of the Paradise you are promised. We are your supporters and friends in the worldly life and the hereafter; therein you shall have all that your souls desire and all for which you ask as a hospitable gift from the Forgiving, the Compassionate.'"[20]

Mīrzā-ye Shīrāzī and Mīrzā Husayn Qādī—Hallowed be Their Graves

On a Thursday night, October 25, 1967, a few worthy friends and I were in the blessed presence of Master 'Allāmah Tabātabā'ī. Amid his lecture he spoke of his master, the late Qādī, and his teachers and students. He said his deceased mentor had many teachers and named a few. Then he stated, "His father, the late Hāj Mīrzā Husayn Qādī wrote an exegesis of Sūrat al-Fātihah and Sūrat al-An'ām. I read them but I do not know who currently has them in their possession...

Hāj Mīrzā Husayn Qādī was a pupil of the late Mīrzā-ye Shīrāzī and when he went to say farewell to the Mīrzā and go to Tabrīz, the late Mīrzā said to him, 'Now that you are going, put aside one hour every 24 hours to meditate.' After some time, the late Mīrzā asked about Hāj Mīrzā Husayn Qādī. He was told, 'He has increased that one hour to twenty-four in which he is constantly in meditation, self-consciousness, and seclusion.' However, seclusion of the following kind:

Have you heard of being at once among others and absent? I am among the crowd but my heart is elsewhere.

On a Thursday morning, November 23, 1967, I had the honor of

---

[20] Sūrat Fussilat 41:30-32.

visiting the late Āyatullāh Hāj Sayyid Husayn Qāḍī Ṭabāṭabā'ī, the cousin of Āyatullāh Hāj Sayyid 'Alī Qāḍī (hallowed be his grave).

I kept notes of what he said, among which was the matter of the constant meditation and self-awareness of Hāj Sayyid Husayn Qāḍī and his talk with Mīrzā-ye Shīrāzī just as I quoted from Master 'Allāmah Ṭabāṭabā'ī.

On Wednesday night, 27th of Dhū al-Hijjah 1968 CE, I had the honor of visiting with Master Āyatullāh 'Allāmah Ṭabāṭabā'ī. Amid his discussions he said, 'All that I have of such real (i.e. mystic) matters I have of the late Mr. Qāḍī—both that which I learned from him when he was alive and was in his presence and that which I received from the late Qāḍī by my own means.' Contemplate upon this."

Telling of a Dream and the Resulting Statement of the Late Āyatullāh Āmolī Regarding 'Allāmah Ṭabāṭabā'ī

The next day I left Qum for Tehran and had the honor of visiting Āyatullāh Hāj Shaykh Muhammad Taqī Āmolī (may God be pleased with him) and I related a dream I saw of him, wherein he had said to me, "Tawḥīd is to forget all but Allah". When he heard this monotheistic utterance from me in explanation he recited for me the following verse from "Golshān-e Rāz" by 'Ārif Shabestarī: They gave you instructions in a drinkery,[21] that tawḥīd is relinquishing the extras.

Then, I talked of the late Mr. Qāḍī and Master 'Allāmah Ṭabāṭabā'ī and his honorable brother, Āyatullāh Sayyid Muhammad Hasan Ilāhī. The late Mr. Āmolī said to me, "Sir! If a person must become something under perfect authority and education, I do not know

---

[21] This is a literary allusion to the place where dervishes live and worship because that is where they realize mystical ecstasy. [trans.]

anyone better for you than Mr. Tabātabā'ī, the author of "Al-Mīzān". Associate with him more for he and Sayyid Ahmad Karbalā'ī Kishmīrī were the best students among all the students of the late Mr. Qādī. Mr. Tabātabā'ī had many mystical revelations during that time."

Master 'Allāmah Tabātabā'ī's "Risālah Muhākimāt"

On Friday morning, the first of Dhū al-Qa'dah 1392 AH, I was honored by visiting Master 'Allāmah Tabātabā'ī. Talk led to his Risālah Tadhyīlāt in which he appraised the correspondences between the lofty mystic, Sayyid Ahmad Karbalā'ī and the prestigious sage, Mr. Kompānī (hallowed be their graves). These missives relate to a verse from the exalted mystic Shaykh 'Attār (hallowed be his grave):

The mystic cannot, of himself, apprehend that which is Him. How can the collective consciousness attain that which is Him?

In this treatise he imparts mystical subtleties and grand philosophical views.

'Alī wa al-Falsafah al-Ilāhiyyah, a Work by 'Allāmah Tabātabā'ī

One of the works of Master 'Allāmah Tabātabā'ī is the extremely dear compendious book, "'Alī wa al- Falsafah al-Ilāhiyyah" ('Alī and Divine Philosophy). In a paper that the Master sent to the Nahj al- Balāghah Millennium Symposium in Tehran, he expressed his wish to finish this book.

He expressed a sublime point regarding the fact that among all the

Companions [sahabah] of the Prophet of Allah (S)[22], other than Amīr al-Mu'minīn 'Alī ('a), no one has transmitted or revealed such great divine truths as exemplified in "Nahj al-Balāghah".

At the beginning of this compendious book, Master 'Allāmah Tabātabā'ī presents a solid important principle regarding religion and philosophy: in truth, it is surely a great injustice to differentiate between divine religion and divine philosophy.

This utterance issues from the heart of divine research and whoever has heard it exclaims: the speaker of this is a great gem of God. Indeed, considering divine religion and divine philosophy to be separate is surely a great injustice.

At the end of his great book, "Tahsīl al-Sa'ādah" (Acquiring the Bliss), Abū Nasr Fārābī, celebrated as the Second Teacher [mu'allim-e thānī] (after Aristotle), expresses a noble philosophical report which leads to this valuable statement, "A perfect philosopher is an imām." In Asfār, Mullā Sadrā wrote, "Death to a philosophy whose laws do not coincide with the Book and Tradition."[23]

---

[22] The abbreviation, "s", stands for the Arabic invocative phrase, sallallāhu 'alayhi wa ālihī wa sallam [may God's blessings and peace be upon him and his progeny], which is mentioned after the name of the Holy Prophet Muhammad (S). [Trans.]

[23] Asfār, vol. 4, p. 75.

Introduction

The Chain of Exponents of the Practical Mysticism of 'Allāmah Tabātabā'ī

In 1966 CE, I benefited from the presence of Āyatullāh Sayyid Muhammad Hasan Ilāhī Qādī Tabātabā'ī—the noble brother of Master 'Allāmah Tabātabā'ī (may Allah, the Exalted, greatly raise them both in rank)—who had taken residence in Qum to receive and impart blessings.

On a Thursday, March 16, 1967, we talked of the exponents of his and his brother's practical mysticism. He stated, "Our master was the late Qādī—that is, Āyatullāh Hāj Sayyid 'Alī Qādī Tabātabā'ī (may Allah be pleased with him)—in turn, his master was Hāj Sayyid Ahmad Karbalā'ī, and his master was Ākhūnd Mawlā Husayn Qulī Hamadānī, and his master was Hāj Sayyid 'Alī Shūshtarī, and his master was Mullā Qulī Jawlā.

We do not know who Mullā Qulī Jawlā's master was and we do not even know who Mullā Qulī Jawlā truly was. Even Hāj Sayyid 'Alī Shūshtarī did not know who he was.

The Meeting of Hāj Sayyid 'Alī Shūshtarī with Mullā Qulī Jawlā

Hāj Sayyid 'Alī Shūshtarī lived at the time of Shūshtar. A dispute arose regarding a mortmain [waqf] section of land. Some held that the land was not mortmain and they had secretly buried the mortmain deed [waqf-nāmah] in a chest. Others claimed that the land was mortmain though they did not have any evidence.

Anyway, for a few days Shūshtarī was baffled at judging upon the matter. The litigants were insistent and came every day and demanded a judgment from Shūshtarī. During all this, a man came and knocked on his door. Someone went to the door and asked, "Who are you?" The man replied, "Tell the man of the house that one called Mullā Qulī Jawlā wants to see you."

When he entered the house and came to Shūshtarī, he said, "Sir, I have come to tell you that you must leave here and travel to Najaf and take up residence there. Also, know that the mortmain deed of the land is buried in such-and-such place and the land is mortmain."

Though Shūshtarī did not know Mullā Qulī Jawlā, he instructed that they dig the indicated place and there they found the mortmain deed. After this he withdrew from judicature and left Shūshtar and took up residence in Najaf.

There he attended Shaykh Murtadā Ansārī's (may Allah be pleased with him) lectures on jurisprudence and in turn the Shaykh attended Shūshtarī's lectures on ethics. At that time, Ākhūnd Mullā Husayn Qulī Hamadānī embarked upon a quest for truth and went in search of a mystic guide.

He left Hamadān and stayed with a savant for some time but he did not find what he sought with him.

He departed for Najaf and came into the presence of Shūshtarī and

Ansārī. There he learned much.

After Shaykh Ansārī's death, Ākhūnd Hamadānī endeavored to write a composition of Ansārī's doctrines and jurisprudence. Shūshtarī forbid him to do so and said, "This is not your duty; there are others to do this. You must find the gifted."

Thereupon, Ākhūnd Mullā Husayn Qulī (may Allah raise his rank) strove to guide the gifted such that he instructed some from morn to dusk, some from dawn to forenoon, and some from eventide to midnight. Thus, he was successful in edifying three hundred individuals such that they each became great saints [awliyā'] of God, among them Shaykh Muhammad Bahārī, Sayyid Ahmad Karbalā'ī, Mīrzā Jawād Malikī Tabrīzī, Shaykh 'Alī Zāhid Qummī, and Sayyid 'Abd al-Ghaffār Māzandarānī.

And this is just a part of the information Master Ilāhī Tabātabā'ī conveyed on that day in Qum regarding the chain of exponents of their mysticism.

Humans Before this World, in this World, and After this World

Among the works of Master 'Allāmah Tabātabā'ī are the three valuable books: "Al-Insān Qabl al- Dunyā'" (Humans before the World), "Al-Insān fī al-Dunyā'" (Humans in the World), and "Al-Insān ba'd al-Dunyā'" (Humans after the World). As I mentioned at the beginning of this paper, the Allāmah's masterpiece is the great "Tafsīr al-Mīzān" which comprises many of the important issues of his other works; for example the treatise "Wilāyat" which is contained under the exegesis of the following verse:

"O you who believe! Be mindful of your selves (souls): A person who has gone astray cannot harm you, provided

you are rightly guided. Unto Allah is your return, every one. Then He will inform you of what you did."²⁴

Also, the treatise "Al-Insān ba'd al-Dunyā'" is contained under the exegesis of verse 2:213. These individual works are also important for the significant effort that was put in authoring them; thus, such works must also be given weight and heed.

Here it is apt for us to mention the notable French astronomer Camille Flammarion. Flammarion has valuable works on various subjects including a three volume work named, "La Mort et Son Mystere" (Death and its Secret).

The volumes are named respectively "Avant la Mort" (Before Death), "Autour de la Mort" (About Death), and "Apres la Mort" (After Death). An Egyptian scholar, Muhammad Farīd Wajadī, translated this book into Arabic and has named it "'Alā Ītlāl al-Madhhab al-Māddī" (On Refuting the Materialist Doctrine) which is also, like its original, a valuable book. It seems that the 'Allāmah has named his treatises in accordance with Flammarion's books; however, we would have to ask him to be sure.

The Aim of Divine Ambassadors is Educating and Edifying Humanity

I have found the education and edification of Master 'Allāmah Tabātabā'ī such as the Second Teacher, Abū Nasr Fārābī, wrote in "Tahsīl al-Sa'ādah"²⁵, "Educating is formation of theoretical excellence in societies whereas edifying is the method of forming moral virtues

---

²⁴ Sūrat al-Mā'idah 5:105.

²⁵ Tahsīl al-Sa'ādah, p. 29, Haydarābād Publications.

and scientific activity among the people. Education comes about through pure verbal expression. However, edification is realized through accustoming societies and individuals to act according to scientific norms such that their will drives them towards performing these actions and the scientific norms and their ensuing actions dominate their beings and people become eager to perform thus—like lovers. "

Each and every one of the publications of Master 'Allāmah Ṭabāṭabā'ī is noteworthy in these two principles and contains deep and exact critiques. That this master educated and edified gifted souls in the university of divine truths, i.e. the Qum Theological Seminary, at a time when attachment to worldly affairs and material pleasures has bewitched the majority is a blessing from Allah, the Exalted. A blessing with a notification to all that:

"That is the bounty of Allah. He gives it to whom He wills and Allah possesses great bounty."[26]

This master has a long legacy of knowledge and piety and many of his ancestors were great and notable personages in their own time (may Allah be pleased with them all).

The Most Noteworthy Oeuvre of 'Allāmah Ṭabāṭabā'ī, Both Prose and Poetry

All the works of this master are knowledge and thought, truth and understanding, discussion and research, love and reason, Qur'an and ḥadīth, and so forth.

---

[26] Sūrat al-Jumu'ah 62:4.

Whosoever joins words with words, lessens a part of their anguish.
The great exegetic masterpiece "Tafsīr al-Mīzān" in twenty volumes
Uṣūl-e Falsafah wa Rawish-e Ri'ālism (Principles of Philosophy and Realism)
Hāshiyah bar Asfār-e Ṣadr al-Muta'allihīn (Commentaries on Asfār of Ṣadr al-Muta'allihīn) Musāhibāt bā Ustād Kurbin (Interviews with Professor Corbin)
Risālah dar Hukūmat-e Islāmī (Treatise on Islamic Government) Hāshiyah Kifāyah (Commentaries on Kifāyah)
Risālah dar Quwwah wa Fi'l (Treatise on Potential and Actuality)
Risālah dar Ithbāt-e Dhāt (Treatise on Substantiation of the Essence (of God)) Risālah dar Ṣifāt (Treatise on Attributes (of God))
Risālah dar Af'āl (Treatise on Actions (of God)) Risālah dar Wasā'iṭ (Treatise on Intermediaries)
Risālah al-Insān Qabl al-Dunyā' (Treatise on Humans before the World) Risālah al-Insān fī al-Dunyā' (Treatise on Humans in the World) Risālah al-Insān ba'd al-Dunyā' (Treatise on Humans after the World) Risālah dar Nubuwwah (Treatise on Prophethood)
Risālah dar Wilāyah (Treatise on Trusteeship) Risālah dar Mushtaqqāt (Treatise on Derivatives) Risālah dar Burhān (Treatise on Logical Reason) Risālah dar Mughāliṭah (Treatise on Sophistry) Risālah dar Taḥlīl (Treatise on Analysis)
Risālah dar Tarkīb (Treatise on Synthesis) Risālah dar I'tibārāt (Treatise on Credibilities)
Risālah dar Nubuwwah wa Maqāmāt (Treatise on Prophethood and Ranks)
Manẓūmah dar Rasm-e Khaṭṭ-e Nasta'līq (Poem on Writing Nasta'līq Calligraphy) 'Alī wa al-Falsafah al-Ilāhiyyah ('Alī and Divine Philosophy)
Qur'ān dar Islām (the Qur'an in Islam) Shī'ah dar Islām (the Shī'ah in Islam)

Muhākimāt bayn-e dow Mukātibāt (Appraisal of Two Missives)
Bidāyah al-Hikmah
Nihāyah al-Hikmah.
Many scientific papers published in scientific articles

The final two books ("Bidāyah al-Hikmah" and "Nihāyah al-Hikmah") are very important philosophical texts; they are the greatest evolvement of divine philosophy available—written by the same prudent hand that wrote "Tafsīr al-Mīzān". Currently, these two books are part of the Islamic seminary curriculum.

The One from the friendship land, knows where my goods come from.

I hastily wrote these few paragraphs as well as my knowledge could avail regarding 'Allāmah Tabātabā'ī and handed them over. I confess that I did not do justice to the Master.

However, I have hopes that I may fulfill my duty of gratitude regarding His Holiness and his brother (hallowed be their graves) and present it upon the people. They were both my masters and I am much indebted to them for their education and edification.

Amīr al-Mu'minīn ('a) has declared:

"Verily, the Prophet of Allah (S) taught me one thousand doors (subjects), every door of which opens one thousand other doors."[27]

Zurārah and Abī Basīr cited regarding Imām al-Bāqir ('a) and Imām al-Sādiq ('a) that:

"They told us, 'We taught you the principles and it is for you to elaborate on them.'"[28] 'Allāmah Hasan-zādah Āmolī

---

[27] Bihār al-Anwār, vol. 7, p. 281.

[28] Majma' al-Bahrayn, māddah f r '.

Discourse One: The Spirituality of the Shi'ism

The Method of Apprehending Truth

One of the extraordinary distinctions and beauties of the divine religion of Islam is that its teachings have been propounded so as to be wholly assimilable by all human societies. Of course, to understand this concept and its invaluable results, deep contemplation is necessary.

Many who are wallowing in worldly thoughts and have withdrawn completely from spiritual life consider this, as well as other statements that evoke spiritual issues and praise spiritual life, a poetic notion lacking any real value.

They are people with limited knowledge who, upon hearing materialist scholars say, "Religion is a relic from the Age of Legends", have neglected to look closely at Islam's call and the veracious teachings of this impeccable religion.

Needless to say, one should not expect a better and more profound opinion or a more clear and logical outlook from such people and there is no need for their acceptance or endorsement because if our view is righteous and justified it does not rely on the judgment of others nor require their approval. Hence, it is better that we leave them be: "Let them die in their vainglorious agony!"

Islam makes assimilation of its teachings easier in every respect through use of: Instruction and guidance of the superior (those with expertise)

Logical exposition and reasoning Conscience and observation

Clearly, these are the only ways for a human to understand and apprehend any type of truth. By way of illustration, sick persons may obtain prescriptions from a competent and sanctioned doctor, deduce the remedy through their own medical knowledge, or realize it by observing the positive effects of a treatment in similar patients.

In the same manner, students of foreign languages may learn the meaning of words from an adept teacher, infer it through grammar and conditions of the sentence, or learn it by observing its use by native speakers of the foreign language.

Therefore, whenever we wish to fathom something as a "rational human", we must apprehend it through one or more of these methods. If possible we learn facts by personal observation. In the event that this is not viable, we deduce through our God-given reasoning.

Finally, if we cannot learn by either observation or reasoning, we must refer to someone else who has grasped the knowledge through observation or reasoning (albeit through one or more intermediaries) and follow their view. Naturally, we must first verify that person's competence through observation or deduction if we ourselves cannot fathom the issue itself by such means.

This is the collection of methods a person uses with the orientation of the system of creation. Islam accredits all three ways, and the Noble Qur'an, which is the divine book of Islam, explicitly bases the call of God on the principles governing the world.

It enjoins and leads us to a series of ideological and practical teachings necessitated by the relationship of humanity with the world and the universal order in general. The human civilization will sooner or later realize the necessity of believing in and effectuating these teachings.

> *"So set thy face toward the pure religion; it is in accordance with the nature [fitrah] of God upon which He has formed the nature of humankind. There is no alteration in the creation of God. This is the enduring (and true) religion, however most humans do not know."*[29]

Based on this, Islam enjoins us to adhere to knowledge and science and has prohibited following irrational and unscientific paths. It warns of speech and actions that are not in line with reason and necessitate following doubt, conjecture, carnal lusts, desires, feelings, and longings.

> *"And follow not that of which you have no knowledge..."*[30]

> *"...surely conjecture will not avail aught against the truth..."*[31]

> *"And do not follow desire, for it shall lead you astray from the path of Allah..."*[32]

---

[29] Sūrat al-Rūm 30:30.

[30] Sūrat al-Isrā' 17:36.

[31] Sūrat al-Yūnus 10:36.

[32] Sūrat Sād 38:26.

Method of the Guidance of the Superior [tarīq-e irshād-e mawlawī]

In the Divine Book, God, the Almighty, directly addresses His servants and speaks with us. He portrays His divinity and pure qualities. He describes the principles of the universal system, which He has created and manages, and the genesis and termination of the cosmos, which He directs. Also, He explains the decrees and instructions that must be carried out in the human world which are founded upon the universal system.

This method of expression seen in religious literature, i.e. the Holy Qur'an and narrations of the Prophet and the infallible members of his Household, is an aspect of "the guidance of a superior" [irshād-e mawlawī]. It shows that humans, who are infinitesimal before God, must submit before the divine presence of the Creator and obey His "canonical" [tashrī'ī] laws just as they by their natures obey His "genetic" [takwīnī] (i.e. natural, hence inviolable) laws.

No doubt, this method of expression is acceptable to true advocates of Islam and disciples of the school of the Qur'an, that is, those who have comprehended the righteousness of Islam and the divinity of the Qur'an through knowledge and conviction. For, on the one hand, the Divine—who has created all laws, reasons, and even the structure of causality—is not restricted by His own creation. He is above these causes, and not limited by them.

When we ask a person, "Why did you do that?" or "Why did you say that?" we are asking for the cause. What we mean is: what external cause gave you the right to do or say that?

Logically, this question or objection is only justifiable regarding a person who is bound by external causes and whose rights derive from external activities, effects, and rules. However, concerning a being that has created the concept of necessity and effect of external causes, this question or objection is completely irrelevant.

If what He commands is of the genetic order, His command is precisely the external existence of the phenomenon.[33] If it is of the canonical order, it is an external virtue or evil that has been given the form of an instruction or prohibition,[34] and this is, of course, according to reason.

On the other hand, with regard to the fact that Islam is a natural [fitrī] religion (meaning that it is in line with human nature not that it is mundane or secular) and that its intellectual and practical substance derives from the universal system of creation, Islam asks only that which conforms to the human make-up.

The existential constitution of humanity is equipped with abilities and mechanisms which yearn for the religious call and, obviously, this does not require comprehensive rationalization.

By way of illustration, a human, who is constitutionally equipped with the faculty of nutrition from head to toe, does not require reasoning to accept the statement of one who prescribes them food. In the same manner, a person who is equipped with a reproductive system and does not suffer from dispositional or mental deviations

---

[33] Contrary to our speech, the speech of Allah is not a set of compiled sounds that signify meaning on account of established conventions and the speech of Allah is in no way similar to the speech of creations. This is due to the fact that verbal expression is not possible without corporeal form and Allah is free of corporeality. Rather, the speech of Allah is the creation of an object, which demonstrates the perfection of the Creator. As Amīr al-Mu'minīn 'Alī ('a) has declared: "His speech is His deed."

[34] Instruction, prohibition, and other ordinary commands are a type of social accreditation that is normally carried out by utterance or signal. Doubtless, it absolutely necessitates the corporeality and sociality of the commander; this is impossible regarding Allah. Rather, the instruction and prohibition of Allah is creation of something that intrinsically expresses the command. For further information regarding speech [kalām] refer to "Tafsīr al-Mīzān".

will never deny the tradition of marriage and will not need an extensive rationale to accept this institution.

It is self-evident, therefore, that genetic equipment makes its needs palpable and acceptable to its host (on the condition that the host does not deviate from the genetic or natural course on account of malady).

This method, pronounced in the statements of the Qur'an—i.e. guidance of the superior—is one of the three methods that were previously indicated. This concise encroachment upon this method was beyond the objectives of this text. In fact, our chief aim is to demonstrate the authority Islam bestows upon the other two methods: "the rational method" [tarīq-e istidlāl] and "the empirical method" [tarīq-e mushāhidah wa 'ayān]. Among these, major consideration is credited to the empirical method or transcendent life of Islam, which is otherwise called "Islamic eschatology".

The Rational Method

We cannot doubt that discourse and curiosity regarding the causes of incidents and rationalization of doubtful or suspect theories is an intrinsic and natural human characteristic.

Humans understand phenomena using all available faculties. They necessarily accept and cannot disregard them. They comprehend that knowing and understanding something that has causes and means depends upon knowing those causes and means. Thus, when they intend to understand something, first they discuss and enquire into its causes.

Humans are realists due to their God-given fitrah and do not depart from the fortress of thought for as long as they are alive and healthy. Whatever they comprehend is due to thought, something for which they never asked. They eternally desire independence from thought and do not regard it to be objective. They are forever seeking external truth and independent of thought.

Consider a man who peers at himself though a mirror. Even though he knows the mirror creates disruption in his appearance—such as inversion, magnification, reduction, etc.—he is concerned with his own face not the illusory image that is portrayed in the mirror.

In any event, humans are naturally realists. Even when those who deviate from this belief through discourse or other factors and become sophists or skeptics summarize the essence of their beliefs and say "we doubt everything", "we doubt everything external to ourselves", or "there is nothing but our thoughts", it is evident that these statements are presented as scientific and definite information in a realist perspective.

In addition, in their daily lives they treat their thoughts realistically like everyone else. When they encounter an external advantage, they hurry to achieve it and when they come across disadvantage, they try to avoid it and never treat their thoughts as unreal. As a result, in practice, they confirm that they are realists.

Additionally, even when advocates of "pragmatism", who have negated the value of realism in thought and only give credence to realism in practice, define the essence of their thought: "thought only has practical value", they put forth this statement as something with real value.

It is evident that they want us to believe that in reality thoughts only have practical value and this itself is a practical truth. If their intent is only the practical value of this thought, then they are a type of skeptic. If so, like true skeptics they would also give credence to thought in words and deeds (as previously stated). Therefore, humankind cannot escape from realism.

Obviously, we must not go too far and conclude that any thought, even one deriving from human senses, completely corresponds with reality and that reality is exactly what we perceive externally without human cognitive processing.

What we mean is that the distance between self and the external world is not completely obstructed and, in short, the human mind can access external reality. (Further elucidation of this matter will come at its proper place.)

These two issues, meaning "human realism" and "human rational intellect", which derive from human nature and genesis, have drawn the attention of Islam—which is based upon the system of creation. As a result, even though Islam has conveyed its teachings though divine revelation (guidance of the superior), it has also traversed the path of free reasoning and in this way encourages and emphatically recommends following Islam.

For example, among the (over six thousand six hundred) verses of the Holy Qur'an, many verses may be found that express the theoretical and practical teachings of Islam in a ratiocinative manner. These verses present their objectives with sufficient reasons to the realist instinct and rational intellect of humanity.

None of these verses demand that their ideas be accepted without dispute and the Qur'an does not reason about them as a pastime; rather, the Qur'an requests: "Freely refer to your sound judgment. If you confirm these assertions though the reasons and evidence provided (and you will surely confirm them) accept and submit to Islam. (This is the philosophical and free rationality outlook.)"

As a further example, amid the holy Qur'anic verses, there are many that rebuke ignorance and rigidity of mind, praise knowledge and understanding, and instruct humans to think, contemplate, plan, weigh, debate, and inquire into every nook and cranny of the world of creation.

These verses are so profuse and clear that quoting them does not seem necessary. However, there are some practical precepts that rise from the superior knowledge of God, such as the following statement:

"...That is better for you, if you know."[35]

These verses combined with other verses that enjoin intellection and thought indicate that every Muslim must understand the good and evil which give rise to religious precepts, even if they cannot understand their details and characteristics.

Many hadīths regarding this issue may be found in the traditions of the Prophet (S) and statements of the noble members of his Household [ahl al-bayt] ('a).

Advantages of the rational method in Islam

The Advantages of This Approach in the Lofty Teachings of Islam are as Follows:

When placed on the path of thought and free logical reasoning, the teachings of Islam are assimilable for humans, who instinctively tend toward philosophical contemplation and rational thought.

Apart from divine revelation, the rational method is another support that keeps Islamic teachings alive for all people and all time and the objectives of this pure religion will always be more consistent and novel through the eyes of logic.

By opening this path, even after discontinuation of revelation and termination of prophethood, religious teachings will never be vague or abstract and will never be put aside as relics of a bygone age.

In order to better understand the important effects of this enlightening Islamic method, we must inquire deeper into Islamic teachings and especially inspect the two issues of "divinity" and "Islamic eschatology" in more detail.

---

[35] Sūrat al-Tawbah (or Barā'ah) 9:41.

Using both methods (revelation and reasoning), Islam asserts that the Lord of the Cosmos has absolute knowledge, power, and life. It also asserts that all phenomena, in all aspects of their being, existentially rely on His existence—like a shadow that follows an indicator—and are "absolute need" before His "absolute needlessness".

Logically, this infinite being is unique and the existence of more than one such being is inconceivable.[36] Because in their limited existence all phenomena, whether tangible or not, and also the world as a whole depend on His infinite and unlimited existence.

He exists and is evident in all aspects of every object's existence. Therefore, if some creature is cut off from Him, it will lose its existence and dissipate into nihility and nothingness like a shadow that detaches from its object.

In order to keep the uninformed from simple mindedly misunderstanding these truths and thinking of the Divinity's true sovereignty [qayyūmiyyat-e haqīqī-ye ulūhiyyah] in the world as a type of "incarnation" [hulūl], existential "mingling" [ikhtilāt], or "incorporation" [imtizāj], the Infallibles ('a) have broached this subject by negating "anthropomorphism" [tashbīh] and making use of negative theology.

They maintain that God has life but not like ours; He has knowledge but different than ours; He has power but unlike the power we have; etc.

It can be said that the reason that "Allāh-u Akbar"[37] is like a slogan in Islam is to protect this truth from misinterpretation and prevent it from being understood in terms of immanence or union [ittihād] and in this way divest divinity of its infinitude in the minds of people.

---

[36] This issue is easily understood from Qur'anic verses and the assertions of the first Imām of the Shī'ah, Amīr al- Mu'minīn 'Alī ('a). It is also discussed to some extent in "the Shī'ah" Journal and in the 6th volume of the "Tafsīr al- Mīzān" of the Qur'an.

[37] Allāh-u Akbar means 'God is the Greatest', meaning that nothing can supersede God or be better than Him.

Even if the intellectual form of divinity in our minds manifests as good and righteousness, the pure essence of God is even greater than this finite and limited concept.

In accordance with this principle, the Holy Qur'an clearly states: The Divine is Infinite and All-encompassing and shall never be limited or contained.

> **"Know that surely He encompasses all things absolutely."**[38]

In this same manner, absolute authority and sovereignty are particular to the Divine and He has no partner in the creation and management of the cosmos or in the emanation of command.

> **"This is Allah, your Lord, Creator of all things; there is no god save Him..."**[39]

Even though the general law of causality links the existence of objects to each other and makes causes necessary for effects—and Islamic teachings verify this—Islamic teachings refute the absolute independence of causes. Strictly speaking, God has created causes and effects, the relationship between them, and the superiority of cause over effect and He reigns supreme over them.

The wheels of existence are in continuous rotation. Through the relationship and union among objects, a stable system has been created. God has created this system using the correlations He has made dominant between objects and He guides all things toward the specific purpose of their creation by means of these associations.

---

[38] Sūrat Fussilat 41:54.

[39] Sūrat al-Mu'min (or Ghāfir) 40:62.

Furthermore, human social life cannot be maintained without a set of rules and regulations. However, according to Islam only the commands of God, the Honorable, the Glorious, must be obeyed. This is because absolute proprietorship is His and no one has the right to expropriate command of His creations except by His leave. Therefore, any command that He issues and issued commands that He validates must be carried out and all other commands are rejected.

Prophets: The Epitome of Divine Manifestation

As we previously stated, because the Absolute Existence completely encompasses the world of contingents, His relationship with creation cannot be explained in terms of incarnation [hulūl], unity [ittihād], or dissociation [infisāl]; rather, the most proximate and suitable term is "manifestation" [tajallī or zuhūr].

This term has also been utilized in the Qur'an and repeatedly in the speech of the Infallibles, specifically the first leader of the Shī'ahs.

Regarding God, the Infinite, who existentially encompasses the world of creation, we cannot say that He has become incarnated [hulūl] into a worldly object; that He has been limited and contained in the framework of existence; or that He has transformed his necessary essence into the essence of a contingent being [mumkin] and has become like one of His creations!

Also, we cannot say that this Unlimited and All-encompassing Essence has taken a place in a corner of the world in rank with His creations and rules the domain of creation like a king.

Instead, as an explanation of the relationship of the Divine with this world we may declare: the Boundless Existence of the Truth, who absolutely encompasses everything, is perpetually manifest in all things and places and shows Himself without soiling His divinity with corporeality [māddah], temporality [zamān], or locus [makān].

All beings, with their explicit essential differences, are like mirrors that show His pure existence to the extent of each of their capacities. It is evident that any limitation that occurs derives from the mirror [mir'āt] not the manifestation [mar'ī] and any defect that appears derives from the form [mazhar] not the image [zāhir].

Clearly, this does not entail incarnation, unity, or dissociation all of which necessitate limit and corporeality. Beings are neither one with God nor are they distinct from Him. If the theory of incarnation and unity were correct, there would be no difference between God and creation—in fact, there would be no God.

Additionally, if the theory of dissociation were correct, a limited aspect would exist between God and creation and due to this instance a limitedness in God, and as a result He would lose the divine status. (We shall return to this discussion later on).

Any person who disregards the thoughts and deeds of Muslims—especially the first Muslims—and only refers to the Book of God and the sayings of the Prophet (S) and members of his Household [ahl al-bayt] ('a) would inevitably understand that according to Islam, God does not retain incarnation or association as part of His essence or essential aspects in regard with the world of creation and humanity in particular.

The Qur'an and hadīth expressly assert: even the holy prophets ('a), the most prominent of which were Noah, Abraham, Moses, Jesus, and Muhammad (S), had no rank besides being servants of God.

Their human characteristics are similar to other humans. Ultimately, any power that arises or knowledge that manifests in the framework of prophethood is divine power and divine knowledge and any commandment that issues from this institution is a commandment from God. The only purposes of this institution are mediation and publicization of messages, and prophets have no part in formulating the laws they propound.

The only discernible difference between prophets and other humans is that they possess the eminence of perfect servitude. That is to say, regarding their spiritual lives, prophets and Imāms have attained utter perfection and all other humans fall short of this state.

Emergence of Incarnation [hulūl] in the Church

Even though Islam has greatly endeavored in the promotion of the monotheistic [tawhīd] view of God, His infiniteness, and His encompassment of existence and has accorded no existential independence or legislative or hegemonic rights to the realm of humanity, from the time the Church gained power and became known as the haven of the Christian world, it founded its teachings on incarnation (in the same sense we have used previously).

There is no doubt that this doctrine restricted the Divine, in its entirety, into the limited material existence of the honorable Jesus Christ ('a).

According to this doctrine, the Divine, whether or not it can separate from humans, has the "capacity" to take on the identity of material man and equip itself with human characteristics. In fact, many parts of the contemporary Torah confirm this belief, as is evident in the account of the creation of Adam ('a) and the narratives regarding Noah, Abraham, Lot, Jacob ('a) and others.

This view, i.e. incarnation of divinity in a corporeal human, entails negation of metaphysics. Thus, because in religion the issue of divinity is fundamental and is the fountainhead of all ideological and practical tenets, this view has toppled all other religious issues based upon spirituality and has caused all spiritual issues to be explained in terms of materiality.

This belief spread in the Christian world and became established. Of course, the previous advocates of this belief had a close precedent with idolatry. The issue of triumvirate divinity—which is a type of idolatry—was one of their most deeply rooted religious beliefs and the spiritual and lifestyle effects of this belief could not be so easily forgotten.

At that time, idolatry reigned supreme over a great number of the earth's inhabitants. Belief in Trinity [tathlīth], incarnation, and all their derivative beliefs—the best testimony of which are the histories of creeds and religions—were of the primary characteristics of this idolatry.

In fact, the belief in Trinity entered Christianity from idolatry after minor adaptations in form. Indeed, it can be stated that the only discord between idolatrous creeds and the Church is the issue of prophethood.

Certainly, we do not intend to start a religious debate with advocates of the Church. In pursuit of our aim we merely intend to evoke various historic truths regarding Islam and Christianity.

In short, the incarnation tenet of the Church, the close relationship of Christians with idolatry and triumvirate divinity, the Torah's summative verification of personification, and the contact of Christianity and idolatry at the time all gathered together and laid the foundation of a completely anti-spiritual materialist view in the structure of the Christian World.

From that time, a panorama of a dark and evil materialistic thought was imprinted upon the Christian World.

The Church did not content itself with the degree of incarnation which it allowed for Jesus Christ. It applied this same incarnation to itself, put itself in Christ's place, and introduced itself as a sovereign that must be obeyed without question.

In addition, with rites such as Holy Communion or Lord's Supper ['ishā' rabbānī] they incarnate the flesh and body of Christ (divinity) within everyone!

With the unchallengeable power the Church attained, it limited the gospels, controlled beliefs and thoughts, and banned free debate in religious teachings. The tribunal of belief scrutiny ruled the possessions and lives of people with singular tyranny and the blood of millions was spilt due to the inviolable and obligatory dictates of the church.

The Church sanctified the kings and tyrants of the day, accepted the repentance of and issued absolution for any sinner it wished, and forever deprived whoever it wanted of the benefaction of spiritual bliss and beatific heaven.

In his greatly spiritual utterances, Jesus Christ ('a) affirmed that his pure faith followed the pure faith of the great prophets ('a), that it shall always live, and that it shall never fade from the world. And the Church, which juxtaposed that spiritual Christian faith with an incarnational and material regime, drunk with pride from its increasing power, thought that it would retain this power for as long as the world existed.

However, it neglected the matter that immediately after taking on material features any method or regime, even religious ones, shall necessarily enter the worldly cycle and become limited by natural laws. Thus, like other material phenomena, it shall have a limited lifespan and go through the various stages of childhood, youth and old age, and inevitably one day die.

That which is permanent in the world and shall not pass is spirituality unadulterated by materiality and beyond the jurisdiction of nature. It has no death and shall always, to a greater or lesser extent, accompany humanity.

In any event, after a few centuries—which is nothing compared with the entirety of history—of tyrannical rule, control of thoughts, and suppression of contrary opinions and objectionable understandings, it could not in the end resist the conscientious reason of the people.

Thus, it was defeated and lost its almost boundless power.

A comprehensive record of these events can be found in the history of Christianity's penetration into the great Roman Empire and the historic timeline of the influence of the Church until its downfall.

The Church lost its horrific power and imprinted memories upon the minds of the people of the West that: religion is an ambiguous material regime that rules in the interests of the powerful and is prejudicial to the weak! Religion is a set of incomprehensible beliefs that cannot be explained with any type of logic!

Religion is a series of imitative thoughts that no one has the right to debate or inquire about! Religion is tyranny of a type that the conscience cannot accept but to which the tongue must succumb! And finally, religion is a natural tradition that has embodied a stage in humanity's history after which it will give way to a better and more complete natural tradition!

Naturally, the effect of this development was that some of the Church's adherents turned their backs upon it and others who remained faithful turned the earlier "unconditional obedience" into "empty sanctification and respect" and the Church became a formality.

The power the people attained by overthrowing the Church and the privation from the benefits of life caused by several centuries of suppression by the Church induced the people to take up a way of life exactly opposite to the path of spirituality.

Thus, for the crime of being a method of exploitation of the Church, wherever they came across spirituality they would turn aside from it and lose themselves in the maelstrom of materiality.

Additionally, the people were not acquainted with true spiritual thought due to the incarnational materialist training of the Church that had become established in the depths of the people's minds throughout the centuries.

Hence, spirituality, which the people had inherited as traditions, was gradually forgotten. In addition, the pastime of materialist scholars who coined advancement as being parallel to industrial advancement and the occupation of various governments in world conquest and domination by means of the weapon of antireligious propaganda made an effective contribution against religious beliefs and spiritual thought.

Naturally, in such an environment where popular thought defines existence as nothing but materiality and material laws, religion becomes defined as a social phenomenon that emerges in uncivilized and semi-advanced societies.

Additionally, it could be defined as an intellectual phenomenon that occupies a fragment of human history. Also, according to material evolution, everything will progress into something better and more complete. Therefore, the age of religion shall give rise to a better and more complete age.

Responsibility for this Unfortunate Situation

A person who meticulously considers these historical developments—from the advent of Christianity until present day—or contemplates and analyzes the current situation of the Western World—which is regarded as the cradle of modern civilization—and retrogressively dissects the proximate and distant causes of these historical developments, will have no doubt that the main blame for humanity's moral degradation, abandonment of human spirituality and establishment of completely material life in the place of spiritual life falls upon the Church and its teachings.

The Noble Qur'an explicitly holds religious authorities responsible for the religious disorder and the discord and chaos in human life.

> *"And those who were given the Book were not at variance save after knowledge had come to them, being envious of one another..."*[40]

Moreover, it declares that the issue of Trinity and the statement "Christ is the son of God" [al-Masīh ibn Allāh] is a fabrication of the Church, which has incorporated a type of idolatry into the heavenly teachings of Jesus Christ ('a) and has turned it into a tenet of the Christian call.

> *"And the Christians say, 'The Messiah (Christ) is the son of Allah.' That is the utterance of their mouths imitating the utterances of those who disbelieved before..."*[41]

Following this they embodied divinity into the Church and introduced the word of the clergy as unconditionally binding in order to attain their material desires.

> *"They have taken their rabbis and their monks as lords apart from Allah and Messiah son of Mary; whereas they were not commanded save to serve one God. There is no god but He; He is pure of what they associate (with Him)."*[42]

> *"Surely many of the rabbis and monks consume the wealth of the people unrighteously and debar (them) from the way of Allah..."*[43]

---

[40] Sūrat Āl 'Imrān 3:19.
[41] Sūrat al-Tawbah (or Barā'ah) 9:30.
[42] Sūrat al-Tawbah (or Barā'ah) 9:31.
[43] Sūrat al-Tawbah (or Barā'ah) 9:34.

Furthermore, God, the Exalted, commands His Holy Prophet (S) to encourage followers of other divine books to cooperate with Muslims in two aims: first, that they attribute divinity exclusively to the One God and worship no god but Him.

Second, that they ascribe mastery and lordship solely to God and refrain from choosing one from among themselves, who is generally a peer and has no preference in humanity, as an unconditional sovereign in order to reconcile their livelihoods with the system of creation—the same system that has created all humans with intelligence, freewill, and desire for beatitude and has stamped no person's forehead with the mark "unduly dear".

> *"Say, O People of the Book! Come to a word common among us and among you: That we serve none save Allah and that we associate nothing else with Him and that some of us take not others as lords besides God..."*[44]

Islam's Recommendation to its Followers

In its campaign against incarnation [hulūl] and unity [ittihād], which the Church—and before them the Jews and idolaters—had advocated, Islam has made deep and emphatic recommendations to its followers.

> *In many verses, the Qur'an urges Muslims to be firm in their monotheistic belief [tawhīd], be sincere in their servitude ['ubūdiyyah], follow the Book [kitāb] and Tradition [sunnah] unanimously and wholeheartedly, solve all intellectual disputes through the Book and Tradition, and refrain from egotistical advice, exploitation, and judgment using religious tenets. These*

---

[44] Sūrat Āl 'Imrān 3:64.

matters have been discussed in "Tafsīr al-Mīzān" under the following verses:

"And hold you fast, all together, to the cord of Allah and divide not..."[45]

"O you who believe, enter absolute peace and submission (to Allah) and follow not the footsteps of Satan; surely he is an obvious foe to you."[46]

"Eat of what Allah has provided for you and follow not the footsteps of Satan; surely he is an obvious foe to you."[47]

The Holy Qur'an advises Muslims to limit their spiritual commingling to the Islamic society, which is the society of piety and theism, and to shun spiritual commingling and superior-subordinate relationships with non-Islamic societies including polytheists, idolaters, and followers of divine books such as Christians, Jews, and Magi.

"Let not the believers take unbelievers for friends or superiors rather than believers and whosoever does that has no connection with Allah in anything, unless to dissimulate before them for fear. Allah cautions you to beware of (disobeying) Him and unto Allah is the return."[48]

---

[45] Sūrat Āl 'Imrān 3:103.

[46] Sūrat al-Baqarah 2:208.

[47] Sūrat al-An'ām 6:142.

[48] Sūrat Āl 'Imrān 3:28. There are many such verses in the Holy Qur'an that sternly enjoin Muslims from spiritual mingling with non-Islamic societies. Refer to Mu'jam al-Mufahris, māddah "a kh dh" [ ].

The Holy Qur'an has implicitly and explicitly mentioned in several places the consequences of such spiritual commingling and superior-subordinate relationships. For example, it says: until now (at the close of the Prophet's (S) life) you Muslims have been in danger due to the covetousness of non-Muslim nations.

Every moment you were in peril of downfall, but today the unbelievers have despaired from shattering your organized religious society. So fear outsiders no longer and be at peace for they shall never be able to seize this blessing from you and obliterate your religious establishment, which is the Islamic approach.

Fear the unbelievers no longer but fear God. Because if you deviate from the path that God has set for you (following the Book and Tradition) and take up other paths, God will make the same trade with you that He made with the others—He took away the gift of spiritual bliss and worldly welfare, created division among them, and denied them every kind of material and spiritual supremacy and independence.[49]

> *"Today, the disbelievers despaired of (harming) your religion; therefore, fear them not, fear me..."*[50]

Moreover, in its predictions (which must be considered divine reports), the Noble Qur'an implicitly indicates that due to relationships with non-Islamic societies, the Islamic society will successively abandon the precepts of the Qur'an using various excuses:

---

[49] This was extracted from the following Qur'anic verse (5:3) and several others. More information may be found in the "Tafsīr al-Mīzān" under this verse.

[50] Sūrat al-Ma'idah 5:3.

> *"And (on the Day of Judgment) the Prophet will declare: O my Lord! Surely my people have forsaken this Qur'an."*[51]

Also, due to spiritual commingling with the Christian World, Islamic methods and traditions shall be reversed. People will change religious laws and turn virtue into evil and evil into virtue. They shall deem religious tenets superstition and consider support of religion folly.

On that day, corruption will expand to the seas and deserts and trouble shall succeed plight. Perhaps through this the people will tire of the evil consequences of their unrestraint and ungodliness and return to the natural religion.

Despair of Muslims Before the West

Here we will discuss repercussions of incidents at the advent of Islam (after the passing of the Prophet until circa fourth century anno hegirae (AH)) and the ensuing series of ramifications that expand and deepen with the passage of time.

Discussion about whether or not the foremost agents of these occurrences intended correction or sabotage and whether they were good or evil people are not the aims of this discourse. However, these are singular circumstances and in order to fully examine them we must perforce probe into and analyze the initial roots.

Thus, we are compelled to refer to the dawn of the Islamic era in hopes of locating our objective. Of course, persons who truly intend to learn must not and cannot obscure the truths they uncover or invert in their minds that which they have understood.

In order to elucidate this matter, we must say that today, in terms of disorder in spiritual life, moral corruption, and confusion of

---

[51] Sūrat al-Furqān 25:30.

human mentalities we are similar to the West. Even though Professor Henry Corbin professes that Muslims have yet to sample the flavor of modernity (!), we still have some life left and the extirpating deluge has not wrought destruction upon our spirituality as it has done with the spirituality of the Western World.

Indeed, in loss of spiritual life and moral corruption our situation is very similar to the West. However, it cannot be denied that contrary to the West, we have not created this unfortunate situation ourselves; rather, it happened the day the Western civilization came after its Eastern customers—especially us Muslims—with its bewitching appearance full of décor and finery, first as honored guests and then as powerful hosts, and wriggled its way into our society.

With their effective and penetrating propaganda the West indoctrinated us to think in the following manner:

'We do not possess the necessary human intellect and resolve; therefore, we must throw aside that intellect and resolve, being completely useless, and only consider the path that the West determines for us. We must do what they intend. We must abandon all our characteristics and become westernized in speech and action, heart and appearance!'

As a result of this inculcation, when we reviewed our sad outmoded lives, without distinguishing between harm and benefit, between poison and panacea—because we had initially lost our intellectual independence—we blindly imitated the Western lifestyle.

Hence, every case of Western corruption augmented the existing corruption in our own society and every case of goodness and correction—because we were not ready and did not have the capacity to accept—brought about corruption in our affairs and no beneficial outcome.

As it happens, from among the unfortunate conditions that exist in our Islamic society, those that are similar to the adverse circumstances in the West have come to us though imitation of the West and the undesirable states of affairs that we have are not directly related to the fact of our being Muslims and methods of previous centuries.

Nonetheless, if our foregoing background was not corrupt and mortified, we would never accept this perversion so easily. We would defend the most excellent treasure of our being—spiritual life and ethical virtues—with felicitously and never would our cogitative mind, if we had not lost it, submit to the iniquitous logic of unquestioning emulation!

In any event, in order to understand the root of our present deplorable situation and discover its primal factors, we have no choice but to look back and study past events and examine the general practice of the Islamic society. We must return to the initial centuries of the advent of Islam until we find an acceptable reason for our current situation.

In the first steps in this reminiscence, we realize that the general situation of the Muslim World has been similar for nearly twelve entire centuries (i.e. from the year 60 AH, about 100 years before the European civilization gradually penetrated into Islamic countries).

All this time we have been dwelling in monotonous spiritual torpor and moral degradation. Even though sometimes there were fluctuations in our society because of historical turns, it has been persistently corrupt and has had little similarity to the glistering radiance of the era of the Prophet (S).

Therefore, we must draw our instruments of discourse and inquisitiveness to the advent of Islam which is the era of the rule of the Companions of the Prophet (S) [sahābah] and start our search from that period.

Of course, as we have stated, in this discussion we intend to continually pursue our objective and it is not our intent to examine the character of the religious persons of the advent of Islam or to write the biography of the great sahābah. Even so, there is no choice but to mention this series of historical events in order to clarify the main discussion, which we now return to.

Inception of the Deviation from the Path of the Prophet (S)

By delving into the situation of Islam after the passing of the Prophet (S), we see a similar and even symmetrical situation to the Christian clergy and the powerful Church. The same signs can be seen among the sahābah just as in the first days of the appearance of the Church and the Christian clergy.

The belief of incarnation that the Church promoted regarding Jesus Christ ('a) was not duplicated by the important men of the advent of Islam regarding Prophet Muhammad (S), except in one or two cases (the Uhud battle and the day the Prophet passed away) in which some drew their swords and shouted: "Muhammad has not died and will never die!"

Even so, because conditions were not favorable and because the Holy Qur'an had annihilated this fallacy at the roots with overt statements and had made it clear that the Noble Prophet (S) is a human like all others and is similar to others in life and death, this susurration easily died away and had no effect on the Islamic society.

A similar situation to the Church after Christ, which was referred to as incarnation of divinity in the Church—meaning absolute sovereignty and unquestionable rule—in previous pages and which gives control of both spiritual and material aspects of the people to the Church (dictatorship in its absolute form!), also manifested in the Muslim World in the first days after the Holy Prophet (S) passed away, first in the form of the caliphate and later extending to the sahābah.

This issue emerged with a very simple, relatively understandable, logical statement. At its inception, in declaration of its general program, the Caliphate stated, "The Holy Prophet (S) was assisted by divine revelation [wahy] in decision-making and general administration; however, with the passing of the Prophet (S) divine revelation has been cut off so that we have no choice but to make necessary decisions through ijtihād[52]."

They also declared, "Like you, we sometimes have correct judgment and sometimes we make mistakes. If we make a mistake in something advise and correct us." Of course, this statement seems very simple and reasonable.

At the time the people regarded its apparent and simple meaning and were naturally thankful. However, observation of subsequent events and acquaintance with a series of happenings has cast us into doubt about the meaning of this statement and this compels us to delve deeper.

Incidentally, what is the meaning of the idea, "The Holy Prophet (S) was assisted by divine revelation in his works; however, now that we do not have divine revelation we must perform ijtihād." Also, what are the areas in which the Prophet (S) only relied upon divine revelation and did not interpolate his own judgment and those regarding which a contemporary Caliph might use his own discernment?

Do the Caliphs mean the divine precepts, which according to the explication of the Qur'an are perennially immutable and unchangeable? Or is their intent execution of these commandments, which according the specific wording of the Qur'an brooks no negligence?

---

[52] Ijtihād has been defined as the exertion of a jurisprudent to extract religious laws using specific methods from the Book, Tradition, reason, and consensus of religious authorities. This definition was derived from the "Dictionary of Dehkhodā". [trans.]

> *"And most assuredly it is a sublime book. Falsehood approaches it not from before it nor from behind it..."*[53]

> *"And whosoever judges not by that which Allah has revealed, verily they are the evildoers."*[54]

Or are the judicial codes of the Prophet of God (S) which were issued regarding litigations intended? Clearly by explicit testimony of the Qur'an in these cases, the verdict of the Prophet of God (S) was law.

He would judge according to material evidence and the verdict was not based on divine inspiration. Perhaps the intent was the commands that the Prophet of God (S) issued in general affairs, in war and peace, after consulting with his followers? It is evident that these affairs were based upon consultation and the decision of the Prophet (S), thus they were unrelated to divine revelation.

Or was it meant that the Prophet of God (S) apprehended the Islamic jurisprudential commandments and rules directly through revelation, without thought, and that we must deduce our course of action by subjecting the Book (Qur'an) and Tradition [sunnah] to scrutiny and ijtihād?

There is no doubt that the Prophet (S) was inspired with the divine commandments through revelation and others must comprehend them through ijtihād.

However, this is not limited to the Caliph—any person in the Islamic society [ummah] capable of religious deduction [istinbāt] must grasp jurisprudential precepts themselves through ijtihād.

---

[53] Sūrat Fussilat 41:41-42. Other verses also demonstrate this issue and there is so much evidence pointing to this fact that it cannot be doubted.

[54] Sūrat al-Mā'idah 5:47. According to similar verses, those who do not judge using what Allah has revealed are also oppressive [zālim] and infidels [kāfir].

Furthermore, this topic is irrelevant to the responsibilities and practical agenda of the office of Caliph.

Expedience in the Place of Truth

Indeed, the intent of the Caliphate by this utterance was intricate.

Even so, subsequent events clarified its meaning. It soon became clear that the Caliphate meant to tell the people that it shall exercise its opinion and ijtihād everywhere and in all things even execution of divine commandments and religious precepts and that its policy is expedience [maslihat] regarding the ummah, adaptation of prevalent precepts with current interests, and ultimately, guidance of the Islamic society through leadership driven by expediency.

Thus, this declaration means, 'These religious laws and precepts are for achieving and retaining your interests. Hence, religious precepts are subject to contemporary expedience and interests. Basically, at the time of the Prophet of God (S) discernment of current interests was committed to divine revelation.

However, after the passing of the Prophet (S) and the loss of current revelation, discernment of interests has been relegated to ijtihād and we shall distinguish good from evil through deduction and execute what is perceived as expedient!'

There is considerable evidence confirming this in the actions of the first Caliph in the short period of his incumbency.

After the second Caliph assumed his office, many changes were made in religious precepts which had no reason other than current expedience in the opinion of the Caliph. At the time of the Third Caliph, there was no longer any obscurity regarding the issue of modifying precepts in favor of current expedience.

After this period, with the start of the rule of the Umayyad dynasty and the domination of Muʿāwiyah over the Islamic society this issue is so clear that it can in no way be obscured.

This elevated the caliphate to a status equal to that of prophethood. In consequence, just as the Holy Prophet (S) was the issuer of Islamic precepts and administrator of the Islamic society, the Muslim Caliph also had the same status in issuance of precepts and administration of Muslim affairs.

One difference was that although the Holy Prophet (S) had the authority to make necessary expedient decisions in administration of the affairs of Muslims, he did not have the right to make the smallest change in divine precepts and commandments whereas the Caliphate had plenary authority and free reign in both Islamic precepts and administration of Muslim affairs, and they could make any change they thought was in the interests of the Islamic society!

At first, this was how the state of affairs progressed, i.e. the interests of Islam and Muslims were implied. However, later on, the interests of the Caliphate replaced the interests of Islam and Muslims! As a result, the Islamic policy of the Holy Prophet (S) was lost and execution of Islamic precepts and commandments became completely dependent on the discernment and judgment of the Caliph.

In reply to a protest regarding prohibition of the grater pilgrimage [hajj-e tamattu'], temporary marriage [nikāh-e mut'ah], and other issues, the Second Caliph first said:

"I am the friend and associate of Muhammad."

And then he explained the current expedience that caused the alteration and interdiction of these precepts.

In the six-person council that was assembled by the instruction of the second Caliph to appoint the Third Caliph, after much dispute, which brought down the candidates to two from the original six ('Alī ('a) and 'Uthmān), "'Abd al-Rahmān ibn 'Awf", who had an extra vote in case of a tie in accordance with the decree of the Second Caliph, extended his hand towards 'Alī ('a) and said, "I shall pledge allegiance to you on the condition that you deal with us in the same manner as the Shaykhayn (the first two caliphs)."

'Alī ('a) answered, "I shall only act in the manner of the Prophet of Allah (S)." 'Abd al-Rahmān did not accept and extended his hand toward 'Uthmān and presented him with his pledge with the condition of following the policy of the Shaykhayn. He accepted and thus the matter of allegiance was ended and 'Uthmān took the caliphate.

Obviously, there is no difference between the policy of the Prophet of Allah (S) and that of the Shaykhayn save that the Shaykhayn brought about changes in the execution of God's precepts and the method of the Prophet of Allah (S) according to their understanding of current interests.

Moreover, it is obvious that these changes were not limited to the practical and administrative method of the Prophet (S); rather, it had also spread to religious precepts. The following examples have been chosen from hundreds of similar cases:

In order to resolve the problem of the apostates after the passing of the Prophet (S) the First Caliph sent Khālid ibn Walīd, a Companion [sahābah], with a group of others to war against "Mālik ibn Nuwayrah". After arriving at Mālik's place of residence, Khālid proposed peace and became his guest. On the same day, he took Mālik by surprise, severed his head, and slept with his wife that night! After hearing about this shameful incident the Caliph did not punish Khālid at all and after 'Umar ibn Khattāb insisted that he be punished, the Caliph told the latter, "I cannot sheathe an unsheathed sword of Allah!"

After banning temporary marriage, the Second Caliph decreed the punishment for infraction be lapidation (stoning to death). Also, regarding the six-person council, he decreed that if they do not vote their heads should be cut off.

After Mu'āwiyah seized the office of caliphate, due to the fact that his father Abū Sufiyān had committed adultery with Ziyād ibn

'Ubayd's mother, he publicly summoned Ziyād to Shām (Damascus) and 'related' him to his father Abū Sufiyān! Even though this is against the explicit wording of the Holy Qur'an, he officially pronounced Ziyād his brother.

Many similar incidents have been recorded in history in which the caliphs put current interests before execution of incontrovertible Islamic precepts. Bygone dialectic theologians exerted themselves to attempt to match these actions to religious precepts using incomplete justifications. However, some recent Sunnī experts concede and explicate the fact that the first caliphs [khulafā' al-rāshidīn] sometimes put the interests of the ummah before execution of indisputable religious precepts.

Consummation of Caliph Immunity and Autonomy, and Ramifications Thereof

As can be seen from our previous discussions, the caliphate had absolute authority in 'issuance of precepts'. In modern terms, they had the jurisdiction to legislate or alter articles of the Constitution and they also had the authority to legislate and execute statutes.

A shortcoming of this independency which required amendment was the immunity of administrators and executives, i.e. the caliphate, vassals, and officials, which consisted of many of the Prophet's Companions [sahābah]. An obligatory irrefutable religious dictum was necessary to bring about religious immunity for officials and divest the people of the right to protest against their words and deeds. In this way, the sahābah would become completely autonomous.

This shortcoming was remedied with a narration the sahābah referred to the Holy Prophet (S). In accordance with this narration, the sahābah of the Prophet of Allah (S) were introduced as jurisprudents [mujtahid] such that if their judgment was correct in a certain matter, they would be rewarded by God and even if their judgment was incorrect, they were rewarded and pardoned.

Again, they related another narration regarding the virtuousness of the sahābah, according to which the sahābah of the Prophet of Allah (S) are automatically forgiven and exempt from punishment and God is pleased with them and whatever they do—good or bad, servitude to or offence against God—entails no divine call to account!

This narration reinforced the previous narration (that the sahābah were mujtahids or jurists and thus rewarded regardless), presented an official authorization to the sahābah, and absolutely guaranteed the unrestrained freedom of judgment and action of the sahābah of the Prophet (S).

The direct consequence of the autonomy of the caliphate and the religious immunity of the sahābah—who were the officials of the caliphate—was that the religious and worldly affairs of the Islamic society were completely entrusted to the caliphate. The result of this situation was that the valence of religious precepts, both worship-related and conduct-related, was restricted to "intuitive deduction-social thought".

Moreover, it introduced the practical laws and even theoretical teachings of Islam as phenomena based upon the material life of people which all people can understand.

As a consequence, the spiritual life of Islam fell from its lofty and true status to the social level and became restricted to materiality. According to the respected scholar, Professor Corbin, contrary to the soul of Islam, divinity was incarnated into the Islamic society or in the seat of caliphate and its vicinity.

As might be expected, the effulgence of Islam that had originated at the time of the Prophet (S)—from his appointment to his passing—became ancient history (consider this point carefully).

This eventuality was the fatalistic, natural, and inevitable effect of the meddling of ijtihād in divine precepts. It had nothing to do with the knowledge or ignorance of the original agents and founders and the supporters of the electoral caliphate.

In truth, it must be said that many of the people of that day and even subsequent periods did not understand the nature of this issue as they should have and they were ignorant of its evil repercussions.

As we can see, the challengers of this electoral caliphate, who in objection broke off from the majority on the first day, became widely known as Shī'ah. They were very few at first but at the eventide of the era of the four first caliphs, they had become a significant party.

It is also evident that the majority of Sunnī scholars do not consider ijtihād that is against the wording of the Book and Tradition permissible even though the actions of the first caliphs can never be vindicated without it.

Repercussions of the Autonomy of the Judgment and rulings of the Caliphs

As previously discussed, the general practical method of the caliphate was execution of Islamic precepts by means of ijtihād and judgment. In other words, their policy was to preserve the interests of the Islamic society conforming to the Book [kitāb] and Tradition [sunnah] where possible and putting current interests before the Book and Tradition if not.

Furthermore, as mentioned, this changed the authentic and immaterial spirituality of Islam into a socio- materialist regime which, like all other material phenomena, must naturally retain the general aspects of material beings such as childhood, adolescence, maturity, and old age. For instance, the Second Caliph compared Islam to a camel that passes through various periods and states such as infirmity, strength, and subsequent infirmity.

This method was not the invariable method of the time of the Holy Prophet (S). It was, rather, similar to democratic rule (where democratic rule is incomplete because obviously it cannot conform to all the incontrovertible principles of democracy).

Thus, it embodies an inner turmoil that is contrary to the stability and consistency of an established social convention. Undeniably, each of the four first caliphs came into office in a different manner. The first two caliphs had relatively similar policies and the third and fourth caliphs each had unique methods of office.

Additionally, Mu'āwiyah took the Islamic caliphate in a dissimilar manner to these four caliphs. He then made the caliphate "hereditary" and publicly turned it into "despotic rule".

In this way, the newly-established Islamic government became like its contemporaneous empires, such as the Roman and Persian empires, first in that it put an end to the convergence of social strata, which Islam greatly struggled to establish.

As a result, social division—such as superior and subordinate, master and servant, man and woman, Arab and non-Arab, Companion [sahābah] and non-Companion, Immigrants [muhājirīn] and Helpers [ansār]—quickly caused great rifts among the people. Second in that it used all its power for world conquest and expansion of its control.

In order to incite the people to Holy War [jihād], the Second Caliph even directed that the words "Hasten towards the best of deeds"[55] be dropped from adhān[56] so that people would not prefer ritual prayer [salāt] to jihād.

---

[55] Or "hayya 'alā khayr al-'amal" (Hasten to the best of acts.) which refers to ritual prayer. [trans.]

[56] I.e., the call to ritual prayer. [trans.]

As a result of this intemperance, all of the exalted aims of Islam in refining and perfecting the people were overshadowed. As a matter of course, it cannot be denied that one of the important dictates of Islam is jihād, which is the instrument of struggle against polytheism and expansion of the monotheistic [tawhīd] maxim. Even so, it is evident that the method of Islam is not the method of Alexander or Genghis Khān.

If Islam has given Muslims the mandate of world domination, with it, it has also given the mandate of statesmanship. It is evident in holy Qur'anic verses that the meaning of expanding the sphere of influence is vivification of the word of righteousness, development of social justice, and spiritual edification of the people; not establishment of a Kaiserist dictatorship, world exploitation, extensive slave traffic, taking of immeasurable spoils of war, and amassment of extraordinary treasures.

Accumulation of treasure became so rampant at the time of the Third Caliph that Abū Dharr, the truthful and cherished Companion of the Prophet (S), campaigned against amassing wealth and obtaining treasure and finally was martyred in this struggle.

When the Third Caliph wanted to resolve a problem of differing written versions of the Qur'an and establish a uniform version, he insisted that a "wāw" [] be taken out of the "Verse of Wealth" [āyat ul-kanz] such that he even threatened Abī ibn Ka'b the great Qur'anic scribe with his sword:

> *"O you who believe! Most surely many of the rabbis and monks consume the wealth of the people unjustly and turn them from the way of Allah; and those who hoard up gold and silver and do not spend it in the way of Allah, give them*

tidings of a painful chastisement"[57]

Moreover, to the very end, Muʿāwiyah insisted that the Verse of Wealth proscription regarding amassing wealth was about the followers of other divine books not Muslims.

This is understandable because history bears witness that everything he and his collaborators did and every conspiracy and corruption that they were involved in was effectuated through the force of wealth and the blessing of ijtihād!

In any event, by stating these facts the intention was not to analyze this segment of history at the advent of Islam; rather, the discussion brought us here. Hence, we shall again return to the main aim of this article, which is discussion of "Islamic eschatology according to the Shīʿahs".

The autonomy of the caliphate in issuance of precepts and the privilege of ijtihād—that the sahābah had gained in those days—had substantial effects on the manifestation of Islamic teachings and precepts.

These directly affected the three methods of "transcendent revelation", "logical thought and reasoning", and "guardianship and eschatology", which we discussed at the start of this article. As would be expected, these three methods were altered to match the prevailing situation.

Alteration of Teachings and Precepts

It can be understood from the words of the Qur'an that the theoretical teachings and practical precepts in it have been canonized for everyone and all times and they can never be changed, because the

---

[57] Sūrat al-Tawbah (or Barāʾah) 9:34.

instructional contents of the Qur'an are a series of general principles.

Furthermore, according to the explicit wording of the Glorious Qur'an, the declarations of the Holy Prophet (S) are canonically binding and his explications of precepts are statutory and are the same as revealed verses. It is a clear historic fact that every word uttered by the Holy Prophet (S) was retained by the sahābah and other hearers, word by word.

They would then relate these utterances to each other and publicize them. Also, the Noble Prophet (S) regarded the words of the Ahl al-Bayt ('a) as having this same credibility and canonicalness and has upheld their explication and elucidation of general Islamic teachings and precepts as his own.

Hence, general Qur'anic laws and the Noble Prophet's (S) explanations of religious canons [sharī'ah] (which consist of the prophetic traditions) hold the status of an immutable Constitution.

Only a temporary set of decisions that a Muslim viceroy is authorized to make in accordance with prevailing interests and necessities in the area of observing religious precepts may be altered or replaced. These precepts are temporary and subsidiary rules and are concerned with the short-term interests of the Islamic society. In the span of his lifetime, this authority was held by the Prophet (S).

After the passing of the Prophet (S), the majority of the sahābah and the people held this same opinion in regard with Islamic precepts. However, as we discussed, the caliphate had a different notion. The caliphate believed that the Islamic laws that must be observed in an Islamic monotheistic atmosphere are divine precepts that have been revealed in accordance with current interests and must naturally change with the variation of the interests and needs of the ummah.

In modern terms, we can interpret this by saying that they believed that the Islamic religion has a Constitution which is a set of divine rules and regulations that were revealed upon the Noble Prophet (S).

These rules, which are in harmony with the interests of the Islamic society, are immutable and mandatory unless the viceroy of the society perceives the interests of the society in something else. The tasks of administrating the Islamic society and propagating Islam after the passing of the Prophet (S) were believed to fall to the ummah itself.

Keeping to the interests of Muslims, the society can appoint whoever it wants to administrate its affairs and to hold the caliphate. Naturally, any goodness or perversion that the caliph discerns is authoritative and is equivalent to the discernment of the society. Any alteration in the standing regulations of Islam by the judgment of the caliph is considered acceptable and binding.

Obviously, this ideology is only attentive to divine rules and precepts in the Holy Qur'an which it considers relatively immutable (similar to the articles of the Constitution in democratic rule).

However, rules and precepts uttered by the Holy Prophet (S), especially precepts not linked directly to the Qur'an, are considered temporary and subsidiary regulations such as the practical method of the Prophet of God (S) and the minor, temporary, and local commands he issued. Or at least, the precepts in the Prophet's (S) Tradition [sunnah] are not considered to possess the constancy and solidity of Qur'anic precepts and may easily be defined as current interests of the Prophet's (S) era!

According to a notable hadīth among the Sunnīs and Shī'ahs (the Hadīth of Paper [hadīth-e qirtās]), when the Prophet (S) asked for paper and ink at the last moments of his life to write a comprehensive directive to be followed after him, the Second Caliph declared, "Surely this man is delirious"[58] and later he said, "The Book of Allah suffices us"[59].

---

[58] (Inna al Rajal la yahjor)"For the man to Immigrate"

[59] (Hasbana ketab Allah) "We took into consideration the book of God"

There is no doubt that the second statement means that with the existence of the Book of Allah we do not need the directive of the Prophet (S) and this cannot be justified other than through the theory we previously stated.

Also, in one of his speeches regarding the ban of "the greater pilgrimage" [hajj-e tamattu‘], the Second Caliph said, "God would make things permissible and prohibited for his Messenger. You must consider only the beginning of the Verse of the Greater Pilgrimage [āyat al-hajj-e al-tamattu‘] and disregard the end of the verse and the implementation of the Prophet (S)!" (Contemplate this carefully.)

At the time of the first caliphs, great importance was placed upon memorizing and reciting the Holy Qur'an whereas relating narrations regarding the prophetic traditions and memorizing the Prophet's (S) statements regarding the details of Islamic jurisprudence were brushed aside.

Even though at the time of the Prophet (S), the sahābah expended considerable effort in memorizing and writing prophetic hadīths and jurisprudential precepts, after the Prophet (S) inscription of hadīth was strictly prohibited.

This prohibition lasted until the end of the rule of the Umayyad dynasty. The First Caliph even collected a great many of the hadīths he himself had written and burned them! The Second Caliph even forbade the sahābah from relating hadīth.

The only incident that attracts attention in the issue of hadīth propagation is that after coming into his office and ascendancy over Islamic governance, Mu‘āwiyah made a public declaration that whoever relates a narration [riwāyah or hadīth] regarding the virtues of the first three caliphs shall receive a reward and whoever relates a narration regarding the virtues of 'Alī ibn Abī Ṭālib⁶⁰ shall have no immunity whatsoever and will be held in contempt by the caliphate.

He commanded his functionaries and governors to write down the names of those who related hadīth on the virtues of the Triad Caliphs and give them rewards from the public treasury [bayt al-māl].⁶¹

Subsequently, a pandemonium of hadīths related to virtues of the Triad Caliphs was released!

A result of this policy was that relation of hadīth in non-jurisprudential areas, especially hadīths that were in some way linked to the virtuosity of the Triad Caliphs and other sahābah, developed extensively. However, no interest was expressed in regard to religious laws and Islamic jurisprudential precepts and they largely fell from grace.

Traditionist experts⁶² ['ulamā' al-rijāl] and historians have recorded the names and backgrounds of approximately twelve thousand sahābahs of the Holy Prophet (S) and have stated that this great group of people lived for close to one century after the hijrah with absolute respect from contemporary Caliphs and Muslims and that their 'goods', which were prophetic hadīths, had great worth in the Bazaar of Islam.

When they state that the hadīths regarding Islamic jurisprudence and religious precepts related by these esteemed individuals throughout this lengthy period is only around five hundred hadīths, which means that from every twenty-four sahābahs only one hadīth remains as memorial, a person becomes awestruck and dazed beyond descrip-

---

⁶⁰ Alī ibn Abī Ṭālib ('a) was the first Imām of the Shī'ahs and was elected the Fourth Caliph by the people. [trans.]

⁶¹ The bayt al-māl is the treasury of the Islamic government in which all Muslims have an equal right.

⁶² Traditionist experts are scholars that critically study the biography of relaters of traditions (traditionists) in order to ascertain the validity of traditions. [trans.]

tion!

In addition, some of the religious issues in these hadīths are still obscure, ambiguous, or even contradictory and precepts that should have become necessary and axiomatic due to their myriad frequency have become unsolvable mysteries!

By way of illustration, we could describe the issue of the ritual ablution [wudū]. The Holy Prophet (S) prescribed wudū and made this ablution himself among the people several times a day for over twenty years.

According to the narrations and relations of the sahābah, it is not evident whether he washed his hands from top to bottom or bottom to top; whereas, according to historic records, when the Prophet (S) made wudū people would crowd around him and attempt to take the water of his wudū as tabarruk[63] and would try not to let even a drop fall to the earth.

The issues of inheritance of aunts[64] and wrongdoing in the duties of inheritance could also be cited.

In short, as a result of this ideology, Islamic jurisprudential precepts were lost and syllogism [qiyās] and istihsān[65] were substituted in the place of religious stipulations.

---

[63] A sacred token that increases blessings. [trans.]

[64] I.e., sisters of one's father and mother. [trans.]

[65] According to "Kitāb al-Taʿrīfāt" (The Book of Definitions) of Jurjānī as cited by the "Dictionary of Dehkhodā", istihsān means abandoning deduction and propounding something that is easier for the people to accept. [trans.]

Proscription of Logical Argumentation and Debate

Through their God-given nature, humans intuitively understand that culture is the key to worldly bliss and happiness. Progress in life is linked to cultural progress. Cultural progress is not possible without logical argumentation and free debate.

Even though there was a time when this issue was not as clear as it should have been due to unenlightenment and other unnatural factors, today this issue is considered axiomatic and there is no longer the least dubiety in this regard.

It has become evident through both discourse and experience that if unnatural factors do not hinder them, due to their God-given natures, humans promote open debates and logical thought and advance in this manner. This is true especially in such as the Islamic society, where religion is based upon logical reasoning and the divine Book does not have even the least amount of reservation or negligence in regard with logical thought.

Even so, at the advent of Islam—particularly synchronous with the first and second caliphs when every day Islam was becoming more and more renowned and the Islamic society was progressively developing—there is no apparent trace of Islamic cultural development through discussion and inquisitiveness.

We must most regretfully confess that in this period of its history, the Islamic society manifested no substantial endeavors in this area and they did not even put into "cultural development" one hundredth of the effort that they put into "jihād".

They placed Islamic principles, with all its subtle details and scientific truths, before the simple understanding of the commons even though various hadīths bear witness to the fact that at the time the sphere of education went no further than the level of corporality and the senses.

Among both the commons and the elite the belief reigned that the words of the Holy Qur'an, with its simple meanings understandable to the public, are sufficient for both thought and deed.

In line with this principle, all kinds of critical discussions and free inquiry in doctrine were forbidden and considered religious innovations or heresy [bid'ah] and entailed heavy punishments. For example, a person who debated an issue with the Second Caliph was whipped by the Caliph until blood freely flowed from his body.

In another instance, the Second Caliph explained a Qur'anic verse in such a manner that it seemed to authenticate fatalism. An Arab made an objection and the Caliph verbally lashed out at him and threatened him such that it seemed he intended to kill him, until finally several of those present were able to quell his anger only with great difficulty!

Even so, a series of argumentations regarding religious doctrine could not be avoided because:

First, as a result of Islamic conquests the Muslim society daily grew and scholars of other faiths and creeds came to Muslim gatherings and propounded various discussions regarding Islamic teachings. Thus Muslims were forced to take part in debates and offer answers.

Second, the Islamic society was entangled with a motley of hypocrites who propagated all kinds of doubts and perceived faults in Islam. Also, there were religious minorities who disagreed with the majority in many subsidiary beliefs. Hence, time and again, many scientific discussions and debates would break out.

As a matter of course, a series of discussions that later became known as "dialectic theology" ['ilm al-kalām] were developed and circulated among the people in spite of the aversion and prohibition of officials. Finally, some individuals became experts in these debates and government officials and jurists of the time who strived with all their might to prevent dialectic discussions approved of the science of dialectic theology.

In previous discussions we talked to some extent about the method and style of dialectic theological discussions and there is no need to repeat these arguments. However, we must state the fact that even though the dialectic theology, which discusses the various theoretical teachings of Islam, is a noble science, due to the shortcomings in its original formation, it has been deprived of the true value of a rational technique and completely free argumentation for two reasons:

As perfectly evident from Qur'anic verses, principles of Islamic doctrine are a series of truths and realities that are much beyond the understanding of the unlearned. Because the Islamic society and government functionaries were heedless of or even opposed to free logical debates, they subjected simple commoner beliefs to discussion and advocated a series of mundane social thoughts as the final true doctrines of Islam.

As a result, in their minds "divinity" [ulūhiyyah] and "the metaphysical world" ['ālam-e māwarā' al- tabī'ah], which are pure and flawless, manifested in the form and identity of a material world similar to our universe. In addition, they believed that our tangible world is governed by the laws of "causality" ['illiyyah] but the transcendent realm has no fixed system and is completely uncontrolled!

Also, they held that our material world is subject to the senses and that the incorporeal world, even though it is similar to this world, is imperceptible to the senses and a time will come when all constituents of the spiritual world even ... [sic] will become tangible!

As a result of the prohibition of the practice of free debate, rationalization became a pretense or pastime and the only proof necessary for the thought being analyzed became imitation.

This is why the strongest reason and sharpest weapon among dialectics is consensus [ijmā']. In flailing to authenticate unanimity first they related this narration from the Holy Prophet (S), "My ummah shall not unite in error."⁶⁶ and therefore, they consider unanimity of the ummah to be sound reason.

Then, they substituted the ummah with the scholars ['ulamā'] of the ummah. Later scholars of a group within the ummah such as the "Ashā'irah" or "Mu'tazilah" were substituted for scholars of the ummah. After that, they swapped scholars of a faction with dialectic theologians of that faction!

This ended here and as a result, obviously, the strongest reason of a dialectic theologian [mutikallim] such as Ash'arī in proving an Ashā'irah belief is the unanimity of the Ashā'irah dialectic theologians. It was quite frequent that a claim was repudiated even though it was congruent with the Book [kitāb], Tradition [sunnah], or reason ['aql] because of being contrary to the consensus of scholars and dialectics of the religious faction!

In line with these affairs, we see that:

First, the opposition of adherents to one Islamic faction regarding an exclusive authorized unanimous view of a second faction is not considered problematic for Islam; according to each faction supporters of other factions are not part of the Muslim society!

Second, a person who accepts one exclusive principle of a faction must accept the rest of its exclusive principles without question, whether or not they have sufficient reason. It is clear that this method has completely annihilated the spirit of rational thought and has dried out the roots of free thought in the Islamic community. In this manner, it has given absolute reign to fanatical imitation in all beliefs!

This method went beyond dialectic theology and contaminated other Islamic sciences such as exegesis [tafsīr], jurisprudence [fiqh], methodology [usūl], etc. and even interloped and caused havoc in linguistic sciences such as morphology [sarf], grammar [nahw],

---

⁶⁶ (La tajameea emate aala khatea) "Do not combine my ema on the wrong"

semantics [ma'ānī], and rhetoric [bayān].

With a look at any of these sciences we see strange classifications such as hanafiyyah, shāfi'iyyah, etc. and kūfiyyīn, basriyyīn, etc. and the like. Every faction rationalizes its unique thoughts and allegorically reinterprets the reasons of others.

Third, as a result of the method of "reliance on tribal and factional unanimity", authoritative proofs, i.e. the Book and Tradition, lost their true value and were demoted to formalities. For this reason, we see that to prove their beliefs proponents of each faction first refer to the consensus of its supporters and then they may turn to the Book and Tradition. Also, they expressly and recklessly allegorically reinterpret the proofs of other factions from the Book and Tradition and thus invalidate them.

This style has even spread among literary scholars and every party reinterprets the reasons and proofs of the opposition, which include Arabic verse or prose, definition, collation, and other devices!

Spiritual and Eschatological Development

With the passage of a century, ignorant darkness spread throughout the Islamic society. However, due to the inevitable contact of Muslims with the scientific and cultural societies of the world, they realized their desperate and increasing need for philosophical and logical sciences. On account of their illogical imitation they never thought that there could be authentic and logical wisdom in the content of the Book and Tradition.

Thus, in their reckless need they sought wisdom elsewhere. At the epilogue of the "Umayyad dynasty" and the prelude of the "'Abbāsīd dynasty" many books of logic, philosophy, mathematics, etc. were translated from Greek, Syriac, and other languages into Arabic.

Even though introduction of these sciences into the Islamic society generated great fervor and enthusiasm and contemporary caliphs completely supported these "newly arrived guests", contrary to expectation, due to the clash of divine philosophy and various dogmatic issues in Islam that were rationalized using the dialectic method, a dispute ignited between "dialectic theologians and jurisprudents" [mutikallimīn wa fuqahā]—who were backed by the admiration of the public—and "advocates of philosophy".

Ultimately, "philosophy" [falsafah] was rejected or abandoned and "dialectics" [kalām] gained primacy owing to the merit that (in their opinion) its discussions were in line with religious law [sharʻ].

Those with sufficient literacy regarding spiritual life and inner perfection that have grasped the true aims of this science, clearly understand that the method of "inner advancement" and "spiritual life" is based on the fact that human inner perfections and spiritual ranks are genuine truths that exist beyond the realities of nature and the material world.

In addition, they acknowledge that "the spiritual realm", which is the abode of spiritual life, is a world much more authentic, real, and vast than "the world of corporality and the senses".

Spiritual ranks are genuine truths and conditions of human existence. They have never been formal concepts or social conventions.

Wealth and poverty, prominence and insignificance, mastership and servitude, lords and subjects are a series of prescriptive or conventional concepts or titles that have been proscribed for various social aims and are given to persons through specific social rules.

Accordance of the title of lordship to a lord or vassalship to a vassal does not affect their external nature or change their essence. Wealth is not an essential part of a person who is wealthy and losing wealth does not diminish the human essence nor take anything away from it.

Also, the only relationship between social actions and their consequences (good or bad) is a prescriptive one. Thus, it happens much that actions which at one time have generous rewards entail punishment at later times or might not have any results at all.

Social ranks and titles are usually prescriptive and follow social conventions. Further, the relationships among these titles and the actions arising from them and between titles and their effects in the society are all prescriptive and conventional.

However, the relationship between human actions and mental states, between these states and the inner levels of human advancement, and between these levels and the realm that incorporates these levels are all genuine and real phenomena existing outside the authority and dominion of material and nature. In short, spiritual life and eschatology (in any form) are based on the authenticity of the spiritual realm.

The view we mentioned before—the foundation of "the electoral caliphate"—caused "the Islamic tradition" to become known as merely a "social tradition". Its cornerstones were exclusively the corporal interests, which were discernible through social-based thoughts.

It is clear that this view has no connection with spiritual advancement and eschatology and that effecting reconciliation between this view and eschatology is impossible. This is because "pure materiality" and "pure spirituality" are situated at two opposite poles. Thus, proximity to one is remoteness from the other.

On this account, in the era of the Caliphs at the advent of Islam there is no trace of the method of spiritual evolution. Except for an assortment of religious worshipers and ascetics who were known only for their good deeds, no one demonstrated spiritual evolution in any other context. This continued until the preludes of the 'Abbāsīd dynasty.

Activities of the Shī'ahs for Establishment of Righteousness

The majority of the Muslims of the first era of Islam were as we stated. As a result of this condition, the theoretical and practical doctrines of Islam were falling into decline. In addition, the methods of understanding and advancing these truths, i.e. the free debate method and the spiritual development method, headed towards the valley of forgetfulness.

On the other hand, the Shī'ah minority, which had risen against the majority from day one, did not have sufficient power to strike down the prevailing situation. In their view, restitution of the general circumstances of the Holy Prophet's (S) era did not seem likely.

Thus, they were forced to desist from general and positive resistance and utilize a different approach—an approach in which they could protect the theoretical and practical teachings of Islam and keep alive the legitimate methods of advancement, which were the methods of free debate and spiritual evolution.

The Holy Prophet (S) introduced the Ahl al-Bayt ('a) as the custodians and teachers of Islamic precepts and the spiritual leaders of Muslims. In accordance with this recommendation, the Shī'ahs embraced the Ahl al-Bayt ('a) and endeavored to learn and record religious precepts even in the face of fear and trepidation.

In his twenty-five years of seclusion and arduous five years of office as caliph, the first leader of the Shī'ah, with his extraordinary eloquence and elocution, which both friend and foe recognized as unchallengeable and unrivaled, promoted Islamic precepts and opened the doors to excellent free logical debates.

He fostered men of God, sahābah and tābi'īn alike, such as Salmān, Kumayl Nakha'ī, Uways Qaranī, Rashīd Hijrī, and Maytham Kūfī. It cannot be said that these people, with their special spiritual approach and treasuries of knowledge and wisdom, had no effect upon the Islamic society.

After the martyrdom [shahādah] of the first Shī'ah leader, the dreadful and despotic Umayyad sultanate emerged. During the reign of the Umayyad dynasty Mu'āwiyah and his agents and all other Umayyad sultans battled the Shī'ahs with all their might.

Everywhere they found a Shī'ah, even those who were presumed to be Shī'ah, they would wipe them out and destroy their families. Conditions for the Shī'ahs became more grave and pressures more intense by the day.

Even so, in this period the second, third, and fourth Shī'ah leaders brooked no neglect in vivifying and keeping alive righteousness. They operated in an environment awash in affliction and adversity under the threats of sword, scourge, and torture. Thus, day after day the truth of Shī'ism proliferated and veridical radiance outspread.

The best testimony to this is the time immediately after this period at the close of the Umayyad dynasty leading up to the consolidation of the 'Abbāsīd sultanate, concurrent with the fifth and sixth Shī'ah leaders, i.e. Imām Muhammad al-Bāqir ('a) and Imām Ja'far al-Sādiq ('a), when for a short period the chokehold on the Shī'ahs weakened slightly and the Shī'ahs gained a moderate amount of freedom.

In this interval, personages, scholars, and traditionists [muhaddithīn] gathered around these two great leaders to learn Islamic sciences. These were not non-Shī'ahs who first became Shī'ah at the hand of the Imām and then endeavored in studying the sciences; rather, they were Shī'ahs who by necessity lived in the guise of pretense and dissimulation [taqiyyah] and dropped the façade at the merest of opportunities.

This evolved spirit was not without influence in the majority of the social corpus. To a varying degree, it reflected righteousness and truth in the mirror of the people's minds and made everyone aware of the innate human need for natural religion, free debate, and spiritual evolution.

Furthermore, with the dark times that were progressively becoming darker and the extreme oppression and unrestraint of government agents at the time of the Third Caliph and throughout the Umayyad rule, the Shī'ah leaders made it clear to the people that religion is in no way safe in the hands of the Caliphate; that administration of religious precepts cannot be handed over to the Caliphate; that implementation of these precepts cannot depend on the ijtihād and judgment of the Caliph; and that ultimately, the power of the Caliphate works in its own interests not the interests of the people and the Islamic society!

Consequently, it was clearly established that religious precepts are immutable and eternal and that ijtihād which is against the wording of the Book and Tradition is meaningless.

Only, due to the affection the majority of the people had towards the sahābah and the Traditions that extolled the status of the sahābah and acknowledged their ijtihād, the people refrained from protesting against the first three caliphs and Mu'āwiyah. Even though their incumbency was blatantly based upon the previously-mentioned view and their conduct corroborated this, the people would justify their meddling in Islamic precepts and reinterpret these tamperings to make them seem correct. On the other hand, sometimes they were fair and took part in free debates and became acquainted with Islamic spirituality.[67]

---

[67] This paper was originally published in Farsi in the seventh yearbook, "Maktab-e Islām".

Discourse Two: Trusteeship and Leadership

We human beings have taken up residence on the earth for ages; we procreate and we live out our lives. Due to the fact that we have chosen social life as a requisite of our own nature, we help each other as much as possible, perform collective endeavors, and pile up the fruits of our pooled toils and each of us benefits from them to the extent of their social weight and character.

Of course, such a method cannot come about without the loss of absolute individual freedom. Persons who become part of a community, take up the method of cooperation and collaboration, and amalgamate their choices with the choices of others cannot be completely free and do whatever they desire.

Even so, human life is not possible without a degree of individual autonomy. Human personalities are the substance of the community and society is its form. The human personality relies on individual volitions and passions and with their dissipation it would surely be destroyed. In consequence, the cornerstone of the society—any type of society imaginable—would be eradicated and its pillars would fall to ruin.

Individual Autonomy

While every human being lives in a social fold—advanced or savage—they each use their intellect in their individual endeavors and make suitable choices through their personal volition.

However, it is common for the individual personality, which manages life using its intellect and volition, to become incapable so that it cannot carry the burden of life to its destination self-reliantly—such as among people with dementia or those with less than adequate understanding and volition. Naturally, others must manage the lives of such persons.

Moreover, the same holds for infants and children until they reach maturity. Others, meaning their elders, must manage their livelihoods and gradually draw them level with mature men and women through education and edification.

Also, in every human society there may be some advantages and benefits that are not under the charge of specific persons and naturally do not have a custodian, such as general mortmain [awqāf-e 'āmmah] and similar issues.

Above all this is safeguarding and supporting the society that has come into being from a collective of human beings. Because no imaginable society can continue to exist without a series of rules and norms that all or the majority of the people follow, respect, and sanctify. For instance, if in a transaction between two people neither the buyer nor seller is bound by the effects and conditions of the transaction, no sane person would be found performing such a deal.

Equally, there are innumerable other issues with which social humankind organizes its livelihood and regarding these, all or a majority of the society must acknowledge a set of rules and regulations, and sanction their validity. Thus, no society may continue its existence without a series of norms, rules, traditions, and regulations.

Accordingly, having only a series of norms and regulations can never be enough for the continuance of a society because as it has been shown no two humans are similar in their existential constitution—hence, in their intellect, volition, and methods.

Therefore, even though human individuals may be united in their general thoughts, they are unquestionably at variance in details and would surely not make the same choices. As a result of this certain dissimilitude, at the first step each person tends to rush in a different direction bringing about the collapse of common laws and norms.

In addition, as far as the history of human life shows and observation of various human societies with varying methods of government confirms, survival of every society requires an individual or an office whose intellect and volition governs and controls the intellects and volitions of the citizenry and guards and supports the governmental system that has been implemented in the society.

These conditions are manifest in all societies without exception. Humankind, with its God-given make-up [fitrah], is not ignorant of them and does not remain inactive. Willing or unwilling, the people of each society elect an individual or office to oversee them and administrate their affairs.

They ask their chosen—just as a guardian that is the custodian of an orphan, the head of the family, and responsible for managing the affairs of the young family members—to rule over the people as a king or president.

We name this office, according to which an individual or office becomes in charge of the affairs of others and manages their lives, like a real individual, trusteeship [wilāyat]. It has almost the same meaning that we understand from the words leadership and guardianship.

This is the meaning that is addressed in this discourse and the opinion of the holy religion of Islam will be explicated regarding this matter. However, this matter will be discussed from the viewpoint of the social philosophy of Islam, not in the method of Islamic jurisprudential discussion specific to Shī'ah jurisprudence.

Those, who are well-versed in Shī'ah jurisprudence will see that the methods of reasoning in this discourse are significantly different from jurisprudential ratiocination in canon laws [ahkām-e shar'].

Domain of Trusteeship and Leadership

As we have explained, the domain of trusteeship [wilāyat] consists of a series of necessary affairs that are not specific to a certain individual in the society and that of which no person is normally in charge.

This can be instances where the "proprietor" does not have the ability to manage its affairs—such as charge of the assets of orphans and affairs of the mentally ill, the interdicted, and similar cases—or where the matter is not essentially related to a specific individual, such as general social affairs related to government (public goods); in other words, the type of affairs that are forsaken due to having no one in charge but are necessary and cannot be set aside.

As we have explained, no previous or present human society, advanced or savage, great or small, was ever ignorant of such affairs. Every society endeavors upon this matter in proportion with its situation and establishes wilāyat and leadership. This is the best testimony to the fact that the issue of wilāyat is spiritually innate.

All human beings understand through their God-given fitrah that for every necessary thing that does not have a commissioner, a supervisor must be chosen.

Also, Islam, which is a natural [fitrī] religion and its laws and precepts are based upon creation, has not neglected the issue of wilāyat and leadership—which is an innate or fitrī issue. By ratifying it, Islam has signed and put into circulation an innate human principle. God, the Almighty, has stated in His divine Book:

> *"So set thy face to the pure religion of Allah; this is the fitrah (nature) upon which Allah has created humankind. The creation of Allah is immutable. This is the eternal religion, but most people do not know."*[68]

Explanation: With its awesome vastness and magnitude the wide universe of existence, as it is stated in various holy verses, forms a unitary whole. Its diverse components and aspects from the tiniest particle to the greatest celestial body, and the most multifarious group of stars that form tremendous galaxies all are existentially related and influence each other.

Hence, in every coming into existence or evolution of a phenomenon, whether enormous or minuscule, each and every component of the world of existence has a share. Of course, humankind is also a part of the world and is not apart from the rest.

Like a raindrop that trickles into an immense river, it is consigned to the effervescence and currents of the river and does not retain in itself any individual autonomy or distinguished drive.

Creation Leads its Elements Toward Perfection

With its general endeavors and movements and dynamism on the course of its existence, this extensive universal organization brings about general evolutions. Moreover, it delivers each of the variety of creatures to the perfection of their beings and leads them to the aims of their existence.

As we can see, through their creation and genesis, every one of these

---

[68] Sūrat al-Rūm 30:30.

varieties is equipped with a series of abilities and instruments that are perfectly suited to their existential aims and life goals. Only by activities that utilize these abilities and resources may they resolve their existential needs and transform their flaws into perfections.

The best verification of this issue may be found as a general statement in the following verses:

> *"He said: Our Lord is He who gave to each thing its creation and then guided it."*[69]

> *"He who has created then given order; and who has determined then guided."*[70]

From here we can deduce that humans must perpetually know good and evil and their profit and loss through genetic apprehension and existential guidance. This is because humans are non-independent elements inseparable from general creation, and the general nature of creation conveys and leads each of its constituents to its appropriate existential purpose and perfection.

Due to the fact that humankind is a variety that travels towards its life goals and perfection using its intellect and volition, perforce its aforementioned genetic guidance and apprehension manifests in the form of knowledge and thoughts. This has been stated in the following holy verse:

> *"By the soul and He who (created it and) gave it order; then, inspired it (with consciousness of) wrong and right. Truly saved are those who purify it. And surely lost are those*

---

[69] Sūrat Tā Hā 20:50.

[70] Sūrat al-A'lā 87:2-3.

who corrupt it."[71]

It is clear from the foregoing discussion that through genetic inspiration and the guidance of fitrah and constitution, humans are equipped with an array of information and thoughts that guarantee their bliss throughout life endeavors.

By utilizing these thoughts and knowledge, humans attain harmony with the system of creation and do not conflict or clash with the general and perfectionist movement of the universe—which would precipitate the demise of their own perfectionist system. This is the concept that God, the Glorified, has disclosed in the preceding verse, "So set thy face to the pure religion of Allah…", and affirms that:

First, because the bliss and beatitude of humankind is a genetic reality in their lives, an order must reign over the people that stems from the general creation of the universe and the exclusive creation of humanity.

Second, because the system of creation is constant and established, the perfect religion and lifestyle that springs from it must also be constant and established. It must not be dependent upon passions and desires, change color everyday, and draw it through every cesspool of vileness and adversity and thus afflict humankind with wrong even though it knows the correct path by its God-given nature. In another verse, Allah declares:

> **"Did you see the person who took his (or her) desire as his god and Allah led him astray in knowledge (that he was not worthy of guidance)…"**[72]

---

[71] Sūrat al-Shams 91:7-10.

[72] Sūrat al-Jāthiyah 45:23.

Also, in many verses God notifies that humans must abide by righteousness in their lifestyle not passions and desires. They must accept the judgment of sound reason not the verdict of carnal impulses and sentiments:

"..So what is there after truth save error?"[73]

Third, because defying the laws and precepts of fitrah is in reality opposition and resistance to the universal system of creation and this great system with its awesome power inevitably contends with these minuscule opposing humans, it shall, like it or not, straighten them upon the conforming path by either destroying or dominating them. Humans opposing religion and fitrah must anticipate a terrible juncture and painful retribution—as is indicated in the verses subsequent to verse 30 of Sūrat al-Rūm.

Necessity of Wilāyat and Leadership

According to the general principle that "Islam is based upon fitrah", concepts essential to fitrah are endorsed in Islam and one of the necessities and clear tenets of fitrah, in the manner we have defined, is the matter of wilāyat and leadership.

It was due to the clarity of the issue that at the time of the Holy Prophet (S) and especially after the hijrah, even though all aspects of wilāyat and leadership were practiced, (such as administration of people's affairs, appointment of governors and judges, management of charity and mortmain, general education and edification, dispatching missionaries, etc.)

---

[73] Sūrat Yūnus 10:32.

Muslims did not ask regarding the necessity of this principle even though many less important things were asked about including menstruation and donation. There are verses in the Holy Qur'an regarding these issues and the "Saqīfah incident" is the best testimony to this fact.

On the day of the Prophet's (S) death, before the blessed body of the Prophet (S) was interred, several of the muhājirīn, ansār and sahābah left the body and gathered at Saqīfah banī Sā'idah to choose a caliph. They made many suggestions, one saying the caliph must be chosen from the ansār and another saying from the muhājirīn.

Others would say one caliph from the ansār and one from the muhājirīn. Among this group no one came forward to say that there was no need to appoint a caliph or that there was any reason that caliphate was not necessary. This was because by their fitrah everyone understood that the wheel of the Islamic society could not rotate without a spinner and that the religion of Islam has validated the fact that there must be a government among Muslims.

Another attestation to this fact is the following holy verse:

> "And Muhammad is naught but a messenger. Messengers have passed away before him. If he dies or is slain will you turn on your heels? And whoever turns back on their heels will do no harm to Allah and Allah will soon reward the thankful."[74]

This verse says: Muhammad (S) is a messenger like the messengers that came before him, propagated the religion, and passed away. He is also temporary and will not remain among you forever. The religion is God's religion not Muhammad's. It will not terminate with his

---

[74] Sūrat Āl 'Imrān 3:144.

passing. He has the function of mediation and messengership. If one day he dies or is killed, will you turn on the religion?

It is evident that this holy verse was revealed with reference to the battle of Uhud and the defeat of the Muslims due to the sudden injury that the Holy Prophet (S) received from the enemy when it was rumored that Muhammad (S) had been killed.

Subsequent to this rumor, except for a select few, the army of Islam stopped fighting and retreated with the excuse that after the death of the Holy Prophet (S) there is no reason to continue the battle.

God, the Almighty, revealed this holy verse in regard with this incident and addressed Muslims and reproached and rebuked them due to their flight.

It is evident that they did not return to worshiping idols or repudiate prayer or fasting. The only thing they said, after the death of the Holy Prophet (S), was why one should continue fighting? In other words, they decided to abandon a religious duty that needed an administrator (i.e. the Prophet (S)) after his death.

God rebukes them in this regard and speaks not only of the situation of being killed but also of the condition of natural death and declares:

After the death of the Prophet (S), whether by natural death or killing, the tradition that has been created with his appointment must be absolutely preserved and must under no conditions be abandoned because he is no more than a messenger and religion belongs to God and as long as God is God, religion shall remain His.

After the Holy Prophet (S), the system of wilāyat and leadership must endure until the Day of Judgment.

The Islamic society must have a standing government. Departments of education, propagation, economy, defense, judicature, etc. must all continue their work.

Clearly this holy verse by necessity gives Muslims authority to carry on their social activities in the same manner as at the time of the Prophet (S). That is to say, the trustee or vicegerent must execute the immutable precepts of religion (which are termed the religious law [sharīʿah] of Islam), punish offenders in accordance with clear religious instructions, and manage social affairs of the Islamic society remaining true to the best interests of Islam and Muslims by issuing decrees regarding matters that vary according to circumstance.

Variable and Immutable Precepts

As it is clear from the preceding discussion, rules and precepts that are carried out in the Islamic society are of two types: immutable precepts and variable precepts.

In explanation, we may imagine a man with a specific nationality. He is the head of a household and is responsible to advance the small familial system he has started toward life goals as per his social status. He can, observing prudence, utilize his national rights in the shadow of the inviolable laws of his country, make decisions and enact them.

He can appoint a duty for each of the members of his family or release them from those duties. He can give specific instructions regarding food, clothing, habitation, etc. or cancel them according to expedience. He can call a day off or double the work hours.

He can defend himself and his family against those who infringe upon their property or dignity or he may sit calmly and determine that not engaging in defense is more advantageous, etc. However, he may never violate the mandatory laws of the country nor shirk his legal responsibilities.

Undoubtedly, the rules and precepts that are observed in this small social organization are of two types: first, the mandatory laws of the country that are immutable, modification of which is completely beyond the authority of this organization; and second, mandatory laws that stem from the head and vicegerent of the family, which may be changed according to expedience and the will of the head of the family.

The relation of the office of vicegerent and Islamic government to the religious organization and Islamic society is the same as the relation of the aforementioned head of family regarding the familial organization and members of the family.

The divine Islamic rules and precepts that have been sent down to the Prophet (S) through revelation and that we call Islamic sharī'ah and precepts of Allah are immutable laws on the authority of the Book and Tradition. They are unalterable laws and their execution and the punishment of transgressors is the duty of the office of Islamic wilāyat, vicegerent, trustee, or leader.

In the shelter of and compliance to the laws of sharī'ah, the vicegerent may make a series of decisions and legislations based on expedience and execute them. Such laws would be mandatory and have similar credence to the sharī'ah with the difference that divine laws are immutable and unalterable whereas persistence of legislated laws is dependent upon the expedience that caused them to arise.

Due to the fact that the life of human societies is in continual transition and evolution, these regulations will gradually change and lead to better ones.

Several points may be understood from the preceding discourse, which will be explained in turn: Point one, As we made clear, Islamic regulations are of two types:

The first type is divine precepts or laws of the sharī'ah, which are constant and immutable. They are a series of precepts that have divinely been inspired upon the Holy Prophet (S) as an irrevocable fitrī religion that must be carried out for all time—as indicated in the preceding sūrat (Sūrat al-Rūm 30:30) and also in the Tradition [sunnah]:

The halāl (permissible) of Muhammad is halāl unto the Day of

Resurrection and the harām (forbidden) of Muhammad is harām unto the Day of Resurrection.

Of course, is has occurred to many modern thinkers (!) that in accordance with the laws of nature and evolution, the human populace is continually changing and so generally, standing regulations must also change with the advancement of civilization.

A detailed response to this criticism and elaboration on the eternal soul of each of the articles of the Islamic sharī'ah is beyond the scope of this discourse. However, in short, we must note that regardless of what or how civil laws are, they are nevertheless based on the genetic and real needs of humankind. It is self-evident that all human needs are not variable; rather, we possess a series of real and constant needs.

Among these civil laws there are many instances of constant items such as the necessity of social life, defense of sanctities, personal ownership, necessity of government, and so on. Thus, in every imaginable social order there will always be a series of constants and the constant laws and items recognized by Islam are precepts that are collectively called the sharī'ah.

The second type consists of regulations that arise from the office of vicegerency and are legislated and executed in accordance with present expedience. It is evident that the continuance or collapse of these regulations is contingent upon current means and exigencies and will assuredly alter with the advancement of civilization and variation of benefit and detriment. Indeed, the principle of wilāyat and leadership of the society, because it is a divine precept of the sharī'ah, is immutable.

Point two

Is the Islamic Society Similar to the Democratic Society?

The second point is that the Islamic society is not altogether dissimilar to democratic societies in respect to constant and variable regulations. There are also two types of regulations in democratic societies.

Constant regulations make up the 'Constitution', modification of which is even beyond the authority of the parliament or senate.

Only the nation may annul an item of the Constitution directly by referendum or by forming a special congress. The other type consists of minor laws and regulations that are legislated by parliaments or senates and are implemented by various departments. These may be considered temporary interpretations of articles of the Constitution and are generally mutable.

Notwithstanding, one must not err and suppose that the method of Islam with its mark of freedom is a democratic or communist method as is seen in the words of some theorist writers. The Islamic method is neither democratic nor communist.

It has a glaring difference in its two types of regulations with the aforementioned societal and socialist methods since the legislator of the constant regulations of Islam is God—Glorious is His name—and the constant regulations of other social methods are spawned by the thoughts of the community.

Also, regarding the mutable regulations of the other systems, the main basis is the will of the nation's majority. The freedom or in other words the intellect and will of the minority of "half the people minus one" is sacrificed to the desire and approval of the nation's majority of "half the people plus one" whether their desire is right or not.

However, the basis of the mutable regulations in the Islamic society, even though they are the result of the conference of the nation, is righteousness and not the will of the majority—they must be supported upon realism not desires and sentiments.

In the Islamic society, the true right and good of Islam and Muslims must be carried out whether it is the will of the majority or not. Of course, in the community of knowledge and piety that real Islam nurtures, the majority will never prefer their capricious desires over truth and righteousness.

God, the Glorious, has divinely instructed humans to adhere to righteousness and truth [haqq]. He introduces it as the only guaranty for humanity's happiness and forbids conforming to any other standard, even though it may not comply with the lusts and desires of the majority or entirety of the people. Consider the following Qur'anic verses:

"Such is Allah, your true Lord; so what is there after truth save error? Why then do you turn away?"[75]

"Is then He who guides toward the truth worthier to be followed or those who cannot find the way unless guided?"[76]

"He it is who sent His messenger with guidance and the religion of truth..."[77]

"Verily We have brought you the truth; however, most of you are adverse to the truth."[78]

---

[75] Sūrat Yūnus 10:32.

[76] Sūrat Yūnus 10:35.

[77] Sūrat al-Saff 61:9.

[78] Sūrat al-Zukhruf 43:78.

"Surely humankind is in a state of loss; save those who believe and perform righteous deeds and counsel (each other) unto the truth and counsel (each other) unto patience."[79]

Some jurists criticize this aspect of the method of Islam and say: "Methods are acceptable and implemented by the people that are compatible with the desires of the majority—something that Islam lacks. Also, in practice, we have seen that the laws of Islam were completely implemented only for a very short time.

However, because the method of democracy respects the desires of the people, it has endured. Democracy has managed the civilized world for centuries and it has been fortified and beautified with every passing day.

The most that can be said about the social method of Islam is that it was a complete method suited to the human society fourteen centuries ago. Now, however, after fourteen centuries of human evolution and advancement it is no longer compatible with the modern global circumstances of humankind."

The Role of Government in the Development or Decline of Nations

In reply to this criticism the following must be said:

First: Even though to some extent the positive effect of congruity with the wants of the majority on acceptance of the method cannot be denied, the desires of the majority are doubtless an effect of general education and upbringing. Today, this fact has become axiomatic after plenty of sociopsychological debates.

In the environment of religious piety and theology that Islam creates

---

[79] Sūrat al-ʿAsr 103:2-3.

the majority never abandon sound reason for lusts and desires and never sacrifice truth and reality for wishes and inclinations; in this case, the views of the majority will perpetually be in harmony with truth and righteousness.

In other environments that are shaped in advanced and degenerate societies, the wants of the majority of each society is compatible with the norms and general aims of that particular society. Naturally, initially no method will be compatible with the desires of the majority of the society in which it is implemented.

This is not specific to the method of Islam—all other methods are such. Hence, criticism of the method of Islam for the crime of being incongruous with new age immodest unrestrained education and upbringing is nothing but sophistry—a fallacious argument.

Second: The natural life span of the Islamic method among Muslims did not expire a few years after the time of the Holy Prophet (S). The history of Islam bears witness to the fact that when the Holy Prophet passed away, the method of Islam—specifically the Tradition of the Prophet (S)—was abandoned and other traditions were substituted.

Within a very short period, a completely Arab empire replaced the Islamic method and tradition. One cannot say that the Islamic tradition died away naturally, but that it was murdered or martyred.

Also, Islam cannot be considered "unaccepted" because at its advent it was warmly welcomed and over a span of many years is was slowly subdued.

On the one hand, the true method of Islam must be analyzed from the pure Book and Tradition of the Holy Prophet (S) and, on the other hand, the pages of history regarding the shameful and dishonorable methods of governments attributed to Islam must be carefully studied.

Then we can see when and in what Islamic society the true tradition of Islam was carried out—and only then can we say whether the human society or the majority of people will accept the Islamic method or not.

Can it be said that the unfitness of the deeds of Muslims is the best reason for the unfitness of their religious method?!

Nonetheless, we see similar problems in other methods—especially democratic ones. It has been over half a century that we have accepted the democratic regime and government in line with Western civilized societies.

However, we see that our situation is becoming more critical and calamitous with every passing day. Ergo, from the tree that is fruitful and prolific for others we harvest nothing but the fruits of misery and disgrace.

This problem manifests as a question with a very short answer which is that we do not abide by the Constitution and have sufficed ourselves with democracy in name only. Now why is this answer correct regarding democracy but not the Islamic method? Moreover, why is democracy not responsible for the offences of the people but Islam is? This is a question to which others may have an answer—we do not.

Third: If, due to advances in civilization, Islam has lost its social status and the present age is the golden age of democracy which is accepted by the global majority and this will always be so, why, after the World War One, did some democratic societies turn their backs on this preferable method and choose the communist regime?

Everyday democracy looses a base and gives ground. Why has around half the world's population adopted communism in such a short time?

Is communism the next stage in the evolution of democracy just as democracy was the next stage in the evolution of previous regimes? Furthermore, is democracy, in itself, a stage in evolution?

In order to reach an answer to these questions, we must carry out extensive probes and debates on the issue which are beyond the scope of this article. We can however succinctly note the following:

When we realistically examine the democratic method that is currently implemented in civilized societies of the world and scrutinize its global rationale, we see that what this so-called advanced method has done is that it has taken away the individual aspect from the oppressive tyranny and unrestraint of the Age of Myths and has socialized it:

The injustice, oppression, and obstinacy of Alexanders and Genghis Khāns that were realized through the logic of power are now reenacted en masse by the powerful democratic and civilized nations of the world upon marginalized nations—with the difference that the tyranny and oppression of the past were ignorantly and blatantly performed and thus sooner awakened the desire for vengeance.

This had a more effective role in toppling the oppressive system. However, using technical and psychological principles, modern oppressors expertly execute their work in the veil of reviving truth and righteousness and spreading philanthropy and justice. Whenever a veil is torn and these oppressors become known to everyone, they continue their oppression in a different name: colonization, acquisition, protectorate, support, partnership, humanitarianism, donation, and the like.

Admonitory mementos of democracy from the age of colonization are still apparent in all countries in the Orient! There are still living witnesses such as Algeria, Congo, Korea, and Vietnam. Even now, the French government, "The torchbearer of freedom in the banquet of international freedom (!)", maintains that Algeria is part of France.[80]

Still, the logic of the great and powerful nations regarding the pleading of the oppressed in Algeria for justice is that the issue is internal and outside the jurisdiction of the interference of others.

---

[80] This article was written before the independence of Algeria. [Persian edition]

Ultimately, the results of the global movement of democracy may be summarized thus: democracy in the world may be divided into two categories. One is the group of great nations who are vanguards in matters of civilization (!) and despotic rule of all other nations.

They are sovereign owners of the lives, property and honor of other nations who can do anything they want. The other group consists of backwards democratic nations that are usually branded slaves of those who perform the most shameful of despotic rites in the garb of democracy and world-pleasing liberal laws.

Undoubtedly, a method with such an identity and nature, especially keeping in mind that it has abolished the most important pillar of humanity—spirituality—on the pretext that it has no enforcement mechanism, cannot be considered a stage in the evolution of humanity.

Regarding the aforementioned effects, communism is not much different from common democracy even though they have differences in the method of their world domination.

Calling communism evolution is even stranger because the advancement and evolution of a phenomenon is meaningless without passing through previous stages whereas we see that backward strata and even primitive nations who have never even heard of civilization or democracy welcome this method faster and more enthusiastically than others. Is the emergence of communism a leap of evolution?

The condition that the "dialectic materialist" philosophy specifies does not conform to it!

The truth is that if we regard the matter fairly, our opposers, who attack Islam with democracy, want only the immoderation, indulgence, and carnality from their freedom not social correction, security, and welfare. This is why we learn Western moral perversions so quickly and put them into practice so easily and why rectitude in executing laws that are in the interests of the nation is even rarer among us than the legendary phoenix.

On the other hand, those who support communism are usually underprivileged people who want to take their revenge upon the wealthy and give them a taste of their bitterness, abjectness, and destitution, come what may.

It is clear that such changes cannot be considered social or civil human evolution. The evolution that can be envisioned for individual tyranny (ancient tyranny) and social tyranny (the current method of powerful countries) is that humanity develop on the path of truth, both materially and spiritually, and that the logic of truth take the place of all other types of logic. And this is the method of Islam:

> *"Verily, the earth belongs to God; He bequeaths it to whom He wills among His servants. And the (good) end belongs to the righteous."*[81]

As we have said, this is a lengthy discussion and we will suffice with what has been said to prevent further diversion from our main aim. However, consider the preceding synopsis meticulously.

Point three

Is Islam Silent Regarding Government?

The third point is that the rules and regulations that are issued by a leader are generally alterable and depend upon expedience of the time and therefore they are not part of the sharī'ah; however, the issue of leadership and government is not thus.

Leadership is something that no society can do without regardless of the circumstances. All humans understand a society's need for a

---

[81] Sūrat al-A'rāf 7:128.

leader in even the smallest of societies. Thus, leadership is a constant and invariable natural decree. It is something by which all social methods—tyrannical or lawful, savage or civilized, great or small, even the family social unit—are supported.

Also, Islam, which is based upon nature, establishes humanity's god-given nature as the reference of the generality of its laws. Axiomatic truths never invalidate the laws of nature and will never challenge the credence of leadership, the necessity of which can even be understood by a child.

The fact that various aspects of humanity's social life require an administrator is a general truth understood through human nature. As previously mentioned, Qur'anic verses that base religion upon nature are sufficient in proving that leadership is an immutable religious issue; in other words, leadership is an article of the sharī'ah.

Furthermore, the Holy Prophet (S) personally headed the Islamic community. He would appoint supervisors for all aspects of the lives of Muslims, such as governors for cities, judges for settling disputes, missionaries and teachers for spreading the religion and educating the people, officials for gathering assets of the public treasury, and battle commanders. Historically, when he left Medina for a few days for a battle, he would appoint an overseer to govern the people in his absence.

After reviewing this tradition and the fact that according to the exact words of the Qur'an and the belief of the Prophet (S), Islam is global and eternal and has thousands of social and public aspects that require supervision, how can we believe that the Prophet (S) could refrain from addressing the issue of leadership?!

Is it possible that he explicate obvious life issues such as eating and drinking and insignificant matters that occur naturally such as excretion, giving hundreds of instructions regarding them, but turn a blind eye to the issue of leadership—which is the soul that keeps the society alive? Many verses in the Holy Qur'an verify this issue some of which are as follows:

> *"The Prophet is more worthy of the believers than they themselves are..."*[82]
>
> *"Verily your sovereigns are Allah and His Prophet and those who uphold ritual prayer and give alms while bowing down (in prayer)."*[83]
> *"O you who believe! Obey Allah and obey the Prophet and those among you with authority..."*[84]
> *"And some men and women of the believers are supervisors and sovereigns of the others; they enjoin to good and forbid from evil..."*[85]

Some have mistakenly translated "wilāyah" in these verses into friendship or aid. These people have done no more than strip the word of its true meaning.

Point four

The product of the foregoing discussion is that leadership is an element of the sharī'ah and thus, like other items of the sharī'ah, it must be kept alive in the Islamic society for all time. Of course, as such, the Muslim populous is responsible for upholding this office

---

[82] Sūrat al-Ahzāb 33:6.

[83] Sūrat al-Mā'idah 5:55. It is established that "those who uphold ritual prayer and give alms while bowing down in prayer" refers to Alī ibn Abī Tālib ('a) who gave away his ring to a poor person while bowing in ritual prayer. [trans.]

[84] Sūrat al-Nisā' 4:59.

[85] Sūrat al-Tawbah (or Barā'ah) 9:71.

although at any given time a limited number of people actually occupy the position of leadership.

Now we must see whether or not Islam has designated that individuals manage the society as they desire or see fit. Of course, it is evident that specific groups have been described in Islamic sharī'ah as having a limited amount of leadership and there is no controversy regarding these. For example, the leadership (guardianship) of a father towards his young children and the leadership (guidance) of all Muslims toward one another in enjoining good and forbidding evil are limited.

The Shī'ah believe that the Holy Prophet (S) chose Amīr al-Mu'minīn, 'Alī ibn Abī Tālib ('a), for this office—the office of Imamate—and after him, eleven of his noble descendants in succession.

In order to substantiate their belief, the Shī'ahs—as opposed to the Sunnīs who deny this fact—bring evidence of logic, many Qur'anic verses, and substantial traditions from numerous firsthand Sunnī and Shī'ah narrators. Having been said, citation of this extensive evidence is beyond the scope of this discussion and can be found in many other works.

Leadership in the Age of the Imām's Absence ['asr-e ghaybat-e imām]

It is important to say that this Shī'ah-specific belief does not mean that the Islamic society is left leaderless in the absence of an imām—such as the age in which we now live—to scatter and stray like a flock without a shepherd.

This is because we have reasons that validate the necessity for the office of supreme leadership and the necessity for appointing individuals to this position. It is clear that persons are separate from office and in the absence or death of an officeholder the office is not terminated.

How can one imagine the annulment of this office while it has been proven through natural foundations? Invalidation of this office would be invalidation of nature and invalidation of nature would be invalidation of the very existence of Islam.

In addition, there are many commandments regarding types of punishment in the sharī'ah—the perpetuation of which the Book and Tradition affirm. The leader is responsible for the execution of these laws. Nevertheless, leadership endures in the absence of an imām just as it exists in their presence.

Point five

Is leadership associated with all Muslims, just people ['udūl], or modern so-called jurisprudents [fuqahā]? At the advent of Islam, a person was named jurisprudent who knew all religious sciences consisting of principles, applications, and ethics not just applications as is currently popular.

Also, if the third case is so, does it belong to any jurisprudent with enough authority so as to become inviolable? Or does it belong to the most learned jurist? These issues cannot be covered in our current discussion and must be resolved in the field of jurisprudence.

In respect to the subject matter of this article, however, we can conclude that human nature affirms the need for leadership in any society in order to preserve its interests. Islam goes hand in hand with human nature. From these two premises it is deduced that a person who is foremost in religious piety, prudence, and knowledge of prevailing circumstances is chosen for this position. There is no doubt that ruling officials must be the elite of the society in wisdom.

Now we must attend to whether an Islamic society encompassing many regions, nations, and races—as it does today—must be guided under a single leader and government; ruled by various governments according to region and nationality; or ruled by several governments united under a central administration or something similar to the United Nations.

There is no decree in the Islamic sharī'ah regarding any of these and this is as it should be. This is because the sharī'ah can only guarantee invariable religious matters and the method of government may vary with the changes brought by the advancement of civilization.

Therefore, we can say that in every era the method of Islamic government must be selected using the following articles of Islamic sharī'ah:

Muslims must do their utmost to achieve unity;

Every Muslim must observe the interests of Islam and Muslims;

The boundaries of the Islamic nation are beliefs not natural or conventional borderlines.

An important issue here is that an Islamic leader or government may never transgress, regardless of administrative methods, the Traditions of the Holy Prophet (S), and his methods of leadership must be put into practice in the Islamic society.

In view of the fact that leadership is an invariable in the Islamic society and is thus an article of the sharī'ah, God must determine how it is carried out. God, the Almighty, has endorsed the Prophet's (S) methods in many Qur'anic verses and has not given Muslims leave to deviate from them.

"Surely you have in the Prophet of Allah a fine example..."[86]

There are many traditions from the Ahl al-Bayt in this regard. A reliable hadīth from the Prophet (S) states that:
"Those who deviate from my Tradition are not part of me (my nation)."

Explication of the traditions of the Holy Prophet (S) requires a separate discussion; however, the following is a short outline of the matter.

First, in Islam there is no distinction other than piety, and all class distinctions are null and void. Even though social classes such as master and servant, employee and employer, and men and women are preserved, everyone is equal and there is no discrimination. We must only unquestionably bow down before the magnificence of God. Consider the following Qur'anic verses:

> *"O People of the Scripture! Come now to a word common among us and among you; that we not worship any save Allah and not associate aught with him and that none of us take others as lords beside Allah. And if they turn away, say: Bear witness that surely we are Muslims (those who surrender to God's will)."*[87]
>
> *"O people! Verily, we have created you from a man and a woman and have made you into various races and tribes so*

---

[86] Sūrat al-Aḥzāb 33:21.

[87] Sūrat Āl 'Imrān 3:64.

that you may know one another. Surely the noblest among you before Allah is the most God-fearing. Indeed Allah is All-knowing, All-aware."[88]

Second, everyone is completely equal before the law and not even the least bit of exception is made. Note the following verse:

"(Honor before Allah) neither abides by your desires nor the desires of the People of the Scripture; whosoever does evil will be requited accordingly."[89]

Third, decrees issued by the leader are issued by council and in the interests of Islam and Muslims.

"And consult with them in current affairs. After you make your decision put your trust in Allah. Verily, Allah loves those who put their trust in Him."[90]

It is plain to see that this holy tradition cannot lead to disadvantage in any society and thus it is immutable—a constant ruling of human nature that Islam endorses.

In addition, this tradition itself is derived from the performance of the Holy Prophet (S) and all acts of the Prophet (S) are executable.[91]

---

[88] Sūrat al-Hujurāt 49:13.

[89] Sūrat al-Nisā' 4:123.

[90] Sūrat Āl 'Imrān 3:159.

[91] Extracted from "Marja'iyyah wa Rawhāniyyah".

Discourse Three: The Motive behind Creation

From the first days of life, using their God-given intellects, humans inevitably discover the existence of a series of unknowns. Because of our natural inquisitiveness, we strive to clarify these obscurities. We ask ourselves: does this manifest world have a creator? If there is a creator, what was the motive for creation? If the world has indeed been created, are we charged with responsibilities?

Clearly, if we give a positive answer to any of these questions, a series of subsidiary questions come up regarding the properties of the Creator and the manner and effects of its existence. As we have said, the God-given nature of humankind desires a logical and decisive answer to these questions.

Without a doubt, the matter at hand is one of the most elementary and prominent issues faced by human nature. The human self understands the need to rationally and conclusively solve this problem in the first stages of life.

Analysis of the Question

Certainly that which compels us to inquire about the motive and aim of creation is that we perform social and rational tasks in order to achieve suitable and worthwhile aims. We eat to satisfy our hunger; drink to slake our thirst; clothe ourselves to protect our bodies against heat and cold; build houses in which to reside; speak in order to communicate what is in our minds; etc.

In the things that are done intentionally and thoughtfully, humans—and any intelligent being for that matter—have a motive and aim.

We do not do things that have no benefit whatsoever. By observing intents in our voluntary actions and generalizing our mentality to all intelligent agents we are faced with the following question: what is the motive of the Creator, who is an intelligent agent, for creating the world?

But then, can this amount of observation and generalization guarantee the correctness of this question? Can we extend a relationship or property found in several cases to all cases? The answer is no, and the only definitive solution is through analysis of the meaning of 'motive' because it is not possible to use inductive reasoning or empirical study.

As stated in the previous example, we attain the aim of satiation through eating. Satiation is related to eating because it is the result of this action. By entering the body, food activates the digestive system and frees us of the need for more food. Thus, the body's food requirements are met and we become full which is an effect of eating.

Eating is a special process that starts with us and ends in satiation. Eating also is related to us as the agent in that we do not have the necessary materials within ourselves to go on living without nourishment. In order to preserve our lives, we are equipped with faculties with which the body may absorb necessary nutrition.

When our semi-intelligent internal faculties feel the need, through natural mechanisms they force us to procure necessary nutrition and deal with our existential weakness. Therefore, just as satiety is related to eating, in another way it is related to us.

It is a perfection that completes our existential weakness, resolves our needs, and with its manifestation upon our inner faculties, it forces us to act to get what we need to complete ourselves.

By examining each of our innumerable volitional actions such as drinking, sitting down, standing up, talking, listening, going, coming, etc., the same characteristics that we found by inspecting eating will be revealed–even among actions that are apparently completely aimless.

After careful consideration it becomes clear that we do not perform actions that give us no benefit. When we undertake actions with no motive other than philanthropy, such as giving charity, we are in truth fulfilling our emotional desires and relieving the inner sorrow caused by empathy with the poor and so on.

Therefore, we can conclude that, in general, the motive for a volitional act is an appropriate effect lying within the result of the action and is a perfection that rectifies a fault in the agent and completes it.

Purpose in all Elements of Existence

Even though at first we supposed that motives and aims are specific to agents that are equipped with intelligence and free will, upon closer examination we see that all the effects and properties with which we proved the existence of "motives" for volitional acts and agents also exist in natural actions and agents.

Because, like volitional agents, every natural agent or material phenomenon is equipped with faculties that are used to relieve their existential needs. By performing their specific acts, they resolve their needs and faults thus perfecting themselves. Finally, the effect of their actions is directly and systematically related to the action and themselves as well.

This is the same in voluntary acts; therefore, intelligence is not in the least related to the realization of the result and its relationship with the act or agent.

Even though we name this issue "motive", which occurs in respect to the actions of living intelligent individuals with free will and refrain from using this term for other natural acts, instead using "result" or figuratively utilizing the term "motive", the end result is the same in both terms. What a natural agent does in the dark recesses of nature, a living human may do using the light of intellect without a change in the aforementioned relationships.

Hence, "motive" is common to all elements of the world of creation and as long as it rules over all general laws, such as the law of causality, no act will be performed without aim and no agent is free of a purpose and ideal.

All beings of every kind, whether human, insect, apple tree, wheat, hunk of iron, molecule of oxygen, and so on, adapt to the external environment using their active faculties, harmonize with active elements in their environment, and perform specific actions in order to achieve their evolutional or useful aims.

When this specific action is completed, it is substituted with the result of the action, the natural or intentional desire is fulfilled, and the perfection it sought is annexed to its being.

General types that exist all over the world, such as humans, horses, apple trees, etc. are the same. With the specific acts of their type, they strive to achieve their aims and ideals and by achieving them, they remedy their genetic faults and keep on existing. This same thing can be said of the entirety of world components, among which an indubitable relationship exists.

Basically, any movement that occurs has a direction. This movement is always intermediary and joins one thing or direction to the other. The direction desired by the object is the result and motive that completes the deficiency and aspiration of the agent.

When it is achieved, movement ceases. That is, it gains a static state in relation to its previous state. Even though on a different perspective, this static state is a new movement that aims at a new result and motive.

We cannot imagine the realization of a movement that does not have a direction or that has a direction but the "direction" has no relationship with the movement and is realized solely through happenstance. Or that a force creates movement without being causally related to it. Or that even though the force has a relationship with the movement, its relationship with the result of the movement is accidental.

The awe-inspiring order that is seen throughout the world in causes and agents and the general incontrovertible laws that impartially govern the world of existence demonstrate that this world or existence was not accidental.

A scientist has said that the assumption that ten different elements combine by chance in a certain arrangement is one in ten billion. Causeless occurrence of one possibility out of ten billion minus one other possibilities cannot be considered anything but following of baseless and unreasonable notions.

The intellectual thought and natural reason of humankind can never deny the relationship between actions, agents, and the result of actions, for this would debunk all human scientific reasoning and self-evident thoughts.

Universal motive and ideal

There is an authentic relationship between the components of the wide world of existence, from the tiniest particle to the greatest collection of celestial objects and wondrous galaxies. According to scientific and philosophical theories, this relationship makes the world an integrated unit that transforms and evolves in a general direction.

According to the irrefutable aforementioned theory, when the world reaches the boundary between movement and target, the objective replaces its movement and the turbulent evanescent world transforms into a calm and stable place.

The world of tomorrow will doubtless be calm and stable in relation to the world of today. The deficiencies of this world will be resolved, the world perfected, and all potentialities realized. Yet will this stability and perfection be relative to the current conditions of the world or will it reach ultimate inner stability and the end of evolution?

In other words, will the general movement of the world—which is substituted with its goal after reaching it—gain relative calm and stability like current lesser movements, even though it is still moving and evolving in other dimensions or will the future world attain true internal perfection and stability where evolution—the existential role of all phenomena—is completely terminated; where the compasses of existence reach the starting point, stop turning, and leave a permanent and perfect circle; where, in colloquial terms, the world becomes four dimensional; and where phenomena no longer revolve around time?

The conclusion of this synopsis is compact, complex, and esoteric. There is a stable and complete world in the wake of this mobile and incomplete world. There is a calm stopping-place towards which the caravan of existence strives with all its might and one day, all these wayfarers will realize the result of their endeavors there.

Of course, on the path of understanding this conclusion we are faced with the preceding question and many more. The gloom of these obscurities is far-ranging. In reality, these mysteries form a series of discussions that may be considered the most complex and profound general discussions in philosophy.

This is because general theories that do not have tangible support are difficult to understand. From the first time we opened our eyes we have only seen material things. We are traveling on a path that cannot be retraced. Those who leave this world have gone beyond the bounds of our knowledge.

Nonetheless, by relying on positive reasons based on logical and incontestable premises, critical philosophic discussions answer the bulk of these questions. The theory that "the mobile and fleeting world has a stable and fixed objective" conforms to the issue of eschatological truths imparted upon us through revelations upon religious leaders.

The Motive of God in Creating the World

Therefore, "motive and aim" is related to action in that it transforms active movement into immobility and tranquility and is related to the agent in that it transforms the existential defect of the agent into perfection. In addition, according to logical discussions regarding the Attributes of the Creator of the world, His Pure Essence is Absolute Perfection and contains no defect or need.

By merging these two theories, we can hypothesize and prove a motive for the acts of the Lord of the world. If questions such as "What is the motive behind creation?" and "Why did God create beings external to Himself?" mean "What are the aims of God's actions?" then the "action motive" of this deficient world is a perfect one. However, such questions are erroneous if they mean: "What defect does God resolve within Himself by creation and what perfection or benefit does He desire?"

The answer that is given for the issue of motive in religious discourses is the same as what was discussed above: "The motive of God, the Almighty, in creating the world is bringing benefit to others, not to Himself."

In conclusion, we must note that a motive is possible only when the action or both agent and action have a deficiency that is resolvable through the motive. Therefore, if we presuppose the existence of an act (i.e. creation) that has no resolvable deficiencies—such as, in philosophical terms, an abstract—our premise would be invalid.

Indeed, philosophers have found through careful analyses that the motive of an act is perfection of the act and the motive of an agent is perfection of the agent. To conclude, sometimes acts are gradual and perfection is annexed to them at the end and sometimes they are instantaneous and abstracted from materiality and movement. In this case, the reality of the act is the act and its perfection and motive.

Moreover, the agent is sometimes flawed, attaining its perfection after its act, and sometimes it is perfect; therefore, it is the agent and the motive and aim. Thus, the motive of God in creating the world is His own Essence and the aim of His act, i.e. this imperfect world, is a more complete world. The aim of a more complete world is an even more complete world. As for the aim of the creation of a perfect creature, it is the creature itself.[92]

---

[92] From the quarterly, "Maktab-e Tashayyu'".

Discourse Four: The Role of the Supernatural in Society

Some discourses have been with us from ancient times and still have a place within our thoughts; such as "the effects of destiny and decree" and "the effects of the unseen world".

Admittedly, we cannot say that all inner productions that we call "thought" are made up of right materials and correct formulas or that they have good effects on our lives because in the process of our daily lives we constantly encounter many mistakes and endeavor to correct them. We even find faults in our corrections and strive to put them right.

This point impresses upon us the fact that we are not immune to error in the process of our lives and utilization of our existential resources to attain bliss.

Also, philosophically speaking, if humans were insusceptible to error and completely realistic, we could never achieve existential evolution. Thus, our movement would be blocked, our situation would be fixed, and creation would come to the end of its journey in the second moment of existence.

Also, if all human thoughts were erroneous and utterly unrealistic, life would not conform to the external world and it would be destroyed in the first moments as well. One cannot conceive that the thoughts of humankind or other sapient races are completely faulty or that their conformity to the external world is accidental.

Human evolution is caused by the formation of correct and incorrect thoughts. In other words, evolution exists because of the cline of realism ranging between the positive and the negative. By virtue of this cline, we are drawn toward our ultimate goal.

With our inborn disposition toward gaining knowledge and examining the unknown, we continually discover our errors. We deem our thinking formulas faulty and inadequate in their correspondence with the external world and note in our minds the obscurities we encounter each day. With restored spirit we review and revise our past thoughts, posit novel theories, reach newer conclusions and more expressive views, and make headway in spiritual and material matters of life.

After thinking about this short discussion, the first thing we realize is that humans are perpetually faced with many obscurities upon which our lives depend. What we know of the causes and conditions of our spiritual and material lives is always much less than our ignorance.

In fact the ratio cannot be calculated because there can be no ratio between a finite and infinite amount. Regardless, human life depends upon all its known and unknown causes and conditions and the system that reigns over the whole of creation also governs humanity as opposed to the compact system that humans perceive using their infinitesimal knowledge.

The Relationship Between Life and the Supernatural [māwarā' al- tabī'ah]

Causes and conditions that hide behind the veil of human ignorance are called "the unseen or supernatural" [ghayb or māwarā' al-tabī'ah]. If a series of knowns and unknowns are combined, they would still be veiled and invisible. All that we know of the supernatural world is the existence of a veil and that there is something behind it that is not unrelated to our lives.

Humans cannot disregard the fact that our lives are related to the unseen nor can we content ourselves with only causes and conditions that are known to us.

Even those who ridicule belief in the unseen and supernatural as a superstitious religious belief and insipid relic from the Age of Myths pragmatically accept and are humbled by this truth. In the process of life, they are not exempt from the effects of supernatural causes and cannot be nonchalant about unexpected incidents.

Even so, faithfulness to the existence of unseen effects does not mean that one should give up the effects of knowledge and devices at hand, awaiting supernatural aid. In truth, this is sacrifice of knowledge in favor of the unknown—something that reason cannot sanction.

In fact, our realist mechanism that notifies us of the unknown behind the veil also informs us of the effects of what we know and forces us to use them.

Divine religions invite us to believe in the unseen and supernatural and also endorse the products of work and toil in our lives. The Qur'an repeatedly bids us to believe in unseen effects. In regard to religious calls, such as the invitation of Prophet Noah ('a), the Qur'an states:

"And that humans have nothing save what they make an effort for."[93]

Moreover, regarding the Day of Judgment, the Qur'an declares:

"It is a day in which humans remember their works."[94]

Law Requires Executive Support

Humans can only achieve perfection and bliss if they form societies and cooperate in performing myriad vital activities that one person cannot do alone.

This entails the need of social members for rules and regulations that can protect the rights of individuals and determine the share of each person in the benefits of society. That is, people must work as they are able and barter the results of their endeavors, such that each person should benefit from others to the extent of their work value and such that power and weakness not cause injustice and persecution.

These laws can only be effective if there are penal codes to warn against offence and encourage obedience. Also, a governing power must reign over the society with justice and fairness to guarantee the execution of these laws.

This aspiration may only be realized if the executive power is notified of the crime and has the power to punish the criminal. However, if a crime is committed such that no one is alerted—which is very common—there will be no obstacles in the way of its perpetration.

Also, if the government lacks the power to punish criminals or if it

---

[93] Sūrat al-Najm 53:39.

[94] Sūrat al-Nāzi'āt 79:35.

is negligent, criminal offence and infringement of rights will become prevalent. This is because humans have a propensity for greed and make use of everything in their power to gain personal interests–even if it causes disadvantage to others.

The greatest tragedy occurs when all powers are focused in the executive and ruling body. When this unparalleled power considers the people weak and no power remains among the people to regulate its power, its will shall reign absolutely over the affairs of the people. History is brimming with stories of tyrants and oppressors that exploit and abuse the people. The world is still rife with such cases.

Consequently, even if just laws are formulated and severe penal codes are developed, crimes and offences cannot be obstructed save through virtuous human morality.

We must not be fooled by the order and justice that exist in some advanced nations. We should not assume that rules and regulations necessarily bring about justice because the mentality of these nations is fundamentally different from others.

They think socially and consider their interest and loss the interest and loss of the society; however, they too exploit weak nations and subjugate backward countries.

These same people who give the appearance of justice, deal with subjugated countries in the same way that tyrants of old behaved toward their own people with the difference that, in modern times, individual dictators have been replaced with societies and some words have lost their original meanings becoming the exact opposite.

Liberty, honor, justice, and virtue are attributed to things that represent bondage, abasement, oppression, and vice.

Thus, laws are not safe from violation unless they are based upon virtuous human moralities. Also, morality cannot guaranty human bliss and impel people to act suitably unless it relies upon monotheism [tawhīd].

This means that a person has faith that the vast world, of which humans are also a part, has only one God that exists in all places and all times. Nothing is hidden from His knowledge and nothing can overcome His power. He has created all things according to the most complete system—not because He needs them.

In the end, He will return everyone to Himself. He rewards the righteous well and chastises the evil; the righteous will forever remain in beatitude and the evildoers in torment.

It is evident that if morals are based upon such beliefs, no grief or sorrow will remain except the anxiousness associated with being heedful of the Lord's approval. Thus, devotion to God will prohibit violation of laws and committing prohibited [harām] acts. If morality does not stem from such belief, no

aim will remain for humans but hedonism—pursuit of ephemeral worldly pleasures.

As a result, they will limit themselves only to the extent that keeps the society in existence or causes others to praise them, so that after death their good name remains embossed upon the pages of history.

However, the laudation of the people only pertains to things of which they are aware. Therefore, this cannot be grounds for performing good acts and abandoning evils in secret and far from the eyes of people.

However, perpetuation of one's good name and taking joy from it, which usually involves patriotic selflessness and self-sacrifice in favor of the government, for a person who does not believe in life after death is nothing but a superstitious fallacy that fades with the slightest of consideration. Since, after annihilation, how can anyone take pleasure in the fact that their name is remembered fondly, and what sensible persons would turn their backs on life and bliss for the pleasure of others without any personal benefit?

Therefore, these things neither have any value in comparison with tawhīd and belief in God, nor can they take their place in preventing sins and crimes.

The Role of the Resurrection [ma'ād]95 in our lives

Those who are unfamiliar with Islamic teachings and examine Islamic issues separately from Islamic teachings say: what effect does faith in the Resurrection and Judgment Day have on morality and human actions?

What major aspect of the human society is corrected by it? There is no doubt that the human society lives through the actions of people and the actions of people are motivated by a feeling of need and understanding necessities of life.

Due to the extreme affection humans have for survival and its requisites, we enjoy gaining anything that positively influences this aspiration. We obtain the spirit to work by envisioning life and the advantages we may gain and therefore we indefatigably continue our endeavors.

Those actions that are successful inspire intensity, celerity, and determination in human endeavors. Because of this, from the time society first started its progression, every moment it accelerates and finds newer and more profound activities.

It is evident that though thoughts of death and otherworldly life may not cripple individual resolve and put an end to the escalating development of the society, they have no effect in the process of life and cannot give it new spirit.

To answer this delusive argument, we must say that there is no doubt that divine religions to some extent base the system of their call on individual duty and requital on the Day of Judgment.

Especially, among these, the holy religion of Islam founds its call upon the principles of tawḥīd, nubuwwah (prophethood), and maʿād, such that a person who doubts maʿād—like a person who does not accept tawḥīd or nubuwwah—is outside the boundaries of the religion and the circle of Muslims. This makes obvious the importance Islam puts on belief in the Resurrection—it is side by side with tawḥīd and nubuwwah.

Considering that Islam has established "revival of human nature" and "creating a natural human" as the ideal for education and edification, we realize that Islam views belief in maʿād as one of the critical pillars of the natural human, without which the true human constitution is like a soulless body that has lost the source of all human bliss and virtue.

Moreover, it is certain that Islamic teachings and laws are not dry and soulless items that have been formulated to occupy the people or produce lackluster devoutness and imitation.

Rather, they are a completely systematic series of articles of faith, and spiritual and practical issues that have been formed as humanity's life plan and have taken into account the genetic requirements of human beings. The following Qur'anic verses bear witness to this fact:

> *"O believers! When Allah and the Prophet invite you (to faith and good deeds), accept so you attain eternal life."*[95]
> *"So set thy face to the pure religion of Allah; this is the fitrah (nature) upon which Allah has created humankind..."*[96]

Therefore, Islam is not different from civil laws in advanced societies

---

[95] Sūrat al-Anfāl 8:24.

[96] Sūrat al-Rūm 30:30.

that have been formulated to secure their necessities for survival. However, the perennial difference between the divine religion and human-formed laws is that civil laws consider human life as fleeting material existence and base laws upon the desires of the society's majority.

On the other hand, Islam considers human life an eternal one that does not end upon death such that our beatitude or torment in the next world is relative to the rectitude or corruption of our deeds in this world. This is why Islam designs a logical life plan for humans, not a self-indulgent one.

In the view of civil laws, the desires of the majority is law and absolutely binding; however, according to the divine religion, only right and rational laws are binding, irrespective of whether or not they accommodate the inclinations and sentiments of the majority.

The divine religion declares that the innate insight of the natural human—one free of superstitions and caprice—validates ma'ād. Thus, it sees itself as having an eternal life that must be forever lived with reason, never neglecting this apparatus of realism.

As opposed to the materialistic person, ignorant of the Origin and Resurrection with no logic but the shared logic of animals and no wish but mastery of material pleasures, and faith in ma'ād has a clear effect on all aspects of thought, spiritual morality, and social and individual acts of the realistic natural human.

The Effect on Thought and Morality

In this manner, with the eyes of realism, humans see everything—themselves in particular—the way they really are. They see themselves as limited transitory creatures that are part of this impermanent world.

All components of the world collectively make up a convoy that is advancing day and night toward an eternal world, continually pushed by the hands of creation (the efficient cause) and pulled by the aim and result of creation (the day of ma'ād).

This is why the realistic method of thought mitigates the natural human's inner sentiments and emotions and limits them in a manner appropriate to such an objective and destination.

Persons who see themselves dependent, due to their needs, upon the passing world where they are like a straw in the grip of the waves of this terrible deluge, rising and falling along toward a general destination, can no longer accept the ignorant human self-conceit and insurrection. They can no longer submit to sensualism and hedonism.

They will no longer bind themselves by exertions to gain more provisions necessary for their short stay in this world, which would make of them a will-less automaton. As a result, a significant bulk of their social and individual conflicts would be resolved.

No more will they see their selfless endeavors that necessitate loss of life and property a waste because, even if they lose their lives on the path of benevolence, all they would lose is the short vexing worldly life but they would have their eternal life, there realizing the lofty fruits of their sacrifice and attaining endless happiness.

For their sacrifices, they will no longer need to find a series of beguiling and corrupting superstitions like materialism. They do not need to be brainwashed into believing that sacrificing one's life for social sanctities—such as liberty, law, and country—gives a person an everlasting good name by which they may gain glorious eternal life, for if we truly cease to exist after death, life and glory after death are nothing but a myth.

Here, the unfoundedness of the criticism's culmination is made clear. Contemplating death and the afterlife does not take away the zest for work. The human enthusiasm for work is a result of need and by envisioning ma'ād our need does not go away.

A proof of this is that the Muslims of the advent of Islam, who better followed religious teachings and whose hearts sparkled more than any other time with the vision of ma'ād, had an awesome amount of social activity that cannot even be compared with later Muslim activity. Indeed, envisioning ma'ād stops us from overindulgence in materialism and sensuality and self-destruction for the sake of myths and delusions.

Another benefit of ma'ād is that it vitalizes the human soul with faith. Such persons know that if they are oppressed and cannot reclaim their rights, a day will come when they will be requited and their rights restored—a day when they will be highly commended for their every good deed.

Hence, those believing in ma'ād know that their deeds are constantly being monitored and that the flesh and soul of their deeds—both hidden and visible—are manifest before the Omniscient God.

They know that a day will come when our accounts will be reckoned with utmost care. This belief does something to a person that one hundred thousand undercover detectives and intelligence officers cannot do because they all work on the outside whereas this belief is an internal sentinel from which no secret may be concealed.

Analysis of Belief [i'tiqād], Disposition [akhlāq], and Action ['mal]

We know the literal meaning of the words "belief" [i'tiqād], "disposition" [akhlāq], and "action" ['mal] and in the process of our lives, we find many senses for each of them. Although, many people may not understand these concepts through these particular words, they do nonetheless understand these concepts, using other words to signify them.

A belief is a form of thought in which a person has faith and affirmation. For instance, we may say, "The solar year cycle revolves around the seasons of spring, summer, autumn, and winter", "Genghis Khān was a bloodthirsty man", and as an example for the beliefs of Muslims, "The world of existence and everything within it is the creation of God" and "The Creator of the world is One and everything that exists is from Him".

A disposition is a form of discernment that resides within a person manifesting at appropriate times, compelling motivation to act. For example, brave persons possess an inner property that causes them to get excited, display themselves, and challenge or defend; in contrast, cravens possess an inner property that causes them to lose their nerve and run away when faced with danger.

Therefore, these properties—braveness and fear—are two human temperaments one of which is desirable and the other undesirable. Usually, a person possesses one of these two attributes affecting their behavior.

Even so, sometimes—especially when very young—it happens that the inner slate of a person is clear of both characteristics and neither of them has a consistent impression. Therefore, in the event of certain or probable danger, the individual's condition is not clear such that sometimes the person may stand firm against terrible threats and at other times may make a break for it.

An "action" is a series of movements and pauses or gestures that a person willfully performs upon matter to reach an objective. Naturally, an act may be a combination of thousands of gestures or movements and thus it is not a true unit. However, the singularity of the objective unifies these motions and therefore we consider an action singular.

If we examine one instance of eating, which we consider a single unit or act, we easily realize that eating one morsel requires many gestures of the hands, head, mouth, throat, stomach, etc. which a person needs to sate the fires of the appetite. We use satiation as a measure to expertly regulate the movements of our organs and signify a unified name for it. We intend the collection of these motions and call our act "eating a meal".

When an action is closely related with matter and body parts, it is called an "external act". However, an "internal act" is an activity that is performed within the self, managing innumerable gesticulations and consolidating them though the unity of purpose and stimulation of the will. Such acts are different from external acts, even though it also consists of a multitude of movements.

Clearly, all external acts with their specific names are subject to change. By way of illustration, primeval humans ate raw food but then ate cooked food when they learned more about how to live.

Also, once upon a time, they ate food with their hands, but now they eat with spoons and forks. In all these instances the act is eating food. However, our internal acts, meaning managing the myriad movements of various body parts and unifying them through a chosen aim and instigation of the will, are invariable and unalterable.

Doubtless, when eating, if a person—whether civilized or savage—forgets the unified objective or the process of movements and pauses related to it, in that instant, they will be unable to eat and the relevant gestures will fragment and disintegrate.

Appearance of Disposition and its Relation to Faith and Action

Considering our analysis of "eating", it is clear that regarding all actions, the aim of the act, e.g. satiation, manifests through feelings intermingled with human reason. First, we investigate how to attain the aim—such as the internal and external causes and obstacles.

Then, we consider the nature of our goal and its unity, discern and record suitable gestures for each body part and picture each member in its necessary place—e.g. the hand must perform a task before the mouth, and the mouth before the throat. Finally, we establish the necessary order among the movements and apply our will to perform the action.

As you can see, internal acts require more components and operations than external acts. Even so, in my opinion internal acts, like external ones, gain unity through a unified objective. We call these unified acts "contemplation", "decision-making", and "preparing for action".

Even more amazing is that in every great and small act that we carry out, maybe thousands of times a day, we repeat the internal act. The difference of each act with the previous one is that the more we perform external acts, internal acts become easier and vice versa. Because with repetition the internal operation is facilitated and previous experience is not lost.

When considering an action that has never been carried out nor even thought of, one realizes how hard it is to do that act because the new internal operations must be performed without any preparation and the performer will have to strive hard to formulate the preliminaries.

However, after doing it once, the performer will not have to go through the hardships of the first instance since the necessities and obstructions have already been contemplated, verifying the necessities and invalidating the obstructions, and the operations of the action will not have to be authored and systematized anew.

The action is no longer arduous. A brief reference to previous experience will solve the problem; thus, the more an action is repeated, the less hardship is experienced in new decisions.

By repeating an action, we finally attain a state where the form of the internal act is constantly present in our minds and manifests and provides results with the slightest of thought, as in breathing, using the eyes to see, and speaking to convey intentions.

Indeed, sometimes having faith in something does exactly what repetition does. Regardless, we name such emotion-related mental statements "disposition" and for this reason it is said, "Disposition is the internalization of actions and existence of fixed mental forms such that their related actions are accomplished easily."

For this reason, the disposition is formed though repetition, inculcation of the goodness of the act or both. Sometimes a coward may be faced with one peril after another such that danger loses its significance causing them even to throw themselves in death's way because of powerful suggestion and stimulation.

In reality, the effect of repetition on emergence of the disposition is related to the effect of belief. Repetition imprints on the mind the feasibility, rectitude, and expediency of the action so as to concretize its viability and attractiveness and deter all opposing thoughts such that a horrific conceptualization of the most dangerous of predators may cause a person to completely forget escape and paralyze him of her when encountering such a beast.

Moreover, if an opposing thought enters one's mind in such cases, it will manifest as an illusory and ineffective idea. For instance, a person addicted to opium or alcohol cannot give up his ruinous desires, even though he knows the physical and spiritual harm of his predicament, due to a weak will.

Consequently, disposition fills the gap between knowledge and action. In other words, on one side it borders on belief and on the other side it borders on action. To put it another way, a disposition is an established and internalized drive-producing belief in the rectitude and feasibility of an action.

If a person gives up a belief for whatever reason, they will also lose its relevant disposition. Also, if a person is unable to perform an action or acts in an opposite manner, the relevant disposition will slowly degenerate until completely erased.

Therefore, on one side "disposition" ensures "action" and on the other it ensures "belief and faith". Those who do not believe in the necessity to defend their sanctities will never possess the virtue of bravery. Furthermore, those who allow others to do whatever they want with them, dishonoring and degrading them in any way, will not be able to defend themselves and will forever be deprived of bravery.

That it is sometimes said, "Disposition does not guarantee implementation in society" is inapplicable because the guarantee for implementation of every matter is suited to that particular matter.

In this case, with the direct relationship between disposition and belief, on the one hand, and suitable action, on the other, we can say that the success of disposition may be guaranteed in the best possible manner. By strengthening belief and supervising actions, disposition can be protected and maintained.

One cannot assume that disposition does not guarantee implementation in a society where the people live in an environment of appropriate actions and have faith that their happiness derives from those actions?

Disposition Requires Practical Support

We clearly see that in civilized countries, where national laws are implemented completely and people are aware of and bound by their social responsibilities, the disposition related to laws are established and predominant.

People do not lie to each other; they do not abuse one another; they do not betray their society; they are not xenophilic, treasonous, or uncontrolled; and they do not revile national laws and sancties. This is because, on the one hand, they perform their legal responsibilities and, on the other hand, the suitable environment and unflagging propaganda of the government supports this behavior.

When occasionally an undesirable disposition manifests somewhere, it is anomalous. With the existence of civilization, unlawful acts are uncommonly committed.

However, governments cannot establish a disposition in the society, such as eschewing sexual intemperance, deviant behavior, and drinking alcohol, that does not have practical support, even with powerful propaganda. In fact, even weakening such behaviors may prove problematic and every day will bring a new defeat to the powerful propaganda machines.

It is evident that in societies where, for instance, alcohol is given to swaddled babies and preschool children instead of drinkable water or where millions of bottles of alcohol are produced and imbibed, even the most powerful and comprehensive publicity would be considered nothing but idle prattle.

In these societies, the answer to thousands of public campaigns is one verse describing wine from poets such as Shakespeare and Lamartine.

The reason that the civilized world has become entangled in moral degradation is not that moral behavior is devoid of a guarantee for its implementation. It is because current laws have not been devised to conform to virtuous human behavior.

In a nutshell, in its emergence and persistence, disposition is closely related to faith and belief, on the one side, and action, on the other, and the continuance or degradation of these is directly related to disposition.

Now we must see whether or not actions have the same relationship with and dependence on belief and disposition, and whether belief and faith also have a similar relation with disposition and action. Is their relationship and dependence similar to that of three equal siblings or that of parents and their children?

Moreover, to what extent does Islam observe and give credence to these relationships in its laws? What are the views of other social methods in this regard? These are questions that may be answered in short using the preceding discussion.[97]

---

[97] From the quarterly, "Maktab-e Tashayyu'" and also the journal, "Kitab-e Fasl".

Discourse Five: Is Islam Still Practicable Today?

Some ask if Islam can govern the human world and answer current needs in the light of modern circumstances and staggering advancements. They maintain that it is time for humankind, which delves into the deepest reaches of space and masters the stars, to throw aside antiquated religious ideas, select a new method for its glorious life, and focus its thought and will on expanding its praiseworthy triumphs.

Are all Issues Subject to Change?

We must first note that even though we naturally like new things more than old ones, this is not true in all cases, and we cannot apply this method everywhere.

For instance, we cannot say that 2×2=4, which humans have used for thousands of years, is now old and must be thrown away. We cannot say that social life, which until now has been established among humans, is antiquated and a new plan must be designed where people live solitary lives.

We cannot say civil law, which greatly suppresses individual freedom, is passé and has exhausted the people's patience, or that, in an age that humanity has mastered space and sends out probes to explore the galaxy; we must open new paths and free ourselves of laws, lawmakers, and law-enforcers.

There is no need to explain how baseless and absurd these statements are. Fundamentally, oldness and newness only pertain to phenomena that are liable to change—things that have the capacity to transform and evolve. For instance, an individual that is one day happy and full of joy may encounter hardships the next day and become sad and dejected.

Therefore, in discussions associated with natural requirements that aim at realism and examine genuine world laws—one of which is whether Islam can direct the human world in the current run of affairs—one must not engage in such poetical thoughts spinning stories of old and new.

Every Statement and Every Detail has its Proper Place

As to whether or not Islam can direct humanity in the current state of affairs, the question itself is not free of peculiarity. In fact, it is quite surprising upon bearing in mind the true nature of Islam upon which the Qur'anic call is based. "Islam" is the path that the system of humanity and the world's creation reveals.

"Islam" is the code and practice that harmonizes with the singular human nature. Because of its complete consonance with human spiritual and corporeal nature, it provides for and resolves the true needs of humans as opposed to their fancies or desires.

Obviously, the nature and make-up of humankind will remain the same as long as humans are human. Regardless of the time, place, and condition people live in, they will retain their nature. Nature sets its path before us, whether we chose to follow it or steer clear of it.

Hence in truth, the underlying meaning of this question is: if humanity follows the path shown by its nature, will it find happiness and attain its natural aspirations? For instance, if a tree keeps to its natural course—for which it is naturally equipped—will it reach the desired destination of its nature? Clearly such questions are self-evident and skepticism is meaningless in this regard.

Islam is the path of primordial nature, which is perpetually the true course of humankind. It does not vary in different conditions. The aspiration of nature—as opposed to sentimental and irrational desires—are the true desires of the human race and the final destination of human nature is the abode and journey's end of human happiness and beatitude.

In the Honorable Qur'an, God, the Almighty, declares:

> "So set thy face toward the pure religion; it is in accordance with the nature [fitrah] of God upon which He has formed the nature of humankind. There is no alteration in the creation of God. This is the enduring (and true) religion; however, most humans do not know."[98]

Turn towards and accept the religion, which is the religion that is the special divine genesis upon which Allah has created people, with resolution and moderation. There is no change in the creation of Allah—it is immutable. This is the religion that can manage the lives of people.

A short explanation: As it is manifest and tangible to us, the various types of beings in the world of creation each have a specific life or

---

[98] Sūrat al-Rūm 30:30.

existence and a definite course. In the course of their existence, they pursue a precise destination.

Their happiness and bliss is in attaining their journey's end without being blocked by corruptive and degenerative obstructions. In other words, in order to realize happiness, they must follow the course of their life or existence in accord with the provisions of their make-up, without interference, to its conclusion.

A grain of wheat has a specific course in its plant life. In its make-up it has specific apparatuses and mechanisms that activate in special circumstances. It absorbs and consumes substances which it needs to grow and thrive in determined amounts and ratios. Through a precise path, its primordial nature leads the grass of wheat to its goal.

A wheat plant never alters its path, chosen by internal and external factors, in the course of its growth. For example, it would be impossible for it to change its course to that of an apple tree, grow a trunk, branches, and leaves and start flowering.

It is also inconceivable that it might take up the course of a sparrow, grow a beak and wings and fly

away. This law governs all types of phenomena in creation and humans are not exempted from this general rule.

Humans also possess a natural and compositional path and a journey's end, which is their perfection, happiness, and bliss. The human composition is equipped with faculties that show us our natural path and lead us towards our [99]true benefit.

Regarding this general guidance that is in effect in all phenomena in existence, God, the Exalted, states:

> *"Moses replied, 'Our Lord is He who gave each thing its special creation and then guided it towards its benefit.'"*

---

[99] Sūrat Tā Hā 20:50.

Also, regarding specific guidance in effect for humans, He declares:

"By the soul and That which shaped it, then inspired it with understanding of its wickedness and virtue. Surely, those who virtuously cultivate their souls are saved and those who keep their souls from virtuous development despair."[100]

The Difference Between Islamic and Human Laws

From the foregoing discussion it is clear that the true life path of humankind which entails our happiness and bliss is the course led by nature and fitrah; it is based upon our genuine interests and benefits according to the requisites of our creation and that of the world—regardless of whether or not it accords with our feelings and emotions.

Desires, feelings and emotions should adhere to the guidance of nature and fitrah. Nature and fitrah must not submit to unrestricted desires. The human society, with the feelings and emotions of its people, must found life upon realism not the unsteady foundations of superstitionism and the delusive ideals of feelings and emotions.

This is the difference between Islamic laws and other civil laws. Normal social laws adhere to the desires of the majority of the society (half plus one) whereas Islamic laws conform to the guidance of natural disposition [fitrah]—which reveals the will of the Almighty God. On this base, the Holy Qur'an affirms that lawmaking [tashrī'] and rule [hukm] belong uniquely to the Almighty God. Thus, it declares:

---

[100] Sūrat al-Shams 91:7-10.

"Rule belongs specifically to Allah..."[101]

"Who is better than Allah in terms of rule for the people of sure faith?"[102]

Moreover, that which rules in normal societies is the desires of the majority or a powerful dictator, regardless of whether or not these conform to truth and righteousness and secure the genuine interests of the society. On the other hand, in a truly Islamic society, righteousness and truth rule and the desires of the people must comply with it.

Here, an answer to another criticism becomes clear. That is, Islam does not agree with the unhealthy temperament of human societies, and those that enjoy unbridled freedom and realize every kind of desire will never tolerate the many restrictions in Islam.

Of course, if we envision humankind in its current condition—where moral corruption has pervaded into all corners of its life and it has become tainted with every kind of wickedness and oppression and is threatened with annihilation every moment—and compare it with Islam, we will not see any kind of congruity between luminous Islam and Stygian humankind.

With the continuation of current conditions as they are, we cannot expect the Islamic movement, which is merely a semblance of Islamic laws, to provide perfect human happiness. This expectation is exactly like us expecting the products and benefits of true democracy in a despotic environment that is democratic only in name, or like a sick person who expects to get well as soon as the doctor writes a prescription.

On the other hand, if we envision the God-given nature of the

---

[101] Sūrat Yūsuf 12:40.

[102] Sūrat al-Mā'idah 5:50.

people and compare it with Islam, which is the religion of nature and fitrah, we will see perfect harmony. And, how would it be possible for fitrah to clash against the path it has determined itself, upon which it guides and knows not any other way?

The Struggle Against Deviation

Certainly, due to the deviation and distortion—caused by unrestraint—that has currently afflicted fitrah, the identifying relationship between fitrah and the path it shows has, to some extent, been severed. Even so, in such unfavorable circumstances, the rational thing to do is to make every effort against the unfavorable situation and pave the way for the future, not to validate deviated nature and completely and forever despair of human happiness and beatitude.

History also testifies that at first every new system or government encounters strong opposition from the previous one and only after much strife, which is usually bloody, it is able to open up a place for itself in the society and gradually make the people forget about its bygone rival.

The democratic system, which is in the view of its adherents the most harmonious of methods, caused the bloody French revolution and similar incidents in other advanced countries before becoming established.

Also, when the communist system, which is according to its supporters a synthesis of advanced human movements and the greatest gift of history, first arose in Russia and subsequently in Asia, Europe, and America, it shed the blood of tens of millions of people before becoming established.

On the whole, the initial resistance and dissatisfaction of a society is not a logical rationale for the depravity and unfoundedness of a system. Thus, no matter what, Islam is alive and may be presented to any society.[103]

---

[103] From the annual journal, "Ma'ārif-e Ja'farī".

Discourse Six: The Social Status of Women

From the day the human race appeared upon this globe and lived in a community, it needed the female sex for both the survival of social life and natural generation. Men were never able to do without women.

Human societies—both savage and civilized—have continually followed a course of communal life with a series of regulations that have included customs and traditions, and just or cruel laws. Hence, in every tribe and every nation, specific regulations have been carried out regarding women.

Just as all laws and traditions in human societies stem from a series of natural factors and conditions (such as precedents in climate, regional, and environmental demands), the law of evolution that reigns over nature also manifests itself in and has an effect on social law which is an offspring of nature.

Prevailing laws regarding women are not an exception and evolve in the course of human life and follow—albeit slowly—the course of perfection.

The status of women in societies and its evolution may be summarized in three stages:

Woman, a Human Like Animal!

Stage one: In many nomadic human societies, women were not considered a part of the human society and had no social status or value. Transactions with women were like transactions with dumb beasts.

Because of the mentality of utilization and exploitation and in order to resolve their needs, humans employ wild animals that live in their environments, use them to pursue their natural aims and take possession of them for their mortal interests.

They use the meat, skin, fleece, fur, bones, milk, blood, power, abilities, and even the droppings of these animals. However, although they give them a place in their society and nurture them, they do not allow them any rights.

If humans provide domesticated animals the necessary instruments for eating, drinking, and coupling and resolve their needs, it is for the purpose of obtaining the benefits that they expect of them, not because they are living beings that, like humans, possess understanding and rights.

If a domestic animal employed by humans is mistreated or hurt and the offender is rebuked or punished, it is because the offender has violated the rights of the owner of the animal—a criminal act—not because the animal in question has any rights in the human society.

In addition, in order to achieve welfare and ease, humans kill billions of harmful microbes and insects using chemical toxicants and in order to eat and resolve their other needs, they slaughter millions of birds and herbivores and in doing this they feel not the slightest bit of remorse.

In primeval human societies, women had the same situation. As various segments of history reveal and is also manifest from the remnants of this practice among some tribes, many ages have passed in the life of humankind—maybe millions of years—where women had the status of a parasite and were not awarded membership in human societies.

The thought was that the sole reason for their existence in the society was to meet a series of needs of the society not so that they could enjoy their own social rights. Thus, 'lowly' and 'worthless' tasks were given to women, such as carrying chattels during the tribe's migration between summer and winter settlements, carrying firewood, catching fish, serving men, training children, and nursing the sick.

As long as a woman lived in her father's or guardian's house, not only did she not own anything, she was the sole property of the man. Even her clothes and ornaments belonged to the master of the house.

Any kind of policy or reprimand—even murder—regarding a woman could be carried out with impunity. She was given to others as a gift, as a loan, or to flatter a dignitary. As soon as she was transferred to her husband's house—which was in the form of a transaction (a remnant of which is still the custom that endures in some places) that gave money to the bride's family as payment for nursing her—after having been taken advantage of in her father's house, she had to appease the desires of her husband.

Even now, in the civilized society of modern times, one hears that in some advanced cities, just as public lavatories are necessary for expelling bodily wastes, public brothels are also necessary for discharging the sexual fluids.

These establishments exist so that those who cannot form a family or are temporarily deprived due to various factors, such as distance from their spouse, may release the fluids of lust that have gathered within them. This too is one of the practices of primeval humans, remaining to this day.

In ancient societies, men had no restriction in the number of their wives, whereas women did not have such a privilege. Men had the right to divorce, but women did not. Women had to continually live under the authority of men and had to absolutely devote themselves to the whims of men—to such an extent that in widespread famines the flesh of women was known to be eaten.

In short, in primitive human societies, women were considered only human in form, but were treated like domestic animals.

Woman, Liberated in Chains!

Stage two: In a stage of the social life of women, civil laws appeared within civilized nations. Such as the system of Hammurabi of Babylonia and the laws of ancient Rome, Greece, Egypt, China, and Persia which were similar to modern civil laws.

Even though these systems and laws were very different from each other, a similarity may be found among them: women had rights as a human in society, but they were viewed as a weak type of human that could not run their lives by themselves.

In these societies, women had to be under the authority and guardianship of men. They lived out their lives as followers and had no independence. They were not given the freedom to choose their path in life nor possess property.

They were not given independence of action so that they could ascribe deeds to themselves and enjoy the proprietary rights or profits of the actions. They did not have the right to sue or bear witness in court, and they had no authority whatsoever.

In such societies, as long as a woman lives in her father's house, she must obey her father. A father could do anything he wanted regarding his daughter; he could marry her off to any person or give her away

Discourse Six: The Social Status of Women

or take up any policy he desired.

In these societies, women generally did not possess an official familial relationship—with men or other women—entailing inheritance and other rights. They only possessed natural kinship which sometimes prevented marriage with their father, brothers, and sons.

In ancient Persia, marriage with immediate family was acceptable. In China and the Himalayas, natural relationship came from the woman and lineage was focused on women. As a result, one woman could have several husbands. This custom still prevails among some people. Instead of tracing ancestry from fathers, the line of mothers is delineated.

Among these clans and nations, woman could possess no property except in rare cases where they worked with the permission of their guardians or were given a marriage gift and their guardians did not take it away. A woman's life was managed by her guardian. For this reason, a father or husband had the right to punish their women in any way. They even had the right to murder them if they saw fit.

Also, the hardest of times for a woman was when she was suffering her monthly periods—in such cases she was shunned as an unclean creature—or when she gave birth, especially when she delivered a girl!

If a woman did something good, its benefit and praise went to her guardian and if she performed badly or unbecomingly, she herself was responsible and was chastised accordingly. Exceptionally, through fatherly affection or spousal warmth, she might be willed or gifted with some property or given special privileges. Even so, women were accorded no autonomy, determination, nor accomplishment.

For example, the condition of women within these nations was like that of a young child that is unable to manage its own life and must live under the guardianship of its custodians. For although young children are human, in view of the fact that their wills and intellects are undeveloped, they would cast the social system into a state of turmoil and incapacitate the society if they were given autonomy.

Therefore, they must live under the guardianship of their elders and obey them until they are experienced and worthy of membership in the society.

In these societies, an analogy may be made between women and prisoners who live out their lives in slavery and are deprived of freedom of will and action, as a slave fallen into the hands of a conquering enemy.

Even though they are human and possess all human existential faculties, in the view of the victorious population they are foes and their self-determination would harm the cornerstones of the society.

Therefore, they should be divested of their freedom, dominated, debased, and possessed so the subjugating society may go on living as normal.

Likewise, because of their feeblemindedness, capriciousness, and strong emotions, they are enemies of the society and their autonomous entrance into the society would bear nothing but paralysis of society and enduring regret.

These were the common grounds among the policies and laws of all ancient advanced societies regarding women. In addition, the status of women in the society according to Jews and Nazarenes and their divine books—the Torah and the Christian Gospel—was the same as in aforementioned ancient civilized societies.

This was because even though the Torah and Evangel contain recommendations regarding friendship and moderateness with women, it is evident that these divine books assume that women will never be as good as men and women's social and religious status is much lower than that of men. [104] Moreover, in non-divine religions, the religious actions of women have no considerable value or no value at all.

Women and Islam

Stage three: (This is an abbreviated account.) Islam regards women as human individuals and unconditional parts of the human society. Islam gives women the full value that can be given to any human individual as regards the results of their will and actions.

In order to understand the view of Islam regarding women, it is important to note that we live in an environment subject to opposing political gales and contrary propagandistic tidal waves that amplify anxiety and panic, divesting us of the desirability of correct thought. In the name of following independent and correct thought, these environs have transformed our innate and God-given logic into blind imitation.

Furthermore, in the centuries of illogical teachings, coercion, and despotic and unrestrained methods of the Church in the Middle Ages multitudes of correct thoughts were massacred and millions of humans were undeservedly tortured to death.

In order to preserve the power and status of its feeble and baseless institution, it accused Islam—which it identified as its most dangerous and intractable rival—of anything it possibly could and introduced Islam to its followers with every possible unbecoming belief and method.

---

[104] In 586 C.E., after much discussion regarding the issue of women, the Religious Assembly of France ordained that women were human although they had been created to serve men. Until approximately one hundred years ago, in England women were not considered part of the human society. Additionally, most ancient religions did not consider the deeds of women accepted by God. In ancient Greece it was even said that women were a wickedness created by the Devil.

It misrepresented the beautiful truths of this pure religion in the form of the most monstrous of features. The imprudence and bombast of the Church went on until in recent years the West—due to the independence of thought they found within themselves as a result of their industrial revolution—rounded up the power of the Church and fenced it in within the walls of the Vatican.

The reaction to the Church's many centuries of pretentiousness, tyranny, and imposition of beliefs adversely affected the people's thought to such an extent that they no longer consider religious truths as anything but a bunch of superstitions from the Age of Myths and they equate 'religion' with 'blind imitation'.

Evidently, if they think of their own holy religion in this manner, it is clear after extensive negative propaganda what they would think of other religions, including Islam.

Furthermore, with the awe-inspiring power gained through scientific and industrial advancement, European nations used everything in their power to control the other continents and expand their political and economic hegemony.

Their complete success convinced advocates of this system of their theoretical and practical superiority and assured them that non-European life has no value and is nothing except imitation of ignorant and unenlightened ancestral superstitions. They declared that all sensible humans must throw away their God-given logic and unquestioningly and specifically take up the European lifestyle.

Western propaganda was completely successful in planting the seed of the following logic: that which can truly be called the world is the Western world. That which can truly be called human is the Western human, and the life that entails human happiness is a Western style life.

As a result of these inculcations, the logic of our own intelligentsia—no less—is that our antiquated religious precepts and social laws do not conform to the modern world, and as a result we require world- approved laws the style of which the civilized world of today goes by (in these sentences by world is meant the West and Westerners).

In addition—with utmost grief—we must confess to the truth that due to a thousand years of internal strife and contention and the selfishness and capriciousness of rulers and officials, we have completely lost our intellectual independence and converted our free thought and God-given logic into a series of racial prejudices and vain inflexibilities.

A result of the conjunction of these factors was that in the name of achieving freedom of thought and breaking the shackles of imitation, we threw away our God-given logic and wholly imitated Westerners, choosing no path save that of keeping to their words and deeds.

For instance, we looked to them to explain and interpret for us our own truths, spirituality, and teachings. We learned knowledge that belonged specifically to us from them, whereas their knowledge of the truths of Islam is limited to their previous acquaintances and unworthy memories from the Middle Ages and the strange studies of orientalists.

After examining the writings of these scholars, because of their extensive mistakes, one must emphatically bless the priests and writers of the Crusades! For example, some orientalists write that Muhammad married Khadījah at seven, that ʿAlī became caliph after ʿUmar, that the eleventh Shīʿah Imām is buried in Kāzimayn, and numerous other erroneous accounts.

Based upon the above logic, these more-loving-than-a-mother nannies—no less—identify the social status of women in Islam thus: in Islam women live in captivity and absolute lack of social rights. They are bereft of freedom in will and action, and their value in inheritance and testimony is half of a man's and even that only in name not in practice.

Women are imprisoned within their houses and deprived of literacy. If they leave their house for an emergency, they must wrap themselves in a long black veil so that their fronts cannot be distinguished from their backs!

In light of this situation and its detriments, our mission and responsibility is clear. We must rationally and logically refer to Islam's explications in this regard, and with regard to other religious issues, and refrain from probing just anywhere or listening to just anyone. We must discover the interrelations of rights with one another and their factual rationales.

The Common Foundations of Islamic Laws

Without doubt, the mark of distinction separating us from animals is our intellect, which generalizes the products of our senses, orders them and induces general laws to discover the unknown.

Even though humans possess many inner feelings and emotions—which they use greatly in the course of their lives—considering the enduring human distinction, they must all produce their effects under the management of reason, for all animals possess these same feelings and emotions, and in some aspects they may even be stronger than humans.

In many verses, the Holy Qur'an reminds humans of the gift of intellect and holds humans responsible for their perceptions and intellect:

> *"Say: 'It is He that created you and appointed for you ears, eyes, and hearts; how little you give thanks.'"*[105]

---

[105] Sūrat al-Mulk 67:23.

"And adhere not to that which you have no knowledge. Verily, ears, eyes, and hearts are responsible (before Allah)."[106]

Based on this principle, Islam considers the human society dependent upon reason and delegates social laws to the discernment of the intellect, not the desires of feelings and emotions.

Hence, Islam deems binding only those laws and precepts that reason considers right even if they contradict the inclinations of the majority because, on the path to happiness humans should choose a destination that their intellects judge to be the point of happiness not where their animal urges favor.

"The Qur'an guides people towards Truth and a straight path."[107]

"And if Truth had followed their caprices, the heavens and the earth and all in them would surely have been thrown into confusion and corruption..."[108]

Islam views humanity as a superior unit, and men and women as equally human. Even though they are different in their femininity and masculinity, they are no different in their humanity, since all humans—whether man or woman—come into being by the procreation of two individuals: a woman and a man.

"I shall not leave unrewarded the work of any agent among you, whether man or woman; you are all members

---

[106] Sūrat al-Isrā' 17:36.

[107] Sūrat al-Ahqāf 46:30.

[108] Sūrat al-Mu'minūn 23:71.

of the same race..."[109]

"O people! Surely, I have created you as males and females and have made you into [diverse] races and tribes that you may know one another. Verily, the most noble among you before Allah is the most pious of you..."[110]

Accordingly, Islam presents women—like men—as complete members of the human society and equally considers each to be joint elements of the community. It has decreed freedom of will and action for women; the same as it has done for men. However, being a complete member of the society does not necessitate that all members of the society have identical rights and privileges.

This is because, with regard to membership, the differences between individuals and members in their social benefit entail differences in civil rights.

To the testimony of history, even though there have been numerous societies throughout the history of humanity where men were members, the rank of a scientist has never been given to an ignorant person, the responsibilities of an able and experienced man were never given to an inexperienced and incompetent person, and an unrestrained persecutor has never been given the position of a just and virtuous person.

It is true that all members of the society must be equal before the law yet this equality is equality regarding the execution of the law—i.e. benefiting from justice—not equality in social value and determined rights. How can it be possible for ruler and subject; adult and child; intellectual and ignorant; sage and fool; or oppressor and righteous person to be equal in all social privileges without the community

---

[109] Sūrat Āl 'Imrān 3:195.

[110] Sūrat al-Hujurāt 49:13.

falling apart?

Therefore, membership in the human society is one thing and the manner of membership is another and these two must not be confused with each other. In order to give the human society its due consideration, social justice must completely be observed among its members and each person must benefit from rights fit for them.

The Status of Women in Islam

As we pointed out, before the sun of Islam rose above the azure horizon of this world and brightened the world and its inhabitants with its brilliant radiance, the world was divided into two groups:

The first group consisted of the civilized nations, such as the Roman Empire, the Persian Empire, and other nations such as Egypt, Abyssinia, India, and China. In these societies, women were the same as captives—meaning that they were completely deprived of autonomy and the general privileges of society.

They did not receive inheritance. Their deeds were not respected. They did not have any freedom or independence in food, clothing, residence, marriage, divorce, socialization, property, and many other things. Their every breath and every step had to have the approval of men. If they were oppressed, they had to take their case up with courts governed by men where their litigation, testimony, and words were not heeded.

The other group was comprised of backward tribes and peoples such as tribes in Africa. Among these peoples, women were not even considered human but were parasites of the society in rank with exploited animals.

They carried loads, fished, served men, trained children, nursed the sick, appeased the lusts of their husbands, or whoever their husbands chose, and so on. This was the general situation of the world at the advent of Islam.

The specific environment where Islam emerged was the Arabian Peninsula. Its people were generally Bedouin due to its vast deserts. It was surrounded on the outside by the great nations of Rome, Persia, Abyssinia, and Egypt and on the inside it were associated with the Jews of Yathrib, the Nazarenes of Yemen, and what is now known as Iraq.

The majority religion was Wathanīyyah—a type of dualistic worship.[111] Their customs and traditions were an amalgam of the traditions and regulations of their surrounding nations.

Similar to Rome, Persia, and other nations, women were deprived of rights. Men kept them under absolute custody and no social respect was given them.

Apart from the fact that they fundamentally considered women a cause of shame and loathed daughters, the tribe of Banī Tamīm even buried their daughters alive. Thus, the Qur'an specifically remonstrates against these two problems:

> *"And when one of them was given the good tidings of the birth of a girl, their face would darken in repressed anger. They would hide from the people because of the bad news they received asking themselves whether they should keep it in disgrace or bury it in the earth. Ah! Evil is that which they judge."*[112]

---

[111] Advocates of Wathanīyyah believed in one God as Creator; however, the reason that this creed is considered a type of idolatry is that its adherents deemed beings other than God worthy of veneration. Even so, they did not ascribe divinity to their idols, which were representations of prophets, angels, stars, etc. (Extracted from the "Dictionary of Dehkhodā") [trans.]

[112] Sūrat al-Nahl 16:58-59.

> *"And when the infant daughter that was buried alive is asked for what crime she was killed."*[113]

Within the environment that we have described, Islam made women true and complete members of the society, released them from their captivity, and granted them autonomy. In Islam, like men, women have a share in the legacy left by the departed. They inherit from their fathers, brothers, uncles, spouses, etc.

They are free to have any legitimate work and good lifestyle they choose. Their deeds have value and social respect. They can directly approach qualified and legal authorities. If their rights have been encroached upon they can take legal action and also bear witness. In all these phases, whereby the generalities of a woman's life are completely ensured, men have no dominance, charge, or command over women.

> *"The responsibility of what women do within the confines of religious law and custom is not yours (and they are free)..."*[114]

> *"And women have a share in what their parents and family leave; be it slight or considerable."*[115]

The practice of the Holy Prophet (S) is full of fine points in this matter; however, we cannot give a detailed account in this article.

---

[113] Sūrat al-Takwīr 81:8-9.

[114] Sūrat al-Baqarah 2:234.

[115] Sūrat al-Nisā' 4:7.

Comparison and Contrast of the Rights of Women and Men

1. Regarding inheritance, on the whole, women receive half that of men just as the Qur'an states:

"To the male an equivalent of the share of two females (must be given)..."[116]

Even though in this aspect women have a lower position than men, this deficiency has been resolved in another place. That is, the nafaqah (financial support) of women is on the shoulders of men. The Islamic fundaments behind this law are examined elsewhere.

Doubtless, a woman's natural emotional and sentimental disposition holds sway over that of her intellect. All the states and actions of women are manifestations of various elegant and exquisite emotions and sentiments whereas men, according to their nature, possess an opposite mentality.

As we noted at the start of this discussion, in organizing the affairs of the human society, Islam has given reason superiority over emotions. If we consider the entirety of the human populace, in each age the wealth in the world belongs to the population of that same age. They benefit from their wealth as long as they live and, after they die, they pass it on to their family—the ensuing stratum.

As soon as the current stratum is extinct and the surviving stratum—generally consisting of an equal distribution of men and women—comes into office; so to speak, men receive two thirds of the wealth and one third is withheld from them. The two thirds belonging to men is used equally by both men and women; therefore, two thirds

---
[116] Sūrat al-Nisā' 4:11.

of the world's wealth is used by women and one third by men.

"The precepts that have been ordained to the advantage of women are equal to those that are against them..."[117]

According to this type of division, regarding ownership, administration, and cultivation of property, men control the majority of the world's wealth.

On the other hand, regarding its utilization and benefit, women control and benefit from the majority of wealth. Social justice necessitates that the protection and administration of wealth be in the hands of reason and benefiting from it be in the hands of emotions and sentiments.

1. In connection with respect for deeds and property, Islam gives complete autonomy to women in making use of the products of their deeds. In this case, women possess freedom of will and action without being under the supervision of men.
2. As regards legitimate and correct social interaction, they are not the least different from men. They are free to socialize on the condition that they refrain from showing off their adornments, flaunting themselves, flirting, and inflaming the lusts of men.

"The responsibility of what women do within the confines of religious law and custom is not yours (and they are free)..."[118]

---

[117] Sūrat al-Baqarah 2:228.

[118] Sūrat al-Baqarah 2:234.

1. With respect to religious deeds and privileges, the only source of difference between people in rank is their piety and respect before God. There is no difference between women and men.

"I shall not leave unrewarded the work of any agent among you, whether man or woman; you are all members of the same race..."[119]

"O people! Surely, I have created you as males and females and have made you into [diverse] races and tribes that you may know one another. Verily, the most noble among you before Allah is the most pious of you. Truly, Allah is All-knowing, All-aware."[120]

In an area where no privilege is given to any class and the only mark of distinction is piety and Islamic religious service, men and women are not different and one devout woman is more respectable and preferable to one thousand impious men.

1. As regards the issue of marriage, women are free to marry anyone they want. However, considering that the precepts regarding inheritance and marriage are based upon genealogy, a woman can under no circumstances have sexual relations with anyone save the one husband she has chosen. Nevertheless, a man can

---

[119] Sūrat Āl 'Imrān 3:195.

[120] Sūrat al-Hujurāt 49:13.

take more than one wife on the condition that he is able to behave justly and equitably with all his wives.

It is evident, however, that Islam has not necessitated polygyny rather it has merely given permission for men to marry up to four women and this precept requires background. This means that the situation must be such that social order is not threatened by a shortage of women and congestion of men.

One thing that is clear for men is that because the residence and living expenses of women and children are the responsibility of men and in view of the fact that justice and equity are stipulated, taking such action is feasible for a limited number of men, not all. In fact, nature and external incidents often provide more women fit for marriage than men.

The validity, purposefulness, and reasonability of this precept is made clear by contemplation of the true nature of human societies and unexpected incidents. Supposing an equal proportion of men and women in the world—something that is usually statistically valid—if we set a certain year as starting point and separately add up male and female births, in the first year that the young men reach natural maturity or legal age we would be faced with a much greater number of marriageable girls.

In the sixteenth year the number of women fit for marriage would be seven times that of available men. In the twentieth year, the fit women to fit men ratio would be 11:5, and in the 25th year, which is the average age for marriage, this ratio would be 16:10. In this case, if we assume the ratio of men that have more than one wife to be one fifth, 80% of men would have one wife and 20% would have four and in the thirtieth year, 20% of men would have three wives.

Apart from this, uncontrollable events such as brutal wars and dangerous occupations cause the deaths of countless men. This leads to an abundant population of marriageable widows and women who—if polygyny was forbidden—would have no course but to give up their chastity perhaps even bringing illegitimate children lacking guardianship into the world.

The two recent world wars proved this fact beyond doubt such that the population of spouseless women in Germany requested that—in accordance with Islamic law—the government permit polygamy and in this way appease the population of single women. Regrettably, due to the opposition of the Church, their request was denied.

This incident demonstrates that the opposition of women to polygyny is based on habit not the exigency of nature and fitrah and it was the best answer to censure the assessment within Islam that, 'The decree of polygyny has hurt the feelings of women and dispirited them. It has instigated their desire for vengeance and causes many deplorable incidents.'

This event and similar ones prove beyond doubt that when there is need and a shortage of eligible men, all these opposing thoughts transform into acquiescence.

In addition, polygamy was practiced for ages before Islam without any limit in the number of wives and in Islam with a specific delimitation and it never caused disorder or chaos in the society. Women who went to a wedded man as their second, third, or fourth wife did not grow from the earth or fall from the sky; rather, they were these same women who according to critics, are naturally opposed to polygyny.

Aside from the fact that Islam has not made polygyny obligatory, but has made it permissible—on the condition that the man is not afraid he might act unjustly and is fit to behave equitably—there are methods in Islamic jurisprudence whereby a woman may prevent her husband from marrying another man unless he is willing to divorce her first.

The same thing also exists in the matter of divorce. Even though the authority for divorce is in the hands of the man, in accordance with the sharī'ah, women can resort to methods to separate from their husband or may predict necessary situations and obtain this right so they may enjoy peace of mind and contentment.

The existence of divorce in conjugal life and the fact that it has been entrusted to men on the basis of the sharī'ah is a hallmark of the holy religion of Islam. Even so, there are special ways whereby women can obtain divorce under specific circumstances.

Due to a great deal of suffering and lengthy conflict, civilized nations and legitimate governments all over the world were finally forced to sanction divorce.

However, since they gave the power of divorce directly to both women and men, the rise in the divorce rate—especially as requested by women—has weakened these governments and they are continually seeking a solution to this problem. Some of the reasons that women provide as basis for their divorce which are broadcast in newspapers and mass media especially ratify the correctitude of this Islamic view.

Rule of reason or sentiments?

What is understood from preceding discussions is that women are not inferior to men in affairs of life and social privileges. In all conditions they retain their autonomy and are not under the control of men.

However, one thing that is certain is that a woman must obey her husband in matters of marital relations.

The threefold restriction that women, who are full of love and sentiment, have in Islam are in the domain of rationality which Islam devolves to men, who have a greater tendency for rational thought and decision-making, and must be separated from the environment of sentiments and feelings. These three matters are: leadership, judicature, and jihād.

According to the religious statements and practice of the Holy Prophet (S), women cannot hold governance and leadership in the Islamic society, cannot act as a judge and cannot directly participate in jihād and supervise battles.

> **"Are then those who have been brought up amid adornments and who by nature cannot show their true aims in times of hostility to be considered daughters of Allah and given governance of affairs of state?"**[121]

Therefore, men are responsible for these threefold aspects:

> **"Men are the protectors and supervisors of women."**[122]

The relationship of these three issues with reason and their impairment by the interference of feelings and sentiments is so clear that there is no need for discussion and research and a decisive trial will leave no room for doubt.

I'll never forget early in the recent World War, when the battle came upon French soil and extreme hostilities continued, while fire fell from the skies and blood seethed on the earth, according to the newspapers a high-ranking female member of the French army general staff designed a beautiful female hat with a scissor mark at the front![123]

---

[121] Sūrat al-Zukhruf 43:18.

[122] Sūrat al-Nisā' 4:34.

[123] From the yearbook, "Maktab-e Tashayyu'".

Discourse Seven: Why Did the Prophet Marry So Much?

A criticism made by some regarding the respectable Prophet of Islam (S) is the issue of his many wives. Critics say that having many wives is essentially a sign of evil and unconditional surrender before lust.

They question why the Prophet of Islam did not content himself with the four wives that he had legitimized for his followers and took up to nine wives at the same time.

This discussion has various aspects related to many verses scattered throughout the Qur'an. I will enter into an extensive discussion regarding all these aspects in the exegesis of the related verses elsewhere. Here I will suffice with a concise presentation of the matter.

First of all, critics must essentially realize that the polygyny of the Prophet was not due to excessive attraction to women. The Prophet's marriages were related to other aspects which I will now succinctly discuss.

The first wife of the Holy Prophet was Khadījah[124]. He lived with her alone for over twenty years—two thirds of his life after this marriage—without taking another wife. The Prophet was appointed to prophethood in the period after this marriage. After his appointment, he lived in Mecca for thirteen years. After that, he immigrated to Medina and started his widespread religious promotion.

After Khadījah's death, the Prophet married some women, both maidens and widows, young and old. This liberty in marriage lasted for around ten years and, after this, additional marriages were prohibited for the Prophet.[125]

Therefore, it is evident that the many marriages of the Prophet cannot be due to overt philogyny. The facts that early in his life the Prophet sufficed with only Khadījah and at the end of his life marriage was prohibited for him are inconsistent with the calumny of lasciviousness.

Furthermore, we see that men who have great passion for women, love their beauty and adornments and relish their coquetry and demureness. Such men are mostly fond of young and attractive women who are in the spring of their life. However, none of these characteristics is evident in the spiritual bearing of the Prophet of Islam.

---

[124] The prophet married Khadījah fifteen years before his appointment as a prophet. He was 25 years old when he married Khadījah, who was forty. She was a widow who previously had two husbands. Her first husband was named 'Atīq ibn 'Āyid Makhzūmī and she had a child by him named Jāriyah. Her second husband was called Abū Hālah ibn Mundhir Asadī and she also had a child by him named Hind.

[125] This prohibition was required by the following verse: *"It is not allowed for you to marry women after this, nor that you should change them for other wives, though their beauty be pleasing to you, except what your right hand possesses (your handmaidens) and Allah is watchful over all things." (Sūrat al-Ahzāb 33:52)*

In his marriages he was not bound by any of these matters. Thus, history shows that after marrying a maiden, he also married a widow.[126] Also, after marrying a young and beautiful woman, he also married a feeble aged woman.[127] The history of the Prophet is the best witness to this fact.

History attests that the Prophet's marriage to Umm al-Salamah, who was an elderly woman, and Zaynab daughter of Jahsh, who was fifty, occurred after his marriage to 'Ā'ishah and Umm Habībah, who were young and beautiful.

In addition, the Prophet himself enjoined his wives against adornments and luxuriousness. He gave them a choice between divorce and a life of austerity and abandonment of adornments and luxury. The best witness to this fact is the Qur'an:

> *"O prophet! Say unto your wives, 'If you desire this world's life and its adornment, then come, I will give you a gift and allow you a goodly release. But if you desire Allah and his Messenger and the Last Abode, then surely Allah has prepared for the doers of good among you a mighty*

---

[126] The only maiden wife the Prophet took was 'Ā'ishah. After the death of Khadījah, the Prophet wedded her in Mecca and consecrated the marriage in Medina after the Hijra. The other wives the Prophet took after Khadījah, which were all widows, are as follows: 1. Sawdah; 2. Zaynab bint Khuzaymah; 3. Hafsah; 4. Umm al-Salamah; 5. Zaynab bint Jahsh; 6. Juwayriyah; 7. Umm Habībah; 8. Safiyyah; 9. Maymūnah.

[127] The first wife of the Prophet was Khadījah who—as cited by Ahmad ibn Hasan Hurr 'Āmilī—was forty when she married the Prophet. 'Ā'ishah was six when the Prophet married her after the death of Khadījah; however, as we stated, the marriage was consecrated after the Hijra when she was ten. (I must note that marriage at a young age was customary at the time and this was not considered a young age for marriage [trans.]) None of the women the Prophet married after 'Ā'ishah were maidens and most of them were advanced in years.

reward.'"[128]

In principle, dislike of adornments and luxury cannot be a mental quality of a person who is madly addicted to relations with women.

Reasons for the Prophet's Marriages

A fair researcher has no choice but to justify the many marriages of the Prophet during his middle years on a basis other than lust and hedonism.

Some of his marriages were exclusively to gain influence. He hoped to extend his tribe and kin through marriage in the interests of proselytization.

Certain marriages were for the purpose of appeasing and assuaging various individuals. Though marriage he safeguarded himself against possible dangers to his mission.

In some marriages, his aim was merely to deliver a woman from misfortune and provide her livelihood. In this way he edified his followers in practice and taught them to support the poor and helpless.

In a number of his marriages, the aim was to carry out a divine decree and in this way eradicate some of the unsound thoughts of the Age of Ignorance. This was his intent in marrying Zaynab, the daughter of Jahsh. At first, she was the wife of Zayd ibn Hārithah, who was the adopted son of the Prophet of Allah.

> *Arabs believed that one could not marry the wife of an adopted son just as he could not marry the wife of his own son by birth. After Zayd divorced Zaynab, the Prophet married her in order to oppose this false thought. There are various Qur'anic verses in this regard such as:*
>
> **"So when Zayd took his need of her and divorced her, We**

---

[128] Sūrat al-Ahzab 33:28-29.

wed her to you so that there will be no fault for believers regarding marriage to the wives of their adopted sons after divorce and the command of Allah must be fulfilled."[129]

The Wives of the Prophet

Approximately one year after the passing of Khadījah, the Prophet married Sawdah daughter of Zama'ah.[130] Sawdah's husband died when returning from the second migration to Abyssinia.[131] Sawdah was a faithful woman who had gone to Abyssinia with her husband. She held the glorious title of émigré [muhājarah].

When she lost her husband, if she had returned to her family, who were unbelievers, she would surely have been persecuted and maybe even killed. Moreover, they would have tried to force her to revert to her previous unbelief. Therefore, the Prophet married her so that she would be safe from torment and persecution.

Zaynab, daughter of Khuzaymah, was wedded to the Prophet after her husband, 'Abd Allāh ibn Jahsh, was killed in the battle of Uhud. Zaynab was a great and virtuous woman from the Age of Ignorance.

She was called "Umm al-Masākīn"—literally Mother of the Destitute—since she showed great kindness and compassion to the poor and needy. The Prophet married her to preserve her status and prestige.[132]

---

[129] Sūrat al-Ahzāb 33:37.

[130] The Prophet took three wives in Mecca: Khadījah, 'Ā'ishah, and Sawdah. He married the others in Medina after the Hijra.

[131] According to another narration, he died in Abyssinia. Also, Sawdah died in Medina near the close of 'Umar's rule.

[132] The Prophet's marriage to Zaynab occurred in the third year of the Hijra and after the battle of 'Uhud. After her marriage, she only lived in the house of the Prophet for a few months before she passed away and was buried in the Baqī' Cemetery.

Another wife of the Prophet was called Umm al-Salamah and her original name was Hind. Before she became the Prophet's wife, she was married to 'Abd Allāh Abī Salamah, cousin and foster brother to the Prophet.

'Abd Allāh was the first person to immigrate to Abyssinia. Umm al-Salamah was a virtuous and devout woman and also a religious authority. When her husband died, she was advanced in age and the guardian of her orphans. Under such conditions, the Prophet of Islam took her hand in marriage.[133]

The Prophet married Safiyyah, daughter of Hayy ibn Akhtab, chief of Banī Nadīr, after her husband was killed in the battle of Khaybar. Her father was also killed in the same battle. Safiyyah was among the prisoners of Khaybar and the Prophet chose her for himself and freed her. Then, he married her and thus saved her from abjectness. Also, through this marriage he became in-laws with Banī Isrā'īl.[134]

After the incident of Banī al-Mustalaq, the Prophet married Juwayriyah who was previously named Barrah. She was the daughter of Hārith, the chief of the Banī al-Mustalaq tribe. In the incident of Banī al-Mustalaq, Muslims captured the women and children of two hundred families.

From among them, the Prophet married Juwayriyah. Subsequently, the Muslims freed all the prisoners because they had become the Prophet's kin. Freedom of the prisoners positively influenced the

---

[133] Umm al-Salamah was the daughter of Abī Umayyah Hudhayfah ibn Mughayrah. After Khadījah al-Kubrā, she was the most virtuous of the Prophet's wives. The Prophet married her in the 4th year of the Hijra. She died in 61 AH. It should be noted that except for Khadījah and Zaynab bint Khuzaymah, all the wives of the Prophet passed away after him.

[134] Safiyyah married the Prophet in the 7th year of the Hijra after the battle of Khaybar. She was previously married twice, first with Salām ibn Muslim and then with Kanānah ibn Rabī'.

people of the tribe and the whole of the tribe's considerable population turned to the Prophet and converted to Islam. In addition, this deed had a significantly favorable effect on all Arab people.

Another wife of the Prophet of Islam was Maymūnah. Her previous name was Barrah and she was the daughter of Hārith Halāliyah. After the death of her second husband, Abī Rahm ibn 'Abd al-'Uzzā, she gifted herself unto the Prophet. The Prophet set her free and married her. A Qur'anic verse was revealed with regard to this issue.

Umm Habībah was also among the wives of the Prophet. Her name was Ramlah and she was the daughter of Abū Sufiyān. She was formerly the wife of 'Abd Allāh ibn Jahsh. She and her husband were part of the second hijrah to Abyssinia, where her husband became Nazarene. She, however, kept faith with Islam. During this time, her father was a bitter enemy of the Prophet and continually incited the people against Islam. The Prophet married Umm Habībah and thus put her under his protection.

Hafsah, daughter of 'Umar, was also one of the wives of the Prophet. After her husband, Khanīs ibn Hudhāfah was killed in the battle of Badr, the Prophet married her. The Prophet had also previously married the maiden 'Ā'ishah, daughter of Abū Bakr.

Considering these facts and what we have discussed regarding the customs of the Prophet throughout his life, the fact that he was an austere person and eschewed luxury and that he also enjoined his wives to austerity and against luxury, leaves no doubt that basically, the marriages of the Prophet were not like those of others who marry to appease their lusts.

One must also note that essentially the Prophet's behavior with women was courteous and respectful. On the whole women's rights, which in the dark Age of Ignorance had been destroyed under the caprice of men, were revived by the Prophet.

Thus women, who had lost their legitimate status in the human society after many dark aeons of Ignorance, achieved their true position. It is even narrated that the final testament of the Prophet on the threshold of death was a recommendation regarding women.

Regarding the importance of ritual prayer [salāt], the necessity of giving due consideration to servants, and advice about women he stated:

"Ritual prayer, ritual prayer (is very important). Also, do not burden servants more than they can bear. For the love of Allah, (I advise you to be considerate) of women for they are allies that are always with you."[135]

The Prophet's justice, cordiality, and consideration for women were specific to him. We must also not leave it unsaid that, like continuous [wisāl] fasting, the permissibility for marrying more than four wives was restricted to the Prophet and it was forbidden for his followers to perform these deeds.

It was these characteristics of the Prophet that prevented people—even his enemies who were vehemently seeking his weak points—from any kind of protest.[136]

---

[135] Al-Mīzān, vol. 4, p. 197; also Mīzān al-Hikmah, vol. 4, p. 3241.

[136] From the yearbook, "Maktab-e Tashayyu'".

Discourse Eight: Short Term Marriage

In Bahman of 1342 (January/February, 1964), following the opinion of Dr. Russell Lee that humans are part of the group of creatures that naturally cannot content themselves with a single wife, the Keyhān Newspaper devoted a column for free debate regarding the issue. It also proclaimed that it would print both favorable and conflicting views.

Naturally, the discussion led to the issue of short-term marriage [mut'ah]. Following this, in issue 6169 dated Bahman 24, 1342 AHS, Keyhān printed an article written by Mr. Mardūkh—who is a Kurdish Sunnī scholar. In a section of this article the Shī'ah creed was attacked for permitting mut'ah marriage. The present article was written in answer to Mardūkh's article but for various reasons it was not printed in the newspaper.

Mr. Mardūkh has cast his words in the form of dialectic. However, unfortunately in a controversy that has continued among scholars of the two great creeds of Shī'ah and Sunnī for approximately fourteen centuries, he has based his reasoning on material that Sunnī scholars posited at the start of the controversy which have been proved wrong hundreds of times—the proceedings of which have been inscribed in the jurisprudential and dialectic books of both creeds.

The only way I found to justify this performance is to say that this respectable scholar did not adequately research this extensive debate and due to religious zeal he wanted to bestow a gift upon the honorable readers of the newspaper with the few words that he had heard and accepted on this topic, thinking that Shī'ah scholars are ignorant of these matters.

He took the first part of the narration from an oration by 'Umar, the second caliph, and the second part from a narration by Amīr al-Mu'minīn 'Alī ('a) regarding the prohibition of mut'ah cited in "Sahīh Bukhārī" and several other books and attributed the comical mixture to Shī'ah scholars!

Translation of the original piece from the second caliph's oration is as follows: "There are two types of mut'ah that were permissible [halāl] at the time of the Prophet of Allah and I make them forbidden [harām] and will punish their perpetrators. These two mut'ahs are the mut'ah of hajj (hajj-e tamattu') and the mut'ah of women."

Translation of the original piece that is attributed to Imām 'Alī ('a) states: "The Prophet of Allah forbade mut'ah of women and the meat of domestic donkeys on the day of Khaybar."

Translation of the oration cited by Mr. Mardūkh—the Arabic recorded above—is: the second caliph stated, "There are two types of mut'ah that were halāl at the time of the Prophet of Allah and I make them harām and will punish their perpetrators. These two mut'ahs are mut'ah and the meat of domestic donkeys."

The end result of entering into discussion with a person with such logic is quite clear. For the information of those who have not adequately studied this topic, I will succinctly point out several issues in regard to the statements of His Eminence. If anyone has anything to say in this regard or any objections I will welcome their statements with open arms and I am ready for debate and expatiation.

Mr. Mardūkh maintains, "If the act of mut'ah were not prohibited, the community of Muslims would act in accordance with it and it would not be specific to the Shī'ah branch."

Indeed, before the interdiction of the Second Caliph, the community of Muslims including the sahābah—i.e. Companions of the Prophet—observed mut'ah. For example, the first caliph gave his daughter Asmā' in short term marriage to Zubayr who was a sahābah and 'Abd Allāh ibn Zubayr who was also a sahābah was the product of this mut'ah.

However, after the prohibition of the Second Caliph, his partisans renounced mut'ah while the Shī'ahs did not accept the ban.

All the same, after 'Umar's prohibition some sahābahs such as Imām 'Alī ('a); Ibn 'Abbās, Ibn Mas'ūd, Jābir, and 'Amr ibn Harith, and also some Tābi'īn[137] scholars such as Mujāhid; Suddī; Sa'īd ibn Jubayr; and Ibn Jurayh regarded mut'ah permissible.

Mr. Mardūkh asserts, "It seems that this is also one of the influences of the Jew, 'Abd Allāh ibn Saba'..."

It must be noted that this 'Abd Allāh ibn Saba' is an imaginary person that the Umayyads and their contemporary scholars created to explain away the discord [fitnah] at the dawn of Islam which led to the death of the third caliph, 'Uthmān. They made this fictional person the hero of these tales and the founder of the Shī'ah creed.

However, recently some scholars—even Sunnī scholars such as the late lamented renowned scholar Tāhā Husayn—have historically proved the fictitiousness of the character of Ibn Saba'.[138]

Mr. Mardūkh asks, "How could 'Umar make a halāl, harām or a

---

[137] Those who did not meet with the Prophet but met with Sahābah and cited narrations through them. [trans.]

[138] Refer to Tāhā Husayn, "Al-Fitnah al-Kubrā"; Dr. Wardī, "Wu"āz al-Salātīn"; Askarī, "'Abd Allāh Saba'"; and the yearbook of "Maktab-e Tashayyu'", issue 3—later republished as "Shī'ah".

harām, halāl without license?"

As various recent scholars admit, the Second Caliph had changed religious precepts where he saw fit—even against the clear wording of Allah and the Prophet, as maintained by Ahmad Amīn, author of "Fajr al-Islām", and author of "Tafsīr al-Manār", and as is demonstrated in many historical cases.

The context of the Second Caliph's oration, which Shī'ah scholars cite from the books of Sunnī scholars, clearly shows that the interdiction of mut'ah was not an enjoinment against wickedness, but a decision that he made by himself in accordance with situational politics.

In his oration, the Second Caliph states, "There are two types of mut'ah that were halāl at the time of the Prophet of Allah and I [my emphasis] make them harāmand will punish their perpetrators. These two mut'ahs are the mut'ah of hajj and mut'ah of women."

Any person who understands Arabic realizes that this means: these acts were legitimate [mashrū'] at the time of the Prophet and I now ban them. It does not mean, they were harām and the people performed these acts in spite of this while the Prophet and sahābah stood by and watched and now, in the name of enjoinment against evil, I announce their illegitimacy.

In addition to this, in many citations by the Sunnīs, the Second Caliph established stoning to death [rajm] as the penalty for offence[139] (in the case of mut'ah) and he swore to execute this penalty, even though there were no grounds for the penalty of rajm. Even Sunnī scholars have not dared to proclaim stoning as the penalty for mut'ah. They say, "The Second Caliph said this as a superficial threat, not in earnest."

Also, that Mr. Mardūkh wrote, "At the pulpit the Second Caliph

---

[139] For more information, refer to "Tafsīr Al-Mīzān", vol. 4.

said: I will feel grateful to anyone who notifies me of my slips and errors", does nothing in proving his speculations because the Caliph never claimed that he would accept what others say.

Mr. Mardūkh says, "In 'Sahīh Bukhārī', which is no less than a book of history, it is written that the narrator of the hadīth banning mut'ah is 'Alī himself." First, "Sahīh Bukhārī" is a book of hadīth and in order to use hadīth, one must first determine whether they are authentic or not. One cannot cursorily and unquestionably accept hadīths.

This same "Sahīh Bukhārī" asserts, "The Temple of Jerusalem [Bayt al-Muqaddas] was built four years after the Ka'bah." whereas it is known that Abraham was the builder of the Ka'bah and David and Solomon were the builders of Bayt al-Muqaddas and there are thousands of years difference between them.

He cites that 'Ā'ishah said, "On the Night of the Ascension [laylah al-mi'rāj] the Prophet slept in bed next to me the whole night." whereas it is irrefutable that the mi'rāj occurred before the hijrah and 'Ā'ishah came into the Prophet's house after the hijrah. In contrast to what is written in "Sahīh Bukhārī", "Sahīh Muslim" cites this famous saying from 'Alī ('a):

"If 'Umar had not banned mut'ah, no one would commit adultery except the wretched."

Mr. Mardūkh says, "According to the Shī'ahs, the verse "... and those of whom ye seek content..."[140] does not address mut'ah of women, rather it means that if the marriage was consummated, her marriage portion [mihr] must be paid in full."

This matter is related to Arabic syntax and morphology. I have fully vindicated the matter in the fourth volume of "Tafsīr al-Mīzān" under Sūrat al-Nisā'. I will refrain from a detailed account of the issue. For more details refer to the book.

---

[140] Sūrat al-Nisā' 4:24.

In short, exegetes from the advent of Islam, such as Ibn 'Abbās, Ibn Mas'ūd, and Ubay who were sahābah, and Mujāhid, Qatādah, Suddī, and Ibn Jubayr who were tābi'īn all of whom lived at the time of the Prophet and revelation of the Qur'an, were Arab, and they knew Arabic much better than Mr. Mardūkh who was Kurdish and was born fourteen centuries later. The former personalities understood this verse as referring to normal mut'ah not intercourse.

This is why contemporary advocates of the Second Caliph never claim that the verse does not refer to mut'ah; rather, they allege that it has been abrogated.

In addition, Mr. Mardūkh holds, "Istimtā' and tamattu'[141] mean taking pleasure and they signify sexual intercourse." which is an incorrect definition. These two words have different formations and thus two different meanings. Istimtā' means seeking pleasure and tamattu' means taking pleasure. Therefore, istimtā' would never be used to refer to intercourse, which is taking pleasure.

Mr. Mardūkh claims, "In Islam, marriage has specific effects, none of which exist in mut'ah, such as inheritance, nafaqah[142], 'iddah[143], the four wife restriction, etc.

Therefore, mut'ah is not marriage and because it is not and is also not 'property of the right hand', according to the holy verse "Save from their wives or (slaves) that their right hands possess, for then they are not blameworthy. [144] Which limits legitimate sexual intercourse to marriage and property of the right hand, it is unlawful and an act of

---

[141] These words are derived from the same root as the infinitive, mut'ah. [trans.]

[142] Nafaqah is the financial support of a wife as necessitated by Islam. [trans.]

[143] 'Iddah is the minimum interval a woman is required to observe between the end of her previous marriage (e.g. death of husband, divorce) and remarriage to another man. [trans.]

[144] Sūrat al-Mu'minūn 23:6.

adultery."

This rationale is one of their oldest sophistries. It was concocted around fourteen centuries ago and has probably been answered by the Shī'ahs fourteen hundred times but these gentleman still do not relent and keep on repeating it.

First of all, according to the religious law [shar'], the effects Mr. Mardūkh enumerates for marriage are for lifelong marriage not marriage itself. He himself accedes that, in the time of the Prophet, before the Prophet banned mut'ah—so Mr. Mardūkh says—and it was permitted, it did not have these effects and the citations of the Sunnīs testify also to this fact.

Secondly, the verse that he makes use of indicates that the act of mut'ah is a type of marriage; thus, if mut'ah were indeed forbidden in Islam, it surely happened after the hijrah.

Their own varying accounts from the battles of Khaybar, 'Umrah al-Qadā', and Awtās, the conquest of Mecca and the Farewell Hajj [hajjat al-widā'] testify to this. Also, because Sūrat al-Mu'minūn was revealed in Mecca before the hijrah, when mut'ah was permissible, it was definitely considered a type of marriage.

Mr. Mardūkh maintains, "The act of mut'ah was adultery and due to the force of circumstance the Holy Prophet temporarily gave permission for it and after the need was obviated he proclaimed it harām."

They brazenly accuse the Prophet of such an act to correct the mistake the Sunnīs made on day one! However, from the first days of the advent of Islam, in Meccan sūrahs such as al-Mu'minūn, al-Isrā', al-Furqān, and al-Ma'ārij, God, the Almighty, introduces adultery as an obscene act and has strictly prohibited it.

Furthermore, in some parts of the Qur'an such as Sūrat Isrā'īl and al-Mā'idah, God sharply forbids the Prophet (S) from even the least bit of alteration in Qur'anic precepts. No Muslim should dare to say that the Prophet issued permission for adultery and that the Prophet's own sahābah including Abū Bakr, Zubayr, Jābir, and Ibn Mas'ūd were ahead of everyone else in performing this evil deed! One sahābah gave a daughter, one took the daughter, and one came into being by the taking!

For instance, the sahābah, 'Abd Allāh ibn Zubayr was born of Asmā' daughter of Abū Bakr in her mut'ah with Zubayr. Certainly, no Shī'ah would ever cause such disgrace by attributing such law-breaking and disobedience to the Holy Prophet (S).

Apart from what I mentioned until now, if we look at the human world in a general perspective, we will precisely see that sexual relations cannot be restricted to permanent marriage, considering all other relations unlawful. Permanent marriage can never fully satisfy the carnal instinct.

Even though permanent marriage is prevalent all over the world and public opinion condemns adultery and fornication, official governments of civilized and semi-civilized worlds have not been able to prevent the outbreak of short-term sexual relations and in all cities of the world, great and small, there are public or concealed centers for obscene acts.

In this situation, a religion such as Islam, which is global and eternal and wants to restrict intercourse to legitimate marriage and completely prevent fornication and adultery, must incorporate short-term marriage with specific conditions that obviate the evil of fornication—for instance, the woman must not be mahram[145] to the person she intends to marry, she must not be married, and the duration and mihr must be determined prior to the union—in order to adequately answer the needs of this universal human instinct.

---

[145] Persons who are mahram (plural mahārim) to you are those who are close family such that you may not marry them (e.g. one's parents and siblings). [trans.]

In the "Tafsīr Tabarī" and Shī'ah narrations, it is quoted from 'Alī ('a) that, "If the Second Caliph had not prohibited short-term marriage, the only persons who committed adultery and fornication would be those who were on the verge of destruction due to the extent they had gone astray."

In conclusion, in answer to Mr. Mardūkh's mandatory decree that Shī'ah scholars must reconsider their opinion on this and other controversial issues, we say that, contrary to Sunnī scholars, the Shī'ahs consider ijtihād legitimate and without waiting for their mandate, we continually reconsider our opinions. However, unfortunately, we cannot change our opinion regarding an issue that is as clear as day.

Reciprocally, we entreat Mr. Mardūkh to observe decency and politeness in his writings. In a very short article, he accuses the Shī'ahs of unbelief, corrupt lineage, and illegitimacy. He has extended his foul language to the daughters, sisters, and family of Shī'ah authorities and in no way restrained himself in his adventurism.

If he truly supports the cause of unifying Muslims and resolving internal conflict, he must refrain from such profane and unjust language because, firstly, such unjust statements are aspersions cast upon the holy character of the Prophet of Allah and his eminent sahābah who were the initial legislators and executers of this matter and, secondly, such words are the main cause of all this rancor and spite between these two creeds.

When the public learns of them, such words overturn worlds; otherwise, a difference of opinion in a few minor issues would not start such uproar.

A few days after writing the foregoing article, I received a postal package from one of my friends containing a short booklet by Mr. Mardūkh. This booklet was written regarding the interdiction of mut'ah and to some extent to accentuate and reaffirm the article he published in the Keyhān Newspaper.

This booklet—as is clear to those who read both article and booklet—contains no significant addition to the published article which would require investigation and debate.

However, due to the fact that said author wanted to take the issue from the temporary form of a newspaper article to the permanent form of a book, he altered the appearance of the debate.

Even so, he reused the same groundless logic he had used at the beginning of his article and in no way did he refrain from his bullying, perjury, and calumniation of religious authorities—even Sunnī 'ulamā' and sahābah. Therefore, I deemed it necessary to indicate several parts of this booklet which are the products of said individual's characteristic logic. I will leave the final judgment to my respected readers.

In this booklet, Mr. Mardūkh says, "All precepts may be abrogated when necessary."

If he had reviewed books of jurisprudence or the discussions of exegetes regarding abrogated verses, he would realize that abrogation of a precept means removal of a precept in accordance with the time not in accordance with conditions.

A precept's persistence in normal circumstances and its lapse in special circumstances have both been taken into consideration in the sharī'ah and this has nothing to do with abrogation. For example, in one verse God, the Almighty, states that eating the dead meat of an animal is harām; however, in times of need the unlawfulness of this act is removed—the latter part of the verse does not abrogate the former part.

In the first years of Islam, the marriage of an adulteress with a believing non-adulterer and the marriage of an adulterer with a believer who was not an adulteress was unlawful. After a while, this precept was eternally abrogated and this was not due to necessity or abnormal circumstances. All abrogated precepts in Islam are thus.

Mr. Mardūkh says, "In the terminology of jurists, mut'ah has two meanings: short-term marriage and mut'ah of divorce."

It seems that he has purposefully forgotten that there is also a third meaning and that is mut'ah al- hajj—the same hajj that, according to the Qur'an, had been legislated into the sharī'ah near the end of the Holy Prophet's life.

The Muslims performed it until the reign of the Second Caliph. Halfway into his caliphate, he banned the mut'ah of hajj and mut'ah of marriage at the same time.

Mr. Mardūkh holds, "None of the Sunnī or Shī'ah books consider a mut'ah woman a wife." This is an accusation against the Shī'ahs. In the view of the Shī'ah and jurisprudence of the Ahl al-Bayt, there are two types of wives: First, there is lifelong marriage, which has specific effects. Second, there is temporary marriage, which also has specific effects.

These effects consist of the fact that a wife may only have a single husband, must observe 'iddah after separation, and the offspring resulting from the marriage are attributed to both parents. By way of illustration, at the time of the Prophet of Allah, 'Abd Allāh ibn Zubayr, who was brought into the world as a result of the mut'ah between the daughter of the First Caliph and Zubayr, was attributed to Zubayr and was not introduced as fatherless.

Mr. Mardūkh contends, "In Sūrat al-Ahzāb, which was revealed in Medina, God, the Almighty, says to His Prophet, 'We have made halāl for you, your wife and the property of your right hand.' If mut'ah was halāl at that time, it was necessary that He enumerate that also."

As I have mentioned, wifehood encompasses both permanent and temporary marriages. In addition, according to the general consensus of all Muslim creeds, understanding and specifying Qur'anic precepts through sunnah is permissible and effectuated.

For example in the Qur'an, the Exalted God only names pigs as essentially unclean [najis al-'ayn] and through sunnah dogs have also been annexed to pigs. No one has ever said that if it is true that dogs are essentially unclean God must mention it! Besides this example, there are many similar cases.

Mr. Mardūkh says, "In the eighth year of the hijrah, when the army of Islam was stationed in Mecca, young women and widows adorned themselves and exhibited themselves before the solders of Islam. The fires of their lusts flared due to the length of their stay and their extended celibacy. Therefore, by force of circumstance and in line with the rule of eating dead meat, the Holy Prophet issued permission for temporary marriage."

One must ask him: Had Zubayr temporarily married the daughter of the Caliph in that period? And was 'Abd Allāh ibn Zubayr, who was born from this marriage and considered one of the sahābah of the Prophet of Allah, supposedly one year old when the Holy Prophet passed away in the tenth year of the hijrah?

Apart from this, was the answer to removing the mentioned danger that the Holy Prophet should give

permission for [in Mr. Mardūkh's words] adultery and fornication or should he have prevented the ostentation of adorned woman and their unrestrained socialization, which the Qur'an clearly states to be forbidden, and in this way carry out a mandatory precept of the Qur'an?

> **"Women must not reveal their adornments to men, except their husbands and mahārīm..."**[146]

---

[146] Sūrat al-Nūr 24:31. As previously mentioned, mahārīm are predetermined close family members such as parents, siblings, and siblings of one's parents who one may not marry one another. [trans.]

Even besides this, how many years did the conquest of Mecca take that the army of Islam was faced with such arduous celibacy and were thus bound by necessity? Whereas, considering other troubles of the Prophet of Islam (S) on this journey, such as the battle of Hunayn, the numerous sieges of Tā'if, and additional reformations around Tihāmah, the army of Islam was not in Mecca for more than a few days!

If indeed this short stay brought about necessity and, according to Mr. Mardūkh, sanctioned the permissibility of fornication, must not mut'ah, fornication, adultery with married women and mahārīm—such as mothers and sisters—and even homosexuality be permissible in the modern world which is—in his words—enveloped in bewitching and aphrodisiacal sights, where hundreds of fully adorned women and throngs of half bare girls are seen in the vista of every street and corner and where various strata of impecunious youths, workers or students, exist who are not able to marry and afford the costs of a family?

Could such Islamic precepts as said author maintains still subsist and not be obsolete in such asphyxiating conditions? Also, what is the difference (according to said author who believes that mut'ah is a form of adultery or fornication) between mut'ah and non-mut'ah whereby one is permissible and the other remains forbidden?

Mr. Mardūkh says, "When honorable 'Umar saw that there is no longer any need for the act of mut'ah and uninformed persons still practiced it, he notified the people that the meat of domestic donkeys and mut'ah are harām, and what is the difference whether the Prophet announced them harām or his Caliph?"

First of all, why would an Islamic precept that was legislated so clearly in several Qur'anic sūrahs, such as al-Mu'minūn and al-Ahzāb, at the start of the Prophet's appointment and after the hijrah—according to the said author—and continually read by Muslims throughout time remain obscure in the twenty-three years of the Prophet's life when he engaged in extraordinary promotional activity of religious precepts and after his passing throughout the caliphate of the First Caliph and half that of the second until it was clarified by the announcement of the Second Caliph?

Secondly, the Second Caliph's statement that said author holds to be an announcement of God's and the Prophet's decree is, "There are two types of mut'ah that were halāl at the time of the Prophet of Allah and I make them harām[147] and will punish their perpetrators. These two mut'ahs are the mut'ah of hajj and mut'ah of women." Dear readers, you judge whether this statement is the announcement of God and the Prophet's decree or an original interdiction by the Second Caliph himself.

Thirdly, those 'uninformed' persons that he is talking about are incidentally the sahābah themselves; especially the most prominent of them such as 'Alī ('a), Ibn Mas'ūd, Ibn 'Abbās, Zubayr, and the First Caliph whose daughter was the mut'ah of Zubayr.

Fourthly, the two mut'ahs that the Second Caliph named are "mut'ah of women and mut'ah of hajj" not "mut'ah of women and the meat of domestic donkeys". The Second Caliph's dignity is much higher than not knowing his own Arabic language and naming donkey meat mut'ah. Of course, this from Mr.

Mardūkh is probably a subtle and intentional mistake!

Mr. Mardūkh states, "None of the precepts regarding marriage, such as lineage and 'iddah, pertains to mut'ah."

This is a blatant misrepresentation of the Shī'ahs. Regardless, he must be asked whose son 'Abd Allāh ibn Zubayr was.

Mr. Mardūkh declares, "The meaning of the verse of mut'ah[148] is

---

[147] Emphasis added.

[148] Sūrat al-Nisā' 4:24.

that if 'you take pleasure of your wife and enter her', you must pay her mihr in full, and this holy verse has nothing to do with the meaning Shī'ah 'ulamā' interpret from it."

I must advise him to refer to narrations in books of hadīth and exegesis from eminent sahābah regarding this verse so that he realizes that before Shī'ah 'ulamā', the sahābah themselves, who were Arabs and spoke the language of the Qur'an, interpreted this verse the same.

When Mr. Mardūkh makes snide remarks, they are actually directed at them. Also, he should refrain from giving Shī'ah 'ulamā' lessons in Arabic, saying in contradiction to Arabs and Arabic lexis that "Istimtā' and tamattu'—i.e. the Arabic verbal mode of istif'āl and tafā"ul—mean the same thing in Arabic lexicology." For more information it would be good if my dear readers referred to "Tafsīr Tabarī", "Durr al-Manthūr", and various books of hadīth.

Mr. Mardūkh notes, "Some Shī'ah leaders say: even though the word istimtā' means enjoyment and taking pleasure, in the terminology of religious law it refers to the mut'ah marriage contract." I say that even though in books of jurisprudence or lexis the word istimtā' is not defined as the mut'ah marriage contract, even so, if istimtā' meant that, then the following verse means that, "Whoever does not marry pure and good things and mut'ahs them instead will be an inhabitant of Hell!"

Bravo to this miraculous logic and reasoning that eliminates all relationship between rationale and conclusion! Apparently, in his logic if a word means one thing in a certain place, it should mean the same everywhere. For instance, if the word ajr means mihr in the verse of mut'ah, then in the following verse it should mean the same thing and so the meaning of the verse would be, "To the patient, mihr will be given without reckoning!"

Also, zawj and zawjān sometimes mean wife and husband. If zawjān in the following verse means husband and wife, it would mean that even angels have males and females and wives and husbands!

Apart from this, no one has said that istimtā' means mut'ah marriage contract; rather, it means temporary marriage and there is a great difference between the two.

Mr. Mardūkh holds, "It is even more strange that the Shī'ahs believe in performing mut'ah; however, they eschew letting the women of their family take part in mut'ah."

I must say that this is for the same reason that you believe in permanent marriage but would never give your daughter's hand to a person who you know wants her only for a night's pleasure and will then divorce her or for the same reason that you would not marry your young daughter to an old man who has only a short time to live.

Essentially, what does liking or disliking a precept have to do with its ordainment or lack thereof? God, the Almighty, declares:

> *"And how oft you hate something which is good for you and how oft you love something that is bad for you..."*[149]

> *"You have been commanded to jihād which is loathsome to you..."*[150]

> *"And if Truth had followed their caprices, the heavens and the earth and all in them would surely have been thrown into confusion and corruption..."*[151]

Even a person who cursorily consults the Holy Qur'an would have no doubt that the basis of Islamic precepts is observance of genuine interests and adherence to truth, whether or not this is in accordance

---

[149] Sūrat al-Baqarah 2:216.

[150] Sūrat al-Baqarah 2:216.

[151] Sūrat al-Mu'minūn 23:71.

with the desires of the people.

Mr. Mardūkh states, "The majority of Muslims believe that mut'ah is harām and opposing the opinion of the religious and legal majority is forbidden."

One must ask him: which religion that considers the opinion of the majority to be proof is rightful? In His divine book, God, the Exalted, considers obedience to the truth, exclusively, to be sine qua non and berates the majority's opposition to it.

> *"Verily We have brought you the truth; however, most of you are adverse to the truth."*[152]

If it is required to follow the inclinations of the majority, then the Muslim minority should have accepted idolatry and also the pious who consist of a very small minority in relation to the wicked and wrongdoers should through aside their piety.

Besides, what does a religious discussion have to do with state law? Also, what influence do the legislated laws of a country have in the enactment or annulment of religious issues? It seems that Mr. Mardūkh thinks that the domain of theology and religious law is that of the senate or parliament!

Mr. Mardūkh says, "Because the authorization of mut'ah is against the Qur'an, it necessitates unbelief and heresy. Therefore, those who believe in it are unbelievers." (!)

It is extremely unfortunate for a person to spend his life in religious debates and still not understand that there is no cause for unbelief in the issue of the permissibility or illicitness of mut'ah where one side of the controversy, Shī'ah or Sunnī, is surely wrong, or that he does not understand the two things that necessitate unbelief and apostasy

---

[152] Sūrat al-Zukhruf 43:78.

which are renunciation of one of the three principles of religion [usūl al-dīn]: tawhīd (monotheism), prophethood, and resurrection; or basic repudiation of one of the requisites of religion [darūriyāt-e dīn] such as prayer, fasting, and that the Ka'bah must be faced in prayer because denying these necessitates denial of God and the Prophet.

On top of that, the issues in dispute among the Sunnīs and Shī'ahs, one of which is mut'ah, are not among the principles or the requisites of religion, rather they are religious ancillaries [furū'āt-e dīn] and are as such theoretical not axiomatic and necessary. Even so, it is highly unlikely that he never heard that a Muslim that refutes a theoretical religious issue is not considered an unbeliever.

However, it is evident from his present work that he has no motive but to provoke naïve persons and inflame the fires of fitnah which have been burning for centuries—fires which were being extinguished through the cooperation of a number of scholars. For instance, in his very short treatise he repeatedly claims that in this matter the Shī'ahs have no purpose but enmity towards 'Umar.

Mr. Mardūkh heaps up ten so-called "evils entailed by mut'ah" including assertions that the Qur'an explicitly prohibits mut'ah, the permissibility of mut'ah was caused by necessity, mut'ah is against the rules of lineage, honorable women would never submit to mut'ah, a woman who is made a mut'ah becomes hated, and so on.

Dear readers, put the title "evils entailed by mut'ah" side by side with professed evils and enmity towards 'Umar and judge yourselves.

Mr. Mardūkh says, "If you do not intend to oppose 'Umar, for the sake of precaution, why do you not instead pronounce the formula of marriage and whenever you decide to separate, do so by divorce?"

It would be well if one asked him, "Keeping in mind the evils you enumerated as results of the temporariness of the marriage, where the marriage might last for no longer than an hour, a night, or a week, what is the difference between the two forms of marriage by which you authorize one and forbid the other? Is not such prohibition of mut'ah in truth a mockery of the law of divorce?"

At the conclusion of his treatise, Mr. Mardūkh attacks a scholar who has recently written a book on mut'ah, saying that he has altered the quotation cited from 'Umar in "Tafsīr Kabīr": "Motaatan kanata ala aahed Rasul Allah halalan, wa ana ahramhoma wa oaaqeb aalyhma lahem al hemar al anesa wa motaat al nesaa"

And he has reproduced it thus: "Motaatan, mahlltan aala aahed Rasul Allah, w ana ahramha, wa oaaqeb aalyehma."

It would be well if he had taken note of the said hadīth which he cited in his article in the Keyhān Newspaper: "Mat'ataan, kanata 'ala 'ahd rasulullah ḥalālan, wa ana ḥaramuha, wa a'aaqab 'alayhuma laḥam alḥumur al-unsiya, wa mut'a al-nisaa."

He did not even suffice with this and he repeated his mistake in his treatise.

> *"..And Allah is He whose help is sought..."*[153]

---

[153] Sūrat Yūsuf 12:18. This article was reproduced from the yearbook, "Maktab-e Tashayyu'".

Discourse Nine: The General Framework of Ownership

Beings that we see upon the earth—comprising plants, animals, and humans—are generally engaged in activity and effort. They each endeavor outside the spheres of their selves to preserve their lives and obtain useful and beneficial things.

No inactive, silent creation may be found in the wide expanse of existence. Among all these efforts, no activity is performed without the intention to gain something.

The actions observed in various types of plants are intended to preserve them from harm, induce growth, and help them to propagate. The actions of the varieties of animals and humans are motivated by the aim to acquire benefits—even if these benefits are internal or imagined—and this subject is not open to doubt.

The Grounds for Struggles and Endeavors

Active beings, animals, and humans naturally understand that using available materials for self- preservation and resolving natural needs is not possible unless the materials are allotted to them and they are not in use by others. In other words, a single action cannot have two agents. This is the basis for all these struggles and endeavors.

For this reason, humans and other active beings, whose basis for action we understand, prevent others from appropriating and intruding into that which they earmark as their own. This clear and indisputable principle is ownership; something that no human doubts. This is what the possessive "lām" [] means in Arabic in word groups such as: "Hatha le, hatha lak, le an afaal katha? lak an tafaal katha."

Confirmation of this obvious principle is the conflict seen among animals. They fight with their enemies to protect their nests or lairs and their food or prey and if their mates or offspring are faced with danger they enter into battle.[154]

Another proof is that children fight to preserve their food and other possessions. It is even seen among infants that they battle with their peers over their mothers' breasts.

---

[154] onsider ants and bees. These creatures build themselves nests and through their nature, they regard it as their own. They store their foodstuff in their nest. This shows that these creatures consider themselves the owners of the nests they build and the food they gather. This feature is also clearly seen in other animals. This patent truth can also be perceived in the lives of early humans and nomads—whose lifestyle is similar to that of early humans. Even though nomads live communally and in tribes, they respect and sanctify private ownership and they prioritize the ownership of specific items. In "The History of Ownership", Felician Shanet writes, "Among nomadic tribes the collective ownership of property does not prevent individuals from owning what is theirs. These private properties are comprised of things that the nomad individuals produced or manufactured themselves." Loy Brovel writes that these belongings are part of the existence of nomadic individuals and can never be separated from them. He maintains that there is an unbreakable connection between each nomadic individual and their property, and the results of their personal endeavors such that these effects are not only part of their private possessions, but they are also part of their identity. He says, in other words, that nomadic individuals elevate their identity by having these possessions.

Is Ownership Instinctive [fitrī]?

In accordance with their fitrah and instincts, humans live communally. However, the pillars of human social life, which is born of the faculty of fitrah, cannot be established and stay firm without this faculty. The only thing the society can do is to amend those fitrī principles and arrange them in the form of social norms.

Thus, the fitrī principle of ownership attains various types and designations. For instance, private possessions are called property and non-monetary features are called rights.

People may have differences of opinion regarding various aspects of the realization of ownership. For instance, there is variation in the means whereby one may or may not gain ownership (e.g. inheritance, transactions, misappropriation) and there may be differences in the attributes of the owners (e.g. minors or adults, dull-witted or rational, individual or community).

Even though various contrasting views consider some owners and others not, in short, the essence of ownership is something that humans must necessarily accept. For this reason, schools that oppose ownership, such as communism, take possessions away from the individual and transfer them to the society or government—they cannot and will never be able to completely eradicate people's ownership.

Thus, the essence of ownership is the fitrah and nature of humans and eradication of fitrah is the eradication of humanity.

Ownership of Work

Humans continually work in order to preserve their lives. For this reason they appropriate things in the external world in various manners and use everything to their advantage. This is an undeniable truth for humans need external materials in order to live and evolve. They must resolve this need by possessing and using these materials.

This is why humans consider themselves owners of their own work, the results thereof, and that which they appropriate. Of course, it must be noted that the general meaning of work is meant, inclusive of all actions and reactions. It is a relationship which sociologists consider to have specific effects in the society.

In short, humans regard the materials they use and exert energy upon and the results and products of this use as their own specific property and consider any kind of use thereof completely legitimate.

This principle has value in human societies and it is regarded as an unchallengeable right. In fact, it could be said that this principle is one of the stable pillars of social life.

Moreover, we know that humans cannot singly resolve all their needs through their own work and actions. The domain of human life is so vast that one person cannot carry out all its tasks. For this reason, humans feel the need for society and social cooperation; in order to compensate for this deficit, they collaborate with others.

The result of this cooperation is that every person makes use of the results of the efforts of other people and they procure that which they cannot obtain by themselves through trade. This indispensable need entails an essential requisite for trade and barter. Thus, each person takes on a certain aspect of the necessities of life and advances upon that path.

They take what they need from the products of their own work and trade the rest to satisfy other needs. This is the basis of barter which has been built upon a social need and has been born of the principle of social cooperation.

Money, Indicator of Ownership

A truth that must be noted here is that the goods and chattels which are products of people's work are not of equal worth. Some are greatly needed, some are plentiful, some rare. The effort required to obtain every commodity is not the same. There are also other differences between commodities.

These differences caused complications in trade, and in order to resolve this problem, the principle of value was developed. However, evaluation of commodities requires a standard by which the value may be judged. As a result, money appeared. In other words, to evaluate the worth of items, the concept of money was devised.

This was the only means by which the value of items could be determined, resolving the basic problem of trade. To this end, various valuable and rare items, such as gold, were established as the basis for value, measuring other commodities according to this criterion. For various commodities, units of weight and volume were assigned and the units of goods were valued by the unit of money, basing trade on this standard.

This is considered the mainspring for the invention of money after which various types of money were introduced such as silver, copper, bronze, notes, and so on. These issues are discussed in detail in books on the history of economics. After the spread of buying and selling, the merchant profession appeared. That is, a group of people specialized in trade and barter to gain profit.

These are activities that humans engaged in to resolve their living needs. In this manner money also became considered as a human need and was substituted for all commodities and necessities since people can gain everything—all desiderata and life pleasures—through money.

Therefore, trade and commerce was based upon the exchange of all goods for a certain type of commodity. The need to exchange goods or gain profit induces humans to trade and the difference of goods being exchanged is the basis for human social life.

Usury or Negation of Ownership

The reciprocal exchange of two similar goods where the value and object of sale are equal is considered valid in many human societies. Such an exchange may be performed for various reasons bringing about cheerfulness and friendship in the society and resolving the needs of the disadvantaged.

This entails no evil. However, in the exchange of two similar goods if an additional amount is received from one party under the pretext of interest, the exchange would be usurious and the additional interest would be usury.

Therefore, usury is the exchange of two similar goods where one side of the deal contains an addition in the form of interest. The sale of ten kilograms of wheat for twelve kilograms of wheat or selling a commodity for ten dollars and buying it back at a later date for twelve are instances of usury.

Of course, it is evident that such an exchange occurs only when the customer is in urgent need and has no other alternative. In order to show you the negative consequences of such transactions, I will elucidate the matter in the form of an example:

A man whose daily income is 100 dollars and daily expenditure is 200 dollars is forced to compensate for

this shortage through loan and obtain the rest by paying usurious interest. Let us assume that he gains the remaining 100 dollars by paying a 20 dollar interest rate; that is, he borrows 100 dollars for 120 dollars.

Therefore, the next day he will have 80 dollars and be 120 dollars short. Again he is forced to resolve this deficit by paying usurious interest. This will go on until he is forced to give all his daily income for interest. The matter, however, does not end here. Continuance of this situation leads to where his daily income no longer suffices to pay the interest on his debts.

On the other hand, the entire principal and interest belongs to the owner of the capital. One of the parties has nothing and the other has everything. The whole yield of the endeavors of one person is amassed in the hands of another creating two disparate classes in the society: the wealthy who lend money in the form of usury and the poor who must work so that they might earn enough money to pay the interest on their loans.

Many of the poor are not even successful in procuring the interest for their loans unless they disregard all their necessities so that they may pay a measure of it.

The main reason that wealth is amassed on one side is that exchanges occur without monetary requital and, in addition, money—which is a means for simplifying the exchange of goods—is traded as a commodity with supplemental value as opposed to its exchange for the value of work or a commodity.

Thus, consequences of usury are the ruination of various helpless individuals and the focus of wealth in the hands of another class of people who are sufficiently privileged with the benefits of wealth.

Everyday, the burdens of the lower class increase and the scope of the usurer class's wealth expands until they are able to do what they will with the people's property and even labor, engaging the creativity and toils of people to fulfill their insatiable appetites. Eventually, they use the strength and stamina of the doomed poor for defense, revenge, and battling against other classes leading to great chaos and disorder. Ultimately, the aftermath of this chaos is destruction of civilization and breakup of the social system and communal life.

In addition, it should be noted that the original capital given in usury may be lost due to poverty more often than not since everyone does not have the means to pay high interest and settle such debts.

Usury, the Root of Class Differences

Those who are familiar with economic matters know that the only cause for the rise of communism and spread of misleading communist thoughts was the blatant accumulation of wealth in a handful of people. This amassing gives them precedence in livelihood and life privileges and deepens social gaps among people of the society while the other classes are deprived of the necessities of life. They have everything and the others have nothing.

This privation breeds deep resentment and suffuses the hearts of people in spite and enmity. As a result, the deprived follow any call that rises—even falsely—in the name of the welfare of the afflicted classes in the hope that it may assuage their pains and problems.

Communists greatly utilize such privations. Essentially, the communist bacterium cannot flourish and multiply in any environment except that of poverty. It is in the climate of class differences that they can use the seductive and beguiling words of civilization, freedom, social justice, and equality as an excuse to inject their thoughts into the minds of the afflicted.

Even so, the truth is contradictory to what they say. They use attractive words; however, their only relationship with them and their meanings is propagandistic exploitation.

After hearing this call from the maw of communism, they imagine that a doorway to salvation has been opened. However, before long they will realize that this call was a lullaby which was intended to put them—with their eroded nerves—into a deep sleep to use the power of their aggregate numbers. When these wretched people awaken, the chains of slavery will have already been shackled to their hands and feet preventing them from any kind of free movement.

Indeed, the Lord of the universe is aware of all the secrets of existence. He knows how the life-ruining effects of usury and improper distribution of capital involve accumulation of untold wealth in the hands of a minority. By circulating this wealth in banks they idly recline upon their comfortable thrones and live extravagantly while others are bereft of everything including their legitimate right to make use of the results of their work—something that the human fitrah considers an apparent principle.

In opposition to fitrah, due to great concentration of wealth, some people live without working and others are not able to support themselves even though they work. This is why the Holy Qur'an adamantly opposes usury, attacking the basis of this oppressive exchange and considering it war against God.

> *"O believers! Fear Allah and give up the extra money gained through usury if you are indeed believers. If you do not do this, know that you have declared war upon Allah and His Messenger. If you repent your principal is your own; you neither deal unjustly nor are you dealt with unjustly."*[155]

---

[155] Sūrat al-Baqarah 2:278-279. Journal, "Maktab-e Anbiyā'", issues 1 and 2.

Discourse Ten: Alcoholic Beverages, Cause of Humanity's Decline

As opposed to other religions—the teachings of which are either based upon withdrawal from the society such as Christianity, Brahmanism, and Buddhism, or fix upon the development of a specific tribe or race such as Judaism—Islam has elected its system of enlightenment as a global social system.

It ensures human happiness in the setting of civilization—something that humans can never do without—by inspiring complete harmony among people. Islam intends to set up an organization whose elements consist of superior and pure humans who attain perfect human beatitude by developing and evolving themselves.

On this base, in order to form its intended society, Islam elects the fitrī human or the natural human; that is, the human originated by the system of creation, equipped with the blessing of sound reason by which it is differentiated from other animals, and free of the taint of delusions, superstitions, and other futile imitative thoughts. This has been made very clear throughout the Noble Qur'an.

Islam is aware that the human created by the system of creation and equipped with sound reason understands through its healthy mind, perceptions, and God-given fitrah that even though it and all other creations desire and seek their own happiness in the course of their lives, they are in no way independent in their origination or subsistence, in attaining happiness or resolving their own needs—they are in need of other persons in all aspects.

Moreover, no being in the world of creation has created itself or has sovereignty in managing its existence or maintaining it. The whole of creation, which incorporates humanity and all other phenomena in the cosmos, is dependent upon a point above and beyond nature. An indomitable and unseen will governs and sustains existence in accordance with the general laws of causality.

Intellectual Development, the Most Important Type of Worship

This understanding guides us to the conclusion that we must surrender to the One God—the supernatural Life, Knowledge, and Power—and advance toward the destination anticipated in our existential make-up which has been entrusted to reason.

The Noble Qur'an stresses that:

> *"Indeed, Religion is surrender to Allah..."*[156]

It also underscores that religion is a series of teachings that are harmonious with the special make-up of humans and provides for their existential needs in an absolutely balanced manner:

> *"So set thy face toward the pure religion; it is in accordance*

---

[156] Sūrat Āl 'Imrān 3:19.

with the nature [fitrah] of God upon which He has formed the nature of humankind. There is no alteration in the creation of God. This is the enduring (and true) religion; however, most humans do not know."[157]

After little thought, a person who understands the general and decisive view of Islam—that humans must live collectively in a way harmonious with the human make-up—will conclude that Islam considers preservation of a sound mind the most important of duties and does not give permission for its defilement even for a moment. This is a correct assumption.

Islam entrusts management of the individual and social affairs of humans to sound reason and does not sanction the interference of false sentiments except to the extent that is reasonably acceptable.

Hence, with all its might it prevents anything that unbalances the natural activity of this God-given blessing or neutralizes the efforts of the intellect. Consequently, it forbids gambling (which is based upon blind luck), lying, calumny, dissimulation, fraud, and things of this sort that unbalance social reason and neutralize thought and judgment.

Included in this range of forbidden acts is consuming alcoholic beverages, which is strictly forbidden in Islam such that for drinking even one drop of intoxicant a penalty of eighty lashes has been determined.

---

[157] Sūrat al-Rūm 30:30.

The Corrupting Effects of Freedom of the Use of Alcoholic Beverages

Among acts that cause interference with reason and contemplation, drinking alcoholic beverages is the only one that works directly on the mind and rationality and is solely performed to kill thought and fortify emotions that deny an overseer.

Accordingly, the evil moral, mental, religious, and health-related effects it spreads in individuals and the society are undeniably clear. Due to this act, for every year that passes in the history of humanity, millions are hospitalized with various diseases related to the gullet, lungs, liver, mind, and so on.

No year passes without multitudes of the alcoholic insane being transferred to psychiatric hospitals or millions of people losing their moral control and becoming afflicted with mental deviations and intellectual disorders.

Nor does a year pass that this deadly poison does not lead humanity to innumerable instances of murder, suicide, crime, theft, treachery, pimping, scandal, defamation, betrayal of secrets, vilification, use of indecent language, and harassment. A moment does not pass that it does not enslave noble human individuals such that they are no longer bound by any rules and regulations.

The pure reason that is lost from society everyday due to the consumption of millions of liters of alcoholic beverages is a deplorable and irredeemable waste. In addition, from the intellectual aspect, one cannot have much hope of general goodness and happiness from a human society that leaves behind the greater part of its identifier as human beings—i.e. correct and pure reason.

The first time the Noble Qur'an prohibits alcohol consumption, it briefly indicates its individual and social evils and names this act ithm (sin), an evil act that entails undesirable consequences and various deprivations.

> *"Say: My Lord has forbidden all indecencies in public and private and sin [ithm] and unjust persecution..."*[158]

Then, the last time it forbids this act—with utmost stress—it specifically indicates two of its iniquities, the diffusion of which weakens the pillars of society and ultimately collapses the structure of public happiness.

Elsewhere, the Qur'an states:

> *"Satan seeks to precipitate enmity and hatred among you through intoxicants and gambling, and to debar you from remembrance of Allah and from prayer. Will you then forbear?"*[159]

It is quite clear that the only aim of Islamic teachings is to create an upright society where friendship and conciliation reign. A society where all its members consider themselves responsible before God to carry out the human laws that guaranty their happiness and never forget God or disregard responsibilities.

This is what is briefly mentioned as law in the Noble Qur'an and that which is cited from the Prophet in this area is extensive and explicates all the physical and spiritual detriments of intoxicants.

---

[158] Sūrat al-A'rāf 7:33.

[159] Sūrat al-Mā'idah 5:91.

Islam's Crusade Against Alcohol

The day Islam banned alcoholic beverages the entire human world, excluding a small number of Jews, was afflicted with this deadly poison. It was common in all advanced and primitive societies of the time and drinking liquor had no legal prohibition. In those days, generation after generation, the people grew and multiplied with this unsavory way of thinking and practice.

To be sure, uprooting this practice by Islam was as hard as eradicating the belief of idolatry—if not harder.

This is why in order to carry out the interdiction of alcohol, Islam undertook a lenient and piecemeal method and implemented its aim over the course of several years—the span between revelation of the verse in Sūrat al-A'rāf and the verse in Sūrat al-Mā'idah. At first, the Qur'an vaguely proscribed use of alcohol in Sūrat al-A'rāf introducing it as ithm and then relatively clearer in Sūrat al-Baqarah and finally plainly forbid it in Sūrat al-Mā'idah.

> *"They ask you regarding intoxicants and gambling. Say: In both are great sin and some benefits for people; however, the sin of these two is greater than their usefulness..."*[160]

At the start of the Prophet's appointment, it was proscribed in a simple manner but ultimately it was severely forbidden with "punishment by the lash".

Even though at first Islam had problems in imposing the ban and clearing the atmosphere of the love for alcohol, it was extremely successful in accomplishing this onerous decree and realizing its general acceptance, which is truly astounding.

---

[160] Sūrat al-Baqarah 2:219.

The final verse banning alcohol, which is in Sūrat al-Mā'idah, shows that even several years after the interdiction, people still had not completely given up their ancient practice. However, as historical evidence shows, after the definite prohibition of alcohol, the people promptly drove the desire of consuming alcohol out of their minds and broke all casks and decanters in the streets and poured their contents onto the earth.

There is no mention of the execution of the punishment for drinking alcohol at the time of the Prophet (S), i.e., from the time it was banned and its punishment was determined until the passing of the Prophet (S), even though many instances for the execution of punishments for murder, fornication, and similar sins have been cited.

In the fourteen century long history of Islam, it can be said about the Islamic society that hundreds of millions of Muslims have come and gone without tasting a drop of this deadly poison. In Islamic nations, where countless Muslims live, except for great cities that enjoy so-called modern civilization, where this poison proliferates in line with civilization, it is certain that millions of Muslims have never even seen the color of wine throughout their lives.[161]

---

[161] Extracted from the yearbook, "Maktab-e Tashayyu".

Discourse Eleven: Why Must the Hand of a Thief be Severed?!

The principle of severing the hand of a thief, which is a punishment in accordance with the Islamic sharī'ah, may be broken down and analyzed according to two basic propositions:

First: thieves must be punished for the wrong acts they commit;
Second: the befitting punishment is severance of the hand.

Respecting the Rights of Others

The first issue, i.e. punishment of a thief, is not specific to the holy religion of Islam. According to the known history of humankind, various human societies—including primitive familial communities, tribal societies, feudal societies, and also great and small dictatorships, democracies, and theocracies—assigned punishments for thieves, which were and still are carried out.

It is evident that this decision in the human world is based upon the principle that according to realism, the most important and valuable thing understood by humans is life, and they know no duty more necessary than attaining happiness in life.

They collectively toil and struggle in the society to earn their basic needs—i.e. various types of possessions and wealth—and use them. In truth, as per sociology, humans spend half of their life pool, for which no finite value may be maintained, to procure living capital for the other half.

It is also evident that the value of preservation and protection of an article is equal to that of the article itself. An object that has no protection against termination is considered to be worthless. Consequently, we must conclude that perseveration of the products of human efforts generally has an equal value to half of a person's life, just as the value of mortal safety is equal to that of a person's entire life.

Moreover, breaking or ruining the fence erected around the products of a society is equal to destroying half the life of that society; just as taking away the mortal security of a society is equal to massacring all the people of that society. For this reason, the Qur'an states:

> *"Whosoever kills a person unless to retaliate for a murder or for corruption done in the land, it shall be as if that person has killed all people..."*[162]

Of course, in view of this a thief that strips the society of its property and security must experience severe punishment, the visualization of which will prevent them from encroaching upon the sanctity of the society's property.

---

[162] Sūrat al-Mā'idah 5:32.

Must Mercy be Shown with Regard to Punishment of a Thief?

The second issue is Islam's decree that the hand of a thief must be severed. That which is understood from Islamic decrees regarding retaliation or retribution in kind [qisās] is that, regarding punishment, the harm inflicted by an offender upon the offended is appraised and inflicted upon the offender, in order that it be a penance for their act and a lesson for others.

Surely, a felony, the essence of which is ruination of half the life of the victims (the effort put in to secure one's livelihood), cannot be resolved with a fine—great or small—or a few months in prison. The best testimony to this fact is that execution of such punishments has not had the least effect in preventing this corruption.

In Islam—as per the real value—one hand of a thief, which is approximately equivalent to half their life efforts, is severed.

This shows the baselessness of a series of criticisms by our own alleged intellectuals. Unfortunately, just as theft has completely ruined economic security in our country like a contagious disease, this blight has deeply rooted itself into our intellectual environment and correct intellectual concepts are being stolen from us!

These highbrows ask, "Why should a human individual who must struggle for their own welfare using their God-given hands until the final moment of their life and must solve their problems by their own able hands, be rendered helpless to the end of their life by losing their hand because of a mistake necessitated by economic need?"

The essence of this criticism is acquiescence to the offence and solving the problem by arousing pity and human sympathy. In other words, "It is true that the thief has committed a felony; however, seeing that economic pressure usually forces this offence upon noble humans, pity and compassion prevents us from making them wretched forever by cutting off their hand."

The mistake in this logic is abundantly clear. It is true that there is no problem in abiding by one's emotions regarding personal rights. As per various Qur'anic verses, Islam encourages people to overlook their individual rights in matters such as qisās (retribution in kind) and financial rights, and refrain from causing their brothers pain and hardship.

However, in regard to social rights, compassion regarding a felon and overlooking their punishment is, in truth, a transgression against an entire society in absolute cruelty. Freeing a thief and preserving the honor of a criminal is equivalent to entangling millions of innocent people and shredding their honor.

Mercy upon the sharp-toothed tiger, becomes oppression upon the sheep.

Must the Society be Sacrificed for the Individual or Vice Versa?

In any event, the problem is that the legal decree legislated for punishing an offender must consider the society and a salve must be applied to the wound inflicted upon the body of the society rather than merely training thieves and victims.

Here, the response to another criticism is made clear. The criticism is this: there is an obvious difference between a person who is in desperate need of food, privation and misery forcing them to steal a ewer for instance, and a person whose profession is theft and crime—who abases and cripples a society, everyday afflicting another innocent family with poverty and wretchedness.

Of course, these two have a striking difference whereas Islam considers the two identical and does not differentiate in the manner of their punishment!

The reply to this criticism is made clear by the previous discussion in addition to a short reminder: in Islam, punishment is carried out only for the most extreme instance of acts that are recognized as offences and crimes and necessitate punishment.

For instance, a person who is guilty of fornication is dealt one hundred lashes as punishment. If a person repeats this act several times without the punishment being dealt and is later proven to be guilty, they will only be dealt one penance—i.e. one hundred lashes.

In view of this introduction and the preceding discussion, it is clear that the penance for theft is for the last theft proven by the Islamic executive branch. There is no difference between the greatness or smallness of the theft and the factors and conditions causing the theft are irrelevant. There is no difference between the theft of a veteran thief and the act of a chicken-thief or a ewer-thief in that they have both harmed a pillar of the society.

Does Severing the Hand of a Thief Slow the Wheels of the Economy?

Critics say, "Upon what rational base is burdening the society by cutting off the hand of a person and harming the production factor of the country?"

These persons must be told that severing the hand of a thief means cutting off four of the fingers except the thumb. In a country naturally containing various healthy and handicapped people and involving thousands of diverse needs, there will be no shortage of work for a person who is only missing four fingers of one of his hands.

The burden of the society will not grow heavier and the production factor of the society will not slow down. For this reason, the punishment for the second instance of theft is not severance of the other hand. After the first time and cutting off the right hand of a thief, the left foot of a thief is severed.

Moreover, even if we consider that dissevering the hand of a few persons will truly lead to increasing the load on the society and slowing down the wheels of economy, is not protecting the economic security of a country by a minuscule addition to the social load a thousand times more important than killing half the life force of the society by exterminating the foundation of financial security?!

Indeed, it is an amusing logic that, "If the hands of thieves are severed, they become burdens upon the society; however, if no one protests against them and they are allowed to continue their profession or are put in jail and provided for, they are not burdens"!!

In our own country in its current palpable condition, are not thieves and pickpockets burdens of the society? Apart from the innumerable individuals who take part in great and small thefts by happenstance, the number of professional thieves and pickpockets is in the thousands!

Among these numbers, those who are free and fearlessly continue their professions obtain their livelihood from the produce of other people's endeavors. Over and above this, in newspapers we read of other deplorable and abominable events that occur every day in the course of thefts such as mortal and sexual assault.

Prison, the college of thieves

In addition to the enormous expenses taken out of the pockets of the helpless for building and maintaining the institutes related to these crimes and looking after offenders that fall into the hands of the government, the criminals live easily off the products of the nation and even finish courses on techniques of theft as a result of new acquaintances among prisoners!

Detractors say, "If such things are supposed to serve as examples, in America psychologists made and broadcast detective movies in order to provide examples so that people learn their lesson. However, not only did these not serve as deterrents, people learned crime and delinquency from them. Crimes similar to the movies occurred in the cities where the films were broadcast the same night. Additionally, up to now, public executions have not served as lessons."

There is no doubt that theaters and publishing houses with their romance in detective movies and novels are factors for propagating corruption. They embellish matters such that one supports the antagonist and imagines happiness in life to be dependent upon love affairs and unrestraint.

Even so, the intellect of an intellectual and the conscience of a conscionable person cannot accept that if implemented correctly, education and edification will not have any effect or that public punishments will not serve as examples causing many to conform to the correct path. Of course, like natural causes and factors, social ones also do not always entail the ideal effect—not continuously.

The intended result of an effective legal punishment is for it to mitigate corruption, and make it into an exception rather than completely eradicating it so it never occurs again.[163]

---

[163] Extracted from the yearbook, "Maktab-e Tashayyu'".

Discourse Twelve: Muhammad (S) in the Mirror of Islam

The heavenly character of the venerated Prophet Muhammad, who was appointed fourteen hundred lunar years ago by God, the Almighty, as messenger, leader and guide of the world, and the divine Qur'an, which is a compendium of God's words containing theoretical and practical generalities and is the Prophet's lasting miracle, have defined the lifestyle of hundreds of millions of followers and have claimed the attention of all humanity.

This must be considered one of the most important factors in the refinement and evolution of humanity. In fact, it is the most important factor and has had great effect upon the human society due to the influence it has had on the beliefs and acts of untold millions.

Islam and Other Religions

It is true that Islam is younger than Brahmanism with a history of approximately thirty centuries, Buddhism with a past of around twenty-five centuries, and Christianity that has lived in the human society for close to twenty centuries.

It is true that followers of this religion are more numerous than those of Islam; however, by referring to the Brahmin Vedas and their other religious texts it is clear that all or most of their religious decrees are negative and are only used by a small number of the religion's followers. Most believers neither benefit from the religion's spirituality nor their holy book. In truth, as regards action and reaction beyond its domain, the Brahmin society is futile.

In negative commandments, Buddhism is similar to Brahmanism. Also, as is plain to see from the four Gospels and other major texts, Christianity is almost completely devoid of applied edicts and social laws and is unreservedly skeptical of philosophy and reason.

Fundamentally, the story of Jesus Christ's sacrifices and the forgiveness of all of humanity's sins or those of the Christian persuasion are in no way compatible with positive religious laws. Other religions such as Sabianism and Manichaeism, have either utterly lost their good image or accommodate a specific people and are thus bereft of an increase in followers.

Indeed, only Islam has become accepted and honored by countless millions by virtue of its logical beliefs and its positive individual and social laws. It continually has millions of adherents who put into practice its positive laws throughout their lives. It goes without saying that the positive and systematic lifestyle of one individual can directly and indirectly influence thousands of people or even a large society.

As a result, others are never idle in enacting policies against this pure religion—by their own acknowledgement—and continually attempt to extinguish its light.[164]

> *"They desire to extinguish the light of Allah with their mouths; however, Allah will complete His light though*

---

[164] Sūrat al-Saff 61:8.

***unbelievers be loath.*"**[165]

Of course, understanding a heavenly character requires a heavenly intellect and describing it, a heavenly tongue. Even so, the extent that this pure personage and his attributes may be studied and debated goes beyond the bounds of a single article.

This discussion addresses the virtuous personality of the Prophet (S) through a general analysis of the method in which he imparted his pure teachings upon the human society because following these teachings is a necessity for the true happiness of humanity.

Authenticity of the Individual [isālat-e fard] and Worldview

In order to completely understand these discussions, I must say in introduction that the human nature has no higher purpose than to carry on its existence as much as possible and attain its instinctive needs.

As such, the first step humans take is to get together and form a community and submit to laws in order to safeguard the society whereby depriving themselves of a proportionate degree of individual freedom. This is all because, by depriving themselves of some elements of their freedom, they intend to realize other components of freedom and in this way better secure their survival and inherent desires.

The cardinal issue in human happiness, as per creation, is individual bliss. The prosperity of the society is subordinate, not vice versa. In other words, the purpose of creation is the human nature, which is in fact individual existence, not the social aspect of individuals.

---

[165] Sūrat al-A'rāf 7:44-45.

As necessitated by this elemental aim—i.e. happiness and success in life—we must choose a methodical style of life, which would inevitably be social; to drink, eat, dress, rest, marry, procreate, endeavor to fulfill needs, and level the path of survival using the intellect.

The features of this method and the configuration of this systemic process depends on a person's notion of the truth of the world of existence and one's own self, which is an inseparable element of the universe. Thus, we see that some humans do not ratify a Creator for the world.

They consider the world's origination to be accidental and consider humans to be no more than their material body—whose existence is limited to the time between their birth and death. They order their styles and rules of life such that they only resolve the ephemeral material needs of mundane life and follow the way toward limited worldly success. It is also obvious that those who consider matter and material life to be that which is valid and genuine follow this same method.

Those who believe in a world creator and consider existence and everything in it to be managed by gods do not regard humanity's being to be confined to the physical universe. They arrange their lives to continually satisfy the gods and to keep from incurring their wrath so they may be successful and safe from unpleasant incidents, which are born of the fury of the gods.

Those who believe in monotheism, consider the world to have One Wise and Powerful God, and support the existence of an eternal human life that does not end with death and an ideology that orders their lifestyle so as to guaranty their happiness and prosperity in both worlds—before and after death—attaining everlasting prosperity and bliss.

Thus, it becomes clear that religion is lifestyle and there can be no differentiation between the two. Those who consider lifestyle genuine and religion and its laws formalities are committing a serious error.

> *According to this principle, Islam regards lifestyle as religion and identifies the divine course before humans as the straight path. The right method of living is the straight path and the wrong lifestyle is the deviate way. Thus, God states in the Qur'an:*
> **"Allah's damnation is upon the evildoers; who debar people from the path of Allah and seek to deviate it, and they disbelieve the Hereafter."**[166]

The Worldview of Islam

The concept that the Noble Prophet (S) bases his religion upon is that the entirety of existence is the creation of a single God, who directs each component of the world to its specific perfection.

Accordingly, He guides humans, who have eternal life, towards their particular prosperity and perfection by asking them to follow the path that He shows them. In order to justify his mission, the Noble Prophet (S) portrayed the natural human—i.e. a person possessing pure human nature, equipped with God-given intellect and will, and unadulterated with imitative and superstitious beliefs—as requisite of his religious invitation.

This is because such a person, through their God-given nature, has the competence to understand the concept mentioned above.

This person automatically understands with the least advisement that this world, with all its greatness and expansiveness and its sound system, is the creation of a pure Creator who is the source of all perfection and beauty by virtue of His infinite existence and is free

---

[166] Sūrat al-Ḥujurāt 49:13.

of all evil and ugliness; that the creation of the world and everything in it is not in vain; that there is an afterlife; and that there will be an accounting for the good and bad deeds of humans.

Therefore, a specific style of human life must exist that can ensure this conception. Selection of the natural human for education and edification has the following Islamic results:

The Principle of Equality

This method will be inclusive of all individuals. There will be no difference between black and white, woman and man, noble and commoner, wealthy and poor, king and beggar, powerful and weak, Eastern and Western, those living in the polar or equatorial regions, wise and ignorant, young and old, and also between the present and future generations.

This is because we are all partners in human nature and we enjoy all its trappings. This equality is specific to the pure method of Islam. Other methods all have some extent of bias. For instance, a general difference is marked in the method of "wathaniyyat" between ecclesiastics and lay people, and between men and women; in "Judaism" between the children of Israel and others; in "Christianity" between women and men; and in social methods between citizens and non-citizens.

Only Islam considers the human world to be a balanced unit and has extirpated bias and division at its roots. The Qur'an states:

> *"O people! Surely, I have created you as males and females and divided you into groups great and small that you may know one another (and form societies). Verily, the most*

noble among you before Allah is the most pious of you..."[167]

"I shall not leave unrewarded the work of any agent among you, whether man or woman; you are all members of the same race..."[168]

The Principle of Realism

In view of the fact that humans possess the instinct of realism, the laws and decrees formulated in Islam are based upon realism.

In explanation, in the process of their natural lives, while humans are drawn towards their life aims with the help of their feelings and emotions, they naturally embark upon real aims not imaginative ones. An infant that touches its mother's breast craving milk or cries of hunger wants that which is really milk not its image; it cries due to hunger not imagination or fantasy.

Persons that endeavor to attain benefits really want things that benefit them not the conceptual image of those benefits. Also, when feelings and emotions reveal needs to us and draw us toward desires without heeding their real goodness or evil, our faculty of discernment—i.e. intellect—harnesses our feelings and emotions, mitigating their longings and showing us the real good and bad in them.

Even though a sick person may desire to eat something harmful, it is the intellect that prevents him from doing so. The intellect stops us from doing dangerous things. Ultimately, it takes from us a large portion of our freedom. Intellect is the only advantage we have over other animals and it is out best tool for realism.

---

[167] Sūrat Āl 'Imrān 3:195.

[168] Sūrat Yūnus 10:32.

The rules and regulations that the Prophet brought the people are based upon realism, not desires and fancy. This means that humans must do that which is in their real interests even though they may not want to—rather than doing what they desire—and even though it may not be to their presumed advantage. The nation must do that which is truly beneficial and conforms to prosperity in life even if it is against individual desires rather than doing what the majority wishes regardless of its expedience.

In the Holy Qur'an's parlance, that which conforms to reality or real interests is called haqq (truth). It is the only aim towards which humans must strive in their belief and practice.

"So what is there after Truth [haqq] save error?"[169]

"And if Truth [haqq] had followed their caprices, the heavens and the earth and all in them would surely have been thrown into confusion and corruption..."[170]

After a few days, the skin of an almond that is put into the earth under special conditions cracks and a green sprout emerges from its kernel. It grows roots and continually gathers nutrition from the soil, growing until it becomes a prolific almond tree with a trunk, branches, leaves, blossoms, and fruit.

The embryo that is introduced into a mother's womb, under the influence of special factors, acquires specific form, limbs, and organs, and through its typical processes it grows larger and more complete everyday until it attains perfection. In the same manner, if we

---

[169] Sūrat al-Mu'minūn 23:71.

[170] Sūrat Tā Hā 20:50.

succinctly examine each and every type of creation in the world, it would be evident that every creation in existence evolves on a specified path until it gains perfection.

From the advent of existence they are directed toward their ultimate destination and never deviate from their course. By way of illustration, an almond sapling will not transform into a horse in the course of its evolution and a horse will not sleep at night and wake up in the morning as an almond tree. Rather, every one of these creations is drawn toward its final destination on a trajectory that is commensurate with the faculties and mechanisms with which they were created.

They gain advantages and ward off harms that threaten their existence in the way their means allow. Chickens eat grain, cows and sheep chew grass and wolves, tigers, and falcons hunt for meat because each of them are naturally equipped with a special feeding system that is only suitable for the food they eat.

In order to defend themselves, chickens use their beaks, cows and sheep use their horns, snakes bite, scorpions and bees sting, lions and tigers use their teeth and claws, and deer run away since those are the inherent defense mechanisms of each.

In short, in life each of these creations embarks on a destination and does what its existential resources compel them to do and determine for them. This determination and guidance is the same as fate [taqdīr] and universal guidance indicated in the Holy Qur'an which is attributed to the Creator God:

> *"He said: Our Lord is He who gave to each thing its specific creation and then guided it."*[171]

---

[171] Sūrat al-A'lā 87:2-3.

> *"The Lord who has created (components) then gave them order. And who has given quantity then guided accordingly."*[172]

Of course human beings, who are also a type of creation, are not an exception to the rule. Our specific creation—or make-up—shows us the method we must adopt in our lives and specifies the duties and laws we must observe. The Qur'an proclaims:

> *"From what did He create humankind? He created it from a zygote then He gave it a measure. Then He eased the way (of happiness and prosperity)."*[173]

By contemplating this matter and the previous discussion, it is clear that the results of both are the same. To state it more clearly, the true [haqq] acts that humans must choose using their realist instinct are the same acts towards which the human make-up guides with its special faculties. This is the religion of truth and haqq; it is also called the fitrī (i.e. innate or natural) religion because of its relation to creation and the inherent human make-up.

> *"So resolutely accept the religion of moderateness; do not turn aside from it because this religion is the special divine creation upon which Allah has created humankind. The creation of Allah is inalterable. This is the religion that can secure the will and prosperity of the human commu-*

---

[172] Sūrat 'Abas 80:18-20.

[173] Sūrat al-Rūm 30:30.

nity..."[174]

> *"By the soul and He who created it and gave it order; then inspired it with understanding of its wrong and its right. Truly saved are those who virtuously develop their souls. And surely despairing (of happiness and prosperity) are those who corrupt it."*[175]

From another perspective, since creation is the work of God and all beautiful phenomena that manifest in it are attributable to His Bounty, the requirements of the specific human genesis that bring about human actions are called God's will.

(Of course, I am talking about the mandate will [irādah tashrī'ī] of God which entails His guidance and human responsibility. This is different from His genetic will [irādah takwīnī] which is absolutely inviolable.) The duties and decree obtained in this way are considered the commands and injunctions of God:

> *"And your Lord creates and chooses what He pleases; they have no will before the will of Allah..."*[176]

In light of the fact that this religion is a series of duties and instructions from God, the Creator, for those who follow its theoretical and practical precepts and submit to God, in Qur'anic parlance this religion is called Islam:

---

[174] Sūrat al-Shams 91:7-10.

[175] Sūrat al-Qisas 28:68.

[176] Sūrat Āl 'Imrān 3:19.

"Indeed, Religion is surrender [Islam] to Allah..."[177]

"And whosoever seeks a religion other than Islam (surrender to Allah) it will not be accepted of him..."[178]

The Principle of Balance Between Batter [māddah] and Spirit [maʿnā]

The third result Islam gained by extending its invitation toward the natural human is that in this manner it has selected a median method between materiality and spirituality.

This is one of the unique masterpieces of this divine religion as contrasted with what is understood from Judaism and the Torah, the Jewish Holy Book, which has no relation to human spirituality; Christianity which, according to a statement attributed to Jesus Christ, has nothing to do with the material life of this world;[179] and other religions such as Brahmanism, Buddhism, and even Magianism, Manichaeanism, and Sabianism that deal with spirituality to some extent but separate the path of spirituality from material life, completely severing their relationship. Only Islam is a primordial religion [dīn-e ḥanīf], based upon the human fitrah.

By way of explanation, there are those who, by all accounts, form the majority of the world's population and throughout their lives have no ideal but material advancement. Nothing occurs to them but the fancy of attaining high rank, great wealth, and material pleasures. They

---

[177] Sūrat Āl ʿImrān 3:85.

[178] This point is understood from the questions and answers between Herod and Christ after his imprisonment and it has been noted in the Gospels. In "The Story of Mankind", Hendrik Van Loon cites this from Christ in a historical letter reproduced in the story of Joshua of Nazareth.

[179] Sūrat Āl ʿImrān 3:64.

endeavor night and day to secure their livelihoods and pay not the least attention to anything beyond the framework of their evanescent lives and the passage of this mundane world.

Contrary to this group, there is a small minority who, through contemplation of the truth of this world and faithlessness of its life, understand that every pleasure is linked with a myriad of pains, every nectar a myriad of stings, every happiness a myriad of woes, every possession a myriad of cares and grief, every union by separation, health by illness, and life by death.

They comprehend that beyond the straits of this prison and this deceptive mirage lays an everlasting world that is free of the hardship and suffering of this one and that its happiness and prosperity belong to the beneficent and enlightened.

As a result of this thought, they become reclusive and turn away from the vileness and beauty of the fleeting world where all sweet enjoyment one day turns into despair, resentment, and disappointment. Thus, they crawl into a quiet corner and occupy themselves with observation of the eternal world and the infinite beauty throughout the heavens.

These two groups exist in our age and historically, they have also continually existed in previous ages.

The persistence of these two groups among humans is the best testament to the fact that with their God-given nature, humans affirm the correctitude (or rather the necessity) of traversing both the material and spiritual paths of life since if humans completely abandon social life and cease their endeavors, they must immediately say farewell to life and pass away from material life and in this event spiritual life would be lost as well.

Conversely, if humans abandon spiritual life, they negate reason and intellect which is the only advantage humans have over other animals and, ignoring realism, enter the same rank as beasts!

Consequently, a fiṭrī human can never adopt a one-sided lifestyle and suffice with only matter or only spirit. This is because, on the one hand, it is not possible to live in the material world and be free of matter, and, on the other hand, the awareness and worship of God in the insight of the fiṭrī human is meaningless without spiritual life.

The truth regarding what was said before regarding the faiths of Judaism and Christianity is that each reinforced one aspect of life in accordance with the prevailing conditions at the time of their inception.

In the age of Moses ('a), the Interlocutor with God [kalīmullāh], the Children of Israel who lived under the oppression and in servitude of Egypt's Pharaoh were bereft of all human privileges and they were treated as animals. After saving them, Moses ('a) spent the majority of his time in giving order to internal affairs, promoting social laws, building housing, and so on. He also taught spiritual life to a small extent.

Conversely, in the age of the Messiah's appointment, though the Children of Israel were under the dominance of Rome, they possessed systematic institutions. However, their priests and influential personages had completely left aside the religion of the Torah and had turned spirituality into a tool for material gain and exploitation of the people. As a result, the Messiah was forced to put all his effort into spiritual life and allocate the greater part of his teaching to this aspect.

As indicated, in its teachings Islam has chosen a method that is the median between physical and spiritual life. In fact, it has reconciled between and amalgamated two methods of life that seem to be completely antithetical.

Furthermore, by rights there is no way for the evolution of humanity except this, because obviously all types of creations attain their perfection—the purpose of their existence—through their fiṭrī activities and endeavors and the type of activity depends upon the capabilities and facilities inherent in their beings.

Humans, who are also one type of creation, are subject to this general axiom and law. Humans have a spirit or soul that has been created to live forever. It does not decay or become nonexistent. However, through virtuous endeavors and pursuits it can attain the raison d'être of perfection that is above and beyond any kind of prosperity, happiness, and success.

All the while, this heavenly soul is bound to an earthly body where lay its tools of trade, and the forces that work these tools are related in some manner to this body. In addition, the human make-up guides us towards society and civilization.

Doubtless, the purpose of such guidance is to deliver the recipient to its life aim and perfection. Moreover, the perfection and prosperity of every creation is certainly that which creation has determined for it, not that which imagination and superstitions decide.

The prosperity of a flower tree is in attaining its natural growth and producing that which its botanic nature impels—not being put in a golden flowerpot and set in a palace overlaid with gold.

Therefore, how can humans achieve their real perfection and beatitude and completely realize their true ideals without utilizing the physical means given to them by their genetic constitution and by living outside the environs of social life?

Islam has determined corporeal human life, which is social in the complete sense and uses all material means, as the backdrop for its education and edification. In line with the guidance of the human fitrah and specific creation, it has adopted extensive laws regarding the individual, social, general, and particular actions of humans which constitute the complete program for their education and perfection.

Some of these laws are responsibilities that humans have towards their God involving the expression of surrender and devotion before

His Lordship, indigence and destitution before His Affluence and Needlessness, abjection before His Glory, ignobility before His Greatness and Divinity, ignorance before His Knowledge, impotence before His Power, and submission before His Will and Providence. It also involves the socialization of daily and festival prayers, the greater socialization of Friday Prayer, and the greatest socialization of all which is hajj.

Another part of these laws are the obligations people have regarding each other and in the context of society. Of course, in these commitments (i.e. Islamic laws) the sense of responsibility is solely pertinent to God in that one must only submit to His Governance—i.e. that which His creation necessitates.

This means that all acts must be performed in the radius of the three principles of tawhīd (monotheism), nubuwwah (Prophethood), and ma'ād (Resurrection). The Qur'an states:

> *"O Prophet! Say to the People of the Book, 'Come, let us unite in a common word: that we serve none save Allah and that we associate not aught with Him and that some of us take not others as lords (to whom the destinies of people are consigned and whose will are followed) besides God.' If they do not accept this proposal, say, 'Bear witness that surely we are those who surrender to God, worship none but Him, and adhere only to His Will (which is what is necessitated by fitrah and creation.)'"*[180]

The foregoing discussion completely shows that the lifestyle in the holy religion of Islam is arranged in a way that the social and material life of humans is like a cradle in which spiritual life is fostered.

---

[180] Sūrat al-Baqarah 2:115.

The spiritual effulgence of a Muslim who conforms to Islamic commandments is something that illuminates and purifies all individual and social acts. At the same time that such persons are among people, they are also in the presence of their Lord. When they are in a crowd, they are concurrently in mystical seclusion.

While their physical bodies are striving to realize their material aims, engaged in various sweet and bitter, agreeable and unpleasant, beautiful and repugnant eventualities, and bound by the events of this disruptive world, their hearts are free and they reside in a calm world. Every which way they turn, they see naught but the face of their God:

"Whichever way you turn, you face Allah..."[181]

As we have made clear, devout Muslims extend their spiritual lives throughout their material ones. Wherever they are, everything they do is linked to their Lord. For such persons, all physical occupations are like a mirror that display God.

However, when other people think of spiritual life they see normal and fitrī life as a veil between themselves and the truth they seek. Therefore, they necessarily abandon their normal life and take an abnormal lifestyle upon themselves like Christian monks, Indian Brahmins, or ascetic Yogis. Regardless of the type, such paths are severe and perseverance in them requires steely determination.

On the other hand, a person who pursues spiritual life through regular social life in accordance with the Islamic method knows very well that the ascetic way is easier than the Islamic. In truth, by abandoning normal life, ascetics flee and absolve themselves of the hardship of constant vigilance and struggle.

---

[181] Sūrat al-Zumar 39:9.

In truth, they have precluded themselves from the path of perfection—laid out by their genetic make-up in the form of innate abilities and faculties—and conceive of a different path. That being so, will they realize the purpose that creation has determined for them?

In addition, in view of the facts that the world and all that is in it are creations of God and every phenomenon with their myriad differences are signs of Truth and signs of God, and humans and their various fitrī properties are among these signs, we must be aware of and know God in the process of our spiritual lives and all these mirrors must be used to acquire complete knowledge of the beauty of Truth, else we will realize no benefit from our endeavors but deficient knowledge or complete ignorance.

Knowledge and awareness from the standpoint of Islam

A person who has read about the religions of the world will have no doubt that Islam's honor and reverence regarding knowledge and understanding and its encouragement and eagerness regarding obtaining knowledge cannot be found in any religion whether divine or secular. The Holy Qur'an proclaims:

"Are those who know and those who do not know equal?"[182]

The Holy Qur'an has greatly and lucidly venerated the high status of knowledge. The Noble Prophet declares:

"Seeking knowledge is a religious duty of all Muslims."

---

[182] Sūrat al-Isrā' 17:36.

"Seek knowledge from the cradle to the grave." and *"Seek knowledge even if it is in China (far away)."*

The Holy Qur'an commands its adherents to never leave the path of knowledge and to refrain from following conjecture and accepting anything heard, seen, or conceived without contemplation because the ears, eyes, and minds are responsible:

"And adhere not to that which you have no knowledge because the ears, eyes, and hearts will be interrogated."[183]

Clearly, Islam encourages its followers to attain knowledge with full force. Among the types of knowledge, it deems learning the theoretical teachings and practical laws obligatory:

"All believers must not go out to jihād; rather, from each party a group must engage in learning religious knowledge and undertake religious promotion..."[184]

It is a reality that the ability of various individuals is different in regard to understanding knowledge and scientific truths. Some people do not have great talent for logical reasoning and exist in the workplace and the material level of life.

Others possess analytic thought and naturally enjoy understanding profound intellectual knowledge and scientific theories. Still others turn a blind eye to thought and action and spiritually forfeit the dismal world of matter and its beguiling beauties and ephemeral pleasures. They discover within themselves a special passion for the infinite

---

[183] Sūrat al-Isrā' 17:36

[184] Sūrat al-Tawbah (or Barā'ah) 9:122.

and everlasting beauties of which the charms of this world are just a sample or a shadow.

These individuals can easily apprehend the truths and secrets of the other world using their inner intuition.

Bearing in mind this obvious variance among people, Islam instructs in three different manners and speaks with each of these groups in their own language.

It educates and edifies some using religious forms, others using free reasoning, and the rest by way of jihād of the soul and inner purification. God, the Almighty, gives an exemplum regarding His teachings:

"He sent down water from the sky that flowed in every channel to the extent of its capacity..."[185]

Also, the Holy Prophet stated:

"We, the group of prophets, are charged to speak with the people on a level they can understand."[186]

1. **The Method of Instruction**

Among its adherents, Islam has not given those with little talent for reasoning who are faced with error and deviation in this path, a greater burden than they can bear. It teaches them the threefold principle of religion, i.e. tawhīd, nubuwwah, and maʿād, using simple instructive

---

[185] Sūrat al-Raʿd 13:17.
[186] Usūl al-Kāfī, vol. 1, p. 23

statements—pure commands and injunctions. Such statements are prolific in Qur'anic verses and narrations from the venerable Prophet (S) and the custodians of the religion.

Of course, this threefold principle, which humans can easily reason out with their fitrah, may be only accepted as a result of sure knowledge. In truth, this policy makes rationalistic the other teachings this group has accepted without reasoning, since the rightfulness of prophethood makes all the statements of the Prophet valid and conclusive.

The Method of Reason

Islam trains people who have healthy minds and the talent for understanding scientific theories and logical reasoning by free argumentation. This means that it guides them toward what their realistic, unaffected fitrah understands, as opposed to first imposing and inculcating its ideas and then bringing ostensible reasons to support them.

The Book and Tradition—i.e. Qur'anic verses and the sayings of the esteemed Prophet (S) and the guiding Imāms ('a), which clarify the aims of the Qur'an—are profuse with logical reasoning. In them, Islamic beliefs are explained in detail with the clearest and most decisive of reasons. They also speak of the general interests of Islamic laws and decrees.

Of course, one must not disregard the fact that discussion of the expedience of laws does not signify that a Muslim or the Islamic society should not accept a decree until they understand its benefits. As I previously pointed out, all these precepts have been received from the Prophet and substantiation of prophethood is a compact proof of the validity of these precepts, even though their detailed rationalization may not be available.

Fundamentally, execution of laws that are in circulation in advanced or primitive human societies cannot depend on the theoretical acceptance of the individual. Individuals cannot be considered free in accepting or rejecting rules and regulations whether or not the law itself approves of intellectual criticism. Otherwise, dissolution of the society would be imminent. Indeed, people are free to give their opinions on these matters but they cannot disobey standing regulations unless the legislative authority declares the annulment of a particular law.

Moreover, following a religious leader [taqlīd] [187] cannot be considered inconsistent with the general mandate that an action must only be performed in knowledge and a breach of the aforementioned verse:

"And adhere not to that which you have no knowledge..."[188]

This is because the reality of the aforesaid taqlīd is that uninformed persons who cannot determine their duty should follow an erudite that can. Referral to an expert when a person lacks discernment is an incontestable intellectual principle.

It differs from censurable imitation whereby people unquestionably devote themselves to a person whose scientific competence has not been acknowledged. As per the instinct of realism, humans do not depart upon a path that they do not know and if they are forced to traverse it, they ask a person who knows it and they utilize that

---

[187] Those who cannot elicit the practical precepts and laws of Islam from their original documents must refer to the opinionof a mujtahid—i.e., a person who has the capability and mastery to deduce precepts—and act accordingly

[188] Sūrat al-Isrā' 17:36

person's knowledge as if it were their own. If a sick person is not a doctor, they consult one.

Whenever a person is in need, they take a person as their guide that is an authority in resolving that particular need. No person can be found in the world that is an expert in all things.

The method of edification and purification

Those who possess genuine talent in rending their hearts away from material attachment and turning their backs upon the delusory adornments and phantasmal desires of this fleeting world—those who have come to draw a debunking line through everything besides God [mā sawā Allāh] and turn a blind eye upon all the beauty and ugliness, the sweet and bitter, and the ups and downs of this impermanent existence—have opened their inner eyes towards the everlasting world to perceive the grandeur of the Truth without the veil of matter.

They want to traverse the stages of perfection prior to taking their leave of this transient world, gaining proximity to God. Islam reveals mystic secrets to these individuals in the veiled and esoteric fashion they are familiar with and understand and guides them from the nadir of ignorance to the zenith of knowledge.

Is Islamic mysticism derived from its Hindu counterpart?

Some foreign scholars have made statements such as, "Islamic mysticism has originated from Hindu mysticism and the Islamic tradition is nothing but a series of rigid simple beliefs and dry devotions."

In order to answer these claimants, the following hemistich must be cited:

You are not a knower of words, O dearest, your error is this.

Of course, I do not intend to defend Islamic mysticism and vindicate its various methods of mystical experience or distinguish their methods from that of the Hindu, just as I did not intend, in the discussion regarding the method of reason, to endorse overall everything written by Islamic philosophers or in the discussion regarding the method of religious forms to vindicate all practices of the Islamic masses.

Rather, my aim in this article is only to concisely review the main documents of Islam, which are the Book and Tradition, without refuting or ratifying the words or behavior of each of the aforementioned groups.

The claim by these scholars is founded upon the principle of evolution, upon which they establish their scientific thoughts and by which they account for the transformation and development of natural phenomena. They have generalized this principle to encompass all events even customs and traditions, and instinctual, fitrī, and spiritual manifestations. They seek the source of every event in previous ones.

This approach is the basis they use when they say that Islamic laws have been derived from Roman law or that Islamic beliefs have been adapted from the thoughts of Greek philosophers. They have even gone so far as to claim that religious beliefs are the evolved form of views from the Age of Myths.

These scholars have made two errors:

First, they have taken it for granted that what we call mystical perception is a form of intellectual understanding. As a result, they consider the knowledge gained by mystics through inner purification to be a series of poetic ideas such that a talented poet with a sweet-sounding tongue can spin these thoughts better than a divine sage.

They have made a similar mistake in regard to revelation—which is the heavenly apprehension of prophets and the instrument by which divine knowledge and laws are imparted. This is why they have introduced the Greek thoughts and Roman laws as the root of Islamic beliefs and commandments. This is totally clear from their discussions regarding prophethood and the prophets' way of thinking.

The statements available from the prophets—whether or not they are righteous in their claims—patently impugn and refute this theory.

Second, even if we consider the principle of evolution as definite and valid, we should not relate it to the principle of typical instinct. In the absence of external impediments, the instinct that creation has made dormant in a type or species will manifest in an individual of that species, whether or not the species has any antecedents.

For instance, we could say that Arabs learned variety in foods and the making of diverse meals from non-Arabs; or that democracy and its administrative institutions were transmitted to the East from the West. However, this cannot be said of the principle of society and government.

It was made clear in previous discussions that self-edification and self-purification—spiritual life and mystical intuition [dhawq]—is a natural human instinct.

With the existence of talent and dissipation of obstructions, this instinct awakens and the person sets out upon this path.

With the advent of religions that more or less involve the eternal and supernatural world, the innate ability of some followers will awaken and rend their hearts away from the attachments of this fleeting, calamitous, woeful world and turn to the world of eternity for the sake of absolute tranquility. In practice, in every religion that contains the name of God we see a group devoted to spiritual life and the path of mysticism.

By comparing the spirituality of the available main texts of various religions, we clearly see that major Islamic texts describe eternal human prosperity and the everlasting world more than any other religion. Therefore, emergence of the method of purification in Islam is natural, without its origination having anything to do with India or any other place.

Besides, history shows that some of the disciples of Amīr al-Mu'minīn 'Alī ('a), such as Salmān, Kumayl, Rashīd, Maytham, and Uways, had spiritual lives under his instruction before Muslims had even set foot in India or had any dealings with Indians. That the various types of Islamic Sufism claim linkage—both rightly and falsely—to Imām 'Alī ('a), makes the foregoing matter certain.

The Difference Between Islamic Mysticism and other Varieties

Indeed, when the elegant statements of Islam are compared with the assertions of others, especially Hindu mysticism, we see that Islam has the distinction that its mystical truths are hidden within general statements that other groups can benefit from to the extent of their understanding and it refrains from divulging secrets whereas other creeds do not possess this distinction. As a result, Islam has remained safe from the detrimental effects caused by the unveiled teachings of others.

For example, if we refer to Hindu mysticism to review the Vedic Upanishads—the sections devoted to divine teachings—and interpret the texts as a consolidated whole and ponder upon every statement, we will see that it has no purpose but a detailed and profound monotheism.

However, it states its valid arguments in such an unveiled manner that any referrer that does not have complete mystic knowledge will see its elegant and valid words as no more than a series of superstitious beliefs. In the least, from statements that describe monotheism in the utmost detail, they will realize nothing but incarnation [hulūl], union [ittihād], and idolatrous beliefs.

This is substantiated by the theories of Sanskritist orientalists regarding Hindu mysticism. After all their inquisitiveness regarding the major Brahman and Buddhist texts, they now declare Hindu mysticism to be a series of superstitions that are the intellectual products of Indians bereft of life privileges. The main reason for these reactions is that the wordings of these texts are intrepidly conspicuous and objectionable.[189]

The Corrupt Results of Hindu Mysticism

The disagreeable method adopted by Hindu mysticism has produced three harmful results:

1. When the mysticism that solely aims at undiluted monism of the pure God enters the awareness of the unenlightened masses,

---

[189] In a book he wrote describing the religion and asceticism of Buddha, an orientalist named Hermann Oldenberg,repeatedly elucidates that the mystic beliefs of Hindus are mingled with folly. He also states that Buddha considers theworld to be independent of God

it becomes the opposite of what it was intended and turns into idolatry. Instead of one God, a number of gods equal to the desires of people are worshiped: angels, fairies, and human saints.

The texts of the Magians show that their mysticism was afflicted with this same doom. Even though making idols was not common among adherents of this religion, they follow the same method as Hindu idolatry in venerating angels, human saints, and the elements—especially fire.

In practice, Christian mysticism, an example of which exists at the beginning of the Gospel of John, is similar to Hindu mysticism. The trinity [tathlīth] in this religion is the same trinity of Wathaniyyah—a type of idolatry.[190]

1. The edicts this mysticism gives to its followers are negative. Therefore, all the positive acts that divine creation has set in the human world, each as a sign of the Creator and each a mirror of His pure attributes, are completely discarded from spiritual life. This is a great deficiency that has befallen this mysticism. Furthermore, the mysticisms of the Magians and Christians have also been afflicted with this flaw. Only Islam has expanded its spiritual life to the human world and all its positive and negative phenomena.

2. Hindu mysticism deprives some strata of people from spiritual life, such as women and some men. Also, in Christianity, women are afforded limited spiritual growth. Only Islam does not deprive anyone and instructs each person commensurate with

---

[190] For more information, refer to "Al-'Aqā'id al-Wathaniyyah fī al-Millah al-Nasrāniyyah" (Idolatrous Beliefs in theChristian Nation)

his or her own individual disposition.

Back to the Islamic Method

The creation of God has put a particular material life within the reach of humans, has equipped everyone with similar mechanisms, and does not discriminate between humans.

It has also made spiritual life, which is beyond the veil of material life, available to all. Just as it has set the perfection of physical human life in the manifestation of our actions and positive and negative works, accomplished by the body, it has likewise extended the perfection of spiritual life to all our actions and positive and negative works.

In line with creation, Islam considers spiritual life as everyone's right and does not discriminate against any group. It also extends spiritual life to all positive and negative aspects of human life, and invites humans to follow a specific transcendent path within the constraints of social life and positive conduct.

While teaching this method, it hints at allusions in its normal and general statements. This is because our literal assertions are born of public opinion, and we use them in the process of our material and social lives for mutual understanding and conveying our ideas and intellectual concepts to each other.

Mystical experience which is rarer than elixir and has never become common throughout the history of humanity is completely apart from this method. A person who wants to express mystical insight using another method—i.e. thought—is like a person who wants to describe various colors to a congenitally blind person using words—i.e. the sense of hearing. A person who puts mystic experience into words is just like a person who carries water with a sieve.

An Outline of the Spiritual Journey

One may think that our claim that Islam expresses the spiritual path using hints and allusions is baseless and just a shot in the dark.

However, adequate contemplation of Islamic teachings and their examination through the passionate and ecstatic state of this group has proven the contrary. In a vague and general manner, it reveals the stages of perfection that the wayfarers of this path traverse. Even so, in order to truly and elaborately understand these stages, there is no way but mystical intuition [dhawq].

This group, who are besotted with the infinite beauty and perfection of the Truth, worship God because of their love and affection, not due to desire of rewards or fear of punishment. Worship of God for attaining paradise or avoiding hell is in truth worship of rewards or punishment, not worship of God. As a result of the love and devotion pervading their hearts, especially after hearing that God, the Exalted, states:

> *"Remember Me that I remember you..."*[191]

and discovering hundreds of other verses that speak of the remembrance of God, such as:

> **"They remember Allah standing, sitting, and laying on their sides (whichever way they face and in whatever state they are)..."**[192]

---

[191] Sūrat al-Baqarah 2:152

[192] Sūrat Āl 'Imrān 3:191.

and when they hear the message of their Beloved that:

> "Surely in the heavens and earth there are (many) signs for the believers."[193]

> "And there is not a thing but celebrates His praise..."[194]

> "Whichever way you turn, you face Allah..."[195]

and find out that all beings are mirrors each of which display the unparalleled beauty of the Truth and that, besides being mirrors, they possess no independent existence of their own; thus, they observe all things with loving eyes and probing hearts and have no intention but to behold the beauty of the true Beloved.

And when they hear God's message that:

> "O you who believe! Be mindful of your selves (souls): a person who is gone astray cannot harm you if you are rightly guided..."[196]

> "O human! Verily you are striving towards your Lord and you shall encounter Him."[197]

They understand that creation has confined them to the enclosure

---

[193] Sūrat al-Jāthiyah 45:3

[194] Sūrat al-Isrā' 17:44

[195] Sūrat al-Baqarah 2:115.

[196] Sūrat al-Mā'idah 5:105

[197] Sūrat al-Inshiqāq 84:6.

of their selves and that they have no way towards God save the way of their selves. Everything that they see or discover from this wide world, they also see and discover through their selves.

In this stage, one finds that they are detached from everywhere and everything; that there is no one but themselves and their God. Such persons are alone even if they are among thousands and even though others may see them among a crowd, they perceive themselves in utter seclusion unattainable by any save God.

At this moment, they look at themselves and everything within themselves, seeing nothing but a mirror in which the matchless beauty of the Truth is manifest. There remains nothing save God.

When they remember God in this manner and stabilize remembrance of God in their hearts, free of vanity, through various devotions, they shall enter the first rank of the people of certitude [yaqīn]. Thus, the following divine covenant will be realized for them. **"And worship your Lord until you attain certainty."**[198]

At this moment, the doors to the kingdom of the heavens and the earth will open to them and they will perceive everything as being from Him. Regarding Abraham, the Qur'an states:

> *"Thus, We show Abraham the kingdoms of the heavens and the earth that he becomes one of those having certitude."*[199]

First, the unity of divine acts [tawḥīd-i afʿālī] will be revealed unto them and they will directly perceive that it is God that directs the world and everything in it; that the innumerable causes and factors in the world of creation that are engaged in various tasks acting in accordance to their attribute—voluntary acts with the attribute of

---

[198] Sūrat al-Ḥijr 15:99.

[199] Sūrat al-Ḥijr 15:99.

volition and compulsory movements true to compulsion—are painted with His (figuratively) capable hands.

Whether it is a cause, an effect, or the relationship between them, all are created and formed by Him:

> "And to Allah belongs the kingdom of the heavens and the earth..."[200]

Then they will start discovering the unity of divine names and attributes [tawhīd-i asmā' wa sifāt] and openly discern that every attribute of perfection that manifests in this vast world and every beauty and grandeur that is seen, including life, knowledge, power, glory, and splendor, are all rays from the never- ending light source of Truth that radiate from the existential windows of the diverse objects in the world:

> "And to God belong names (even) more beautiful..."[201]
>
> Then in the third stage, they perceive that all these various attributes are manifestations of an infinite Essence and are in truth all exactly the same and identical to the Essence:
>
> "Say: Allah is the Creator of all things and He is the One and the Predominant (over all things)."[202]

---

[200] Sūrat al-Jāthiyah 45:27.

[201] Sūrat al-A'rāf 7:180.

[202] Sūrat al-Ra'd 13:16.

Superiority of the Tawhīd of Islam

These were the threefold stages of tawhīd (monotheism) that are allotted to the travelers of the path of Truth. When followers of various Godly religions who love truth journey upon this path, they assign it as their supreme aim. However, in order to instruct its wayfarers, Islam has discovered an apex higher than that found by others, determining it as their ultimate destination.

That which is understood from Brahman, Buddhist, Sabian, Christian, and other texts is merely that they have negated the quality of limitation from the Truth, identifying Him as an infinite truth beyond all status. However, Islam has even negated infinitude—because it is an attribute and all attributes limit their subjects—as a quality of God. It considers the Holy Essence to be above all status and even beyond this description. This stage of tawhīd cannot be found in any place but the holy creed of Islam.

According to a narration cited in the book "Al-Kāfī" from the sixth Imām ('a), he interprets this stage from the following holy verse. In view of the fact that this discussion is beyond the level I have pursued in this article up until now, I will forbear from further explication.

> *"Say: call upon Allah or call upon the Merciful [rahmān]. Whichsoever you call upon, He has names (even) more beautiful..."*[203]

Divine Guidance

From the point they begin to the place where they achieve rest, wayfarers of the path to perfection have many mystic insights that

---

[203] Sūrat al-Isrā' 17:110.

are hidden from the eyes and hearts of the earthbound of the physical world. This topic is beyond the limits of this article. That which is now important is the issue of divine guidance.

When these wayfarers enter the stage of tawhīd and proximity to God, they lose straight away everything they had until then, everything they thought was theirs, and all independence they claimed to be their own.

Seeing all as belonging to the Truth, they forswear their false claims. This is when they realize the greatest tranquility and are freed of all suffering, fear, and sorrow since they do not own anything to be afraid of its possible harm or be sorrowful for harm realized.

> *"Verily upon those who said, 'Our Lord is Allah' then persevered, angels descend saying, 'Fear not nor feel sorrow; receive joyous tidings of the Paradise you were promised. We are your guardians and guides in the world and in the Hereafter'..."*[204]

> *"Lo! Verily the friends of Allah feel no fear nor do they feel sorrow."*[205]

It is then that the bitter and sweet, the ugliness and beauty, and the ups and downs of the world will become one for them. They will attain a different existence, seeing the world and all that is in it in a new light:

> *"Is he who was dead and We brought to life and set for him a light with which he walks among people like his*

---

[204] Sūrat Fussilat 41:30-31.
[205] Sūrat Yūnus 10:62

counterpart in darkness?"²⁰⁶

Ultimately, they and everything they had becomes of God and God becomes of them:

*"Those who are for Allah, Allah is for them."*²⁰⁷

The foregoing discussions have made it apparent that the spiritual life in Islam is more extensive and profound than other religions. Because it encompasses all pauses and motions, positive and negative, performed by humans and its zenith rises above the aims of other creeds.²⁰⁸

1. Regarding the reasons for the advance of Islam and the triumph of Muslims over Christians in the Crusades and other battles, Hendrik Willem Van Loon states in "The Story of Mankind":

"The Prophet promised that those who fell, facing the enemy, would go directly to Heaven. This made sudden death in the field preferable to a long but dreary existence upon this earth. It gave the Mohammedans an enormous advantage over the Crusaders who were in constant dread of a dark hereafter, and who stuck to the good things of this world as long as they possibly could. Incidentally, it explains why even today Muslim soldiers will charge into the fire of European machine guns quite indifferent to the fate that awaits them and why they are such dangerous and persistent enemies."

---

²⁰⁶ Sūrat al-An'ām 6:122.

²⁰⁷ Bihār al-Anwār, vol. 82, p. 197; Wāfī, vol. 8, p. 784

²⁰⁸ Extracted from "Muhammad Khātam-e Payāmbarān".

Discourse Thirteen: About the Knowledge of Imams

Did Sayyid al-Shuhadā'[209] ('a) know that he would be martyred on his journey from Mecca to Kūfah? In other words, did he depart for Iraq with the intention to be martyred or to form a just and totally Islamic government?

Sayyid al-Shuhadā' ('a)—in the belief of the Shī'ah—is a sacrosanct Imām, the Prophet's (S) third successor, and bearer of complete trusteeship. According to narrated confirmation and intellectual rationales, the knowledge of Imāms regarding external events is of two types.

First Type of Their Knowledge

By God's will, the Imāms are aware of the truths of the world of existence in all conditions including that which can be perceived by the senses and that which is beyond them such as heavenly beings and

---

[209] It literally means liege of the martyrs and refers to the third Imām, Husayn ibn 'Alī. [trans.]

past and future events.

Rationale: there are widely transmitted [mutawātir] narrations that are cited in Shīʿah compendiums of hadīth including, "Al-Kāfī", "Basāʾir", "Bihār al-Anwār", Sadūq's books, etc. These innumerable hadīths indicate that Imāms (ʿa) are aware of everything due to divine blessing not personal acquisition. Whatever they want to know, by the leave of God they realize with the slightest attention.

Of course, there are verses in the Holy Qurʾan that determine knowledge of the unseen [ʿilm al-ghayb] to be specific to God, the Exalted. However, the exception in the following verse shows that the exclusiveness of knowledge of the unseen for God signifies that no one possesses such knowledge independently in and of itself, save God.

> *"He is knower of the Invisible and He reveals His knowledge of the unseen unto no one, save those messengers He has preferred..."*[210]

Therefore, it is possible for preferred messengers to know about the unseen through divine instruction and for other elect to know through the prophets' instruction, as many narrations state regarding the Prophet and all the Imāms that they passed their knowledge to the next before their deaths.

There are also intellectual rationales expressing that the Imāms (ʿa), who because of their brilliant status, are the most complete humans of their times, perfect manifestations of divine Names and Attributes, and know everything in the world and every personal incident.

Due to their fundamental nature, whatever the regard, its knowl-

---

[210] Sūrat al-Jinn 72:26-27.

edge is made clear to them. In view of the fact that these rationales are dependent upon a series of complex intellectual matters that are beyond the scope of this article, I will leave them to be examined in their own special place.

Practical Effects of Imamate Knowledge and its Relationship with Obligation

A point that must be especially regarded is that such benedictory knowledge, as per the logical and cited reasons proving its existence, is completely inviolable, inalterable, and irreproachable. In other words, it

is knowledge of that which is recorded in the Lawh-i Mahfūz[211] and awareness of the certain providence [qadā'] of God.

This necessitates that the possessor of such knowledge per se has no duty regarding it because it is inevitable. Also, the person may hold no intention or desire in regard to acting on such knowledge since duty rises from the possibility of action and, where volition is concerned, action and avoidance of action are both facets of responsibility—either action or inaction may be intended.

However, in view of the fact that such knowledge is ineluctable and predetermined, there is no way that responsibility can apply to it.

For instance, it would be correct for God to tell His servant to perform a certain task that is possible to either do or not do. However, it is impossible for Him to command a person to or proscribe them from doing something that will certainly happen due to God's genetic providence since such a demand would be null and void.

---

[211] This literally means the Guarded Tablet, which is a repository of all knowledge. [trans.]

Also, a person can intend to do something that is possible, set it as their purpose, and endeavor to achieve it. However, never can a person intend to do something that will assuredly and providentially happen and endeavor to carry it out since the willingness or unwillingness of a person has no effect on that which will assuredly happen because it will assuredly happen (regard carefully).

This shows that:

1. This benedictory knowledge of the Imāms ('a) has no effect on their actions and no relationship with their specific duties. Essentially, any sure event, because it is linked to certain providence and is inevitable, cannot pertain to commandments or injunctions, or human intention. Indeed, what the certain fate and providence of Truth, the Almighty, does necessitate is contentment with fate. Thus, Sayyid al-Shuhadā' ('a) said amid blood and dust at the final hour of his life:

"With contentment for Your providence and in surrender to Your command. There is no object of worship besides You."

Furthermore, in an oration before he left Mecca he said:

"The satisfaction of Allah is in our satisfaction; that of the Ahl al-Bayt."[212]

1. In regard to divine providence, the certainness of a person's action does not negate the fact that it is voluntary because divine providence regarding an act pertains to all its possible

---

[212] This means that whatever the Ahl al-Bayt are satisfied with, God is satisfied with, because their will and satisfaction has faded into the will and satisfaction of God. [trans.]

circumstances not the act in and of itself. For example, if God wants a person to perform a specific volitional action by his own free will, the external realization of this volitional act will be certain and unavoidable because the will of God has applied to it. Simultaneously, for the human in question it is voluntary and possesses the quality of possibility—as opposed to inevitability (regard carefully).

2. The appearance of the Imāms' ('a) actions should not be considered a reason for their ignorance of the unseen and to debunk the existence of this benedictory knowledge. This is like asking: if Sayyid al-Shuhadā' ('a) knew what was going to happen, why did he send Muslim to Kūfah as his representative? Why did he write a letter to the people of Kūfah through Saydāwī? Why did he get himself killed when God states:

"And cast not yourselves by your own hands into destruction..."[213]

Why, why, why? The answer to all these questions has already been made clear from the foregoing discussion and there is no need for reiteration.

Second type of Imamate Knowledge: Normal Knowledge

According to the Qur'an, the Prophet (S) and the Imāms ('a) of his pure lineage are humans like the rest of us and the actions they perform in the course of their lives are similar to those of other

---

[213] Sūrat al-Baqarah 2:195.

humans–volitional and in accordance to normal knowledge. Like other people, the Imāms ('a) determine the goodness and evil, and advantages and disadvantages of things through normal knowledge intending to do what is worthy of being done and endeavoring accordingly.

If external causes, factors, and conditions are favorable, their endeavors are successful and if causes and conditions are adverse, they fail. The fact that the Imāms ('a) know the details of all past and future events has no effect on voluntary acts—as we have stated.

The Imāms ('a) are like other human servants of God and are obligated to perform religious duties. Also, according to the leadership they have been given by God, which they must carry out by the normal laws governing humanity, they must perform their utmost in revitalizing truth and upholding the religion.

The Movement of Sayyid al-Shuhadā' ('a) and its Objective

With a short study of the general conditions of that time, the reasons behind Sayyid al-Shuhadā's ('a) decisions and measures become clear. The darkest period in the history of Islam for the family of the Prophet (S) and their Shī'ahs was the twenty years of Mu'āwīyah's reign.

After Mu'āwiyah took over the Islamic caliphate through trickery and became the unconditional monarch of the vast Islamic country, he used all his great power to consolidate his rule and destroy the Ahl al- Bayt of the Prophet (S). Not only did he strive to destroy them, he wanted to completely eradicate them from the minds and tongues of the people.

He made a group of the Prophet's (S) sahābah who were respected and trusted by the people his followers and used them to fabricate hadīths advantageous to the sahābah and harmful to the Ahl al-Bayt. Also, at his order preachers cursed Amīr al-Mu'minīn ('a)—as a 'religious duty'—upon pulpits throughout the Islamic nation.

With agents such as Ziyad ibn Abiyah, Samrah ibn Jundab, and Busr ibn Artāh he killed the friends of the Ahl al-Bayt wherever he found them. In order to do this, he used gold, coercion, bribes, persuasion, and intimidation to the utmost extent possible.

Naturally, persistence of this environment would cause the masses to begin to hate the name of 'Alī and his family and those who had any love of the Ahl al-Bayt in their hearts to sever all their ties to them in fear of their lives, property, and family security.

The truth of this can be understood by reviewing the Imamate of Sayyid al-Shuhadā' ('a) that lasted around ten years which—except the final few months—was contemporary with Mu'āwiyah. In this entire period, even one jurisprudential hadīth was not cited from him, although he was the Imām of the Time and clarifier of religious teachings and decrees.

(By hadīth I mean a narration that the people cited from him, showing that the people consulted him, not a narration cited from within his family such as by the next Imām.) This shows that in those days, the doors to the house of the Ahl al-Bayt were closed and the people's referrals to and consultations with Sayyid al-Shuhadā' ('a) had reached zero.

The escalating pressure that had beset the Islamic society prevented Imām al-Hasan ('a) from continuing his fight or revolt against Mu'āwiyah because, firstly, Mu'āwiyah had gotten the fealty of the people and in light of this fealty, no one would follow the Imām. Secondly, Mu'āwiyah had made himself known as one of the great sahābah of the Prophet (S), a Qur'anic scribe, and confidant and right-hand man of three of the first four caliphs.

He had even given himself the title of "Khāl al-Mu'minīn" (literally,

Uncle of the Faithful) as a holy appellation. Thirdly, through his singular intrigue, he easily provoked the killing of Imām al-Ḥasan ('a) by his own relatives then rose in vengeance to kill the Imām's murderers. Then, he was able to hold mourning gatherings for the Imām and grieve for him!

Muʿāwiyah had made living conditions for Imām al-Ḥasan ('a) so bad that the Imām ('a) did not even have the least bit of security in his own home. Then, when Muʿāwiyah wanted to obtain the fealty of the people for Yazīd, he poisoned the Imām ('a) using the Imām's own wife, martyring him.

This same Sayyid al-Shuhadā' ('a), who rebelled against Yazīd without delay after the death of Muʿāwiyah and even sacrificed his own infant child on this path, could not make this sacrifice when Muʿāwiyah was alive because against Muʿāwiyah's deceptive self-righteousness and the allegiance he had extracted from the Imām, his martyrdom would have absolutely no effect.

This was a summary of the woeful conditions Muʿāwiyah had created in this Islamic society in which he had completely closed the doors to the Holy Prophet's (S) house taking away from the Ahl al-Bayt all effect and function.

The Death of Muʿāwiyah and Caliphate of Yazīd

The final blow Muʿāwiyah struck against Islam and Muslims was to turn the Islamic caliphate into a hereditary despotism installing his son Yazīd as his successor though his son did not possess any kind of religious character even in the form of hypocrisy.

He blatantly spent his days in song, wining and dining, lovemaking, and making monkeys dance. He had no respect for religious laws. All this beside, he had no religious belief to the extent that as his soldiers were bringing the Ahl al-Bayt prisoners and the heads of the martyrs of Karbalā into Damascus, he came out to watch and, after having heard a crow squawk (which is held in some places to be a bad omen), he said:

> The crow squawked and I said shriek or not,
> I have surely taken my dues from the Prophet.[214]

Also, when they brought the Ahl al-Bayt captives and the holy head of Sayyid al-Shuhadā' ('a) before him, he sang some verses one of which was:

> Hāshim[215] played with the Land; for no report has come nor divine revelation.

The rule of Yazīd, which was the continuance of Mu'āwiyah's policy, made the duty of Muslims clear. It also made obvious the status of the Ahl al-Bayt's relationship with Muslims in general and the Shī'ahs—who were doomed to be completely forgotten.

Under these conditions, the most effective and decisive factor in instigating the downfall of the Ahl al-Bayt and destroying the foundations of truth was for Sayyid al-Shuhadā' ('a) to swear fealty to Yazīd, declaring him the inviolable caliph and successor to the Prophet (S).

Because of Sayyid al-Shuhadā's ('a) own true leadership, he could not swear fealty to Yazīd in effect taking a potent step in obliterating the religion. His duty was to refrain from pledging allegiance and God expected nothing less from him.

On the other hand, refusal of fealty held a tragic consequence. That terrible unassailable power of the time demanded allegiance with its entire being—it either wanted fealty or a head—and it was not content with anything else. Therefore, the death of the Imām ('a) was

---

214

[215] In full Banī Hāshim, literally Children of Hāshim; he was an ancestor of the Prophet (S). Specifically, in this verse it refers to the Prophet and the Imāms. [trans.]

guaranteed if he did not give his allegiance.

In view of the interests of Islam and Muslims, Sayyid al-Shuhadā' ('a) resolutely chose not to pledge fealty and thus be killed. He dauntlessly preferred death over life and his divine duty was to refrain from giving allegiance and be martyred. This is why some narrations state that the Prophet of Allah said to him in a dream that God wanted to see him dead.

Also, he said to some of the people who advised him against this movement that God wanted to see him dead. In any event, this regards the mandate [tashrī'ī] will of God, not His genetic [takwīnī] will because as we have previously stated, volition has no effect in His genetic will.

Refusal of a Life in Disgrace, Consent to the Red Death (the death of a martyr)

Indeed, Sayyid al-Shuhadā' ('a) chose to reject fealty and thus he chose death. He preferred death over life and the course of events proved that he made the correct choice since the heart-rending circumstances of his martyrdom, affirmed the persecution and righteousness of the Ahl al-Bayt. After his martyrdom, similar movements and bloodshed continued for twelve years.

After that, with the slight calm that transpired at the time of the fifth Imām ('a), the Shī'ahs came in torrents from all around to that same Household that no one paid attention to at the time of Sayyid al- Shuhadā' ('a).

Thus, day by day, the numbers of the Shī'ahs of the Ahl al-Bayt increased and their rightfulness and brilliance began shining and glistering throughout the world. The basis for this was the Ahl al-Bayt's legitimacy in tandem with their persecution, and the pioneer upon this field was Sayyid al-Shuhadā' ('a).

Now we wish to present a comparison of the conditions of the Prophet's Household and their reception by the people in the Prophet's day and the situation—which becomes more revitalized and more deep- rooted with every passing year—after Sayyid al-Shuhadā's ('a) martyrdom during these last fourteen centuries, making the verity of Sayyid al-Shuhadā's ('a) choice clearer than day. A poem recited by

Sayyid al-Shuhadā' ('a)—according to some narrations—is an indicator of this same truth:

And it is not for us to feel fear, because our desires will be realized in the final government.

This is why in his last will and testament, Mu'āwiyah greatly emphasized that if Husayn ibn 'Alī refrained from swearing allegiance to Yazīd, Yazīd should leave him alone and not object.

Mu'āwiyah did not make this final testament as a result of sincerity and love, rather he knew that Husayn ibn 'Alī would not give his fealty and if he was killed by Yazīd, the Ahl al-Bayt would be marked by persecution which would be dangerous for the Umayyad dynasty and the best method of promotion and advancement for the Ahl al-Bayt.

The Imām Indicates His Duty

Sayyid al-Shuhadā' ('a) was aware of his divine duty which was refusal to swear fealty and knew better than anyone the limitless and unassailable power of Banī Umayyah and the character of Yazīd. He realized that an integral necessity of refraining to give fealty was his death and his divine duty necessitated martyrdom.

He explained this matter in various places with differing words. In the gathering of the governor of Medina who asked Sayyid al-Shuhadā' ('a) for his fealty to Yazīd, he said: "One such as me does not give fealty to a person like Yazīd." During his nightly exit from Medina, he quoted his grandfather, the Holy Prophet (S), who said to him in a dream that God wanted—as a duty—that he dies. In an oration before he departed from Mecca, in answer to those who wanted to dissuade him from going towards Iraq, he repeated this.

On the way, in reply to an Arab personage who insisted that he desists from going to Kūfah or else he would surely die, the Imām declared: "This is not unknown to me. However, they will not leave me alone and will kill me regardless of where I am."

Even though some of these narrations have contradictors or are weakly documented, regard and analysis of the prevailing conditions of the day completely substantiates them.

Variance of the Imām's method Throughout the Rebellion

Of course, when we say the purpose of the Imām's ('a) rebellion was martyrdom and that God had asked for his martyrdom, we do not mean that God had asked him to first refrain from giving allegiance to Yazīd and then sit and notify the agents of Yazīd that they should kill him; thus, performing his duty in a nonsensical and irrational manner, naming it rebellion.

Rather, the Imām's ('a) duty was to rise up against the evil caliphate of Yazīd, deny him fealty, and carry out his dissent, which would end in his martyrdom, by any possible means.

This is why the Imām's ('a) method varied in line with prevailing conditions throughout his rebellion. First, when he was pressured by the governor of Medina, he began his nocturnal journey from Medina and sought refuge in Mecca—which was God's sanctum and a religious haven—and stayed there for a few months.

In Mecca he was under the covert surveillance of the caliph's intelligence officers until it was decided that he be killed or captured at the time of hajj and be sent to Shām. On the other hand, a deluge of letters was coming in from Iraq for the Imām ('a). Thousands of letters promised him support and aid, inviting him to Iraq.

In the final letter from the people of Kūfah, which—according to some historians—was clearly sent to finalize their vows, the Imām decided to initiate his blood-filled campaign and rebellion. First, though, he sent Muslim ibn 'Aqīl as his representative to guarantee the truth of their pledge. After a while, Muslim sent a letter explaining the favorable conditions for the Imām's uprising.

In view of these two factors, i.e. preserving the sanctity of the House of God from the secret officers of Shām who had come with the intent of either killing or capturing the Imām ('a) and the apparent readiness of Iraq for rebellion, he set out for Kūfah.

Then, in the middle of the way, when he received news of the horrible assassination of Muslim ibn 'Aqīl and Hānī, he altered his method from an offensive uprising and war to a defensive rebellion. He filtered and purified his assembly, keeping only those who would aid him to their last drop of blood, and proceeded towards the site of his martyrdom.

Question: What is the nature and extent of the knowledge of Imām ('a)? Does the Imām have knowledge of the details of his death, even the exact time?

Answer: According to many narrations, the Imāms ('a) have attained such proximity to God that they can know by the will of God whatever they wish to know. This includes thoroughly detailed knowledge of their deaths and martyrdoms. There are no rational grounds to repudiate this matter and there are also narrations saying that each Imām holds a 'Tablet from God' in which their specific duties are recorded.

Still, they are obligated to preserve the appearance of normal life.

Here an answer to a certain criticism is made clear, that advancing towards certain danger is not logical. Reason demands that a person never does something that they know entails definite danger, especially mortal danger.

Hence, how can one believe that the Imāms ('a), who are the wisest among the wise, will do something that they know will end in their deaths? Essentially, no person willfully does something that he definitely knows is dangerous. In addition, how can an Imām satisfy himself to voluntarily cause his own death whereby divesting the human world of the blessings of his existence?

Answer: The unreasonableness of performing a voluntary act entailing certain danger is because usually people do everything for their own good and therefore, they do not do something that would entail their extermination. However, if one determines that the deed is more important than preserving their own life, they will surely carry it out without fearing their own death. In substantiation, hundreds of examples may be found in various movements and revolutions. A living proof of this is the incident of Karbalā; the Husaynī movement.

Suppose for a minute that the martyrdom of Sayyid al-Shuhadā' ('a) was not voluntary. What about the actions of each of the martyrs of Karbalā which would surely entail death? There is no doubt that they preferred that the Imām ('a) live a few hours more over their own life. Hence, each of them threw themselves into the maws of death to extend the Imām's life.

This makes it clear that this criticism—that basically no person will voluntarily perform an action that they know is definitely dangerous—is unfounded.

In description of the Pharaoh and his people, God, the Exalted, states:

"And they denied the miracles and invitation of Moses ('a)

even though they were certain of their truth..."²¹⁶

According to the Qur'an, the people of Pharaoh knew of their certain demise in the case that they continue to deny certainty and disbelieve. Even so, they still did what they did and were drowned.

Here also, it is obvious that the criticism asking how the Imām ('a) can content himself with voluntarily surrendering himself to death depriving the human world of the blessings of his existence is completely baseless.

Because, as we have indicated, knowing of the importance of his martyrdom in relation to continuing his life, the Imām ('a) preferred martyrdom. No Shī'ah, rather no Muslim, and more precisely no reasonable human being should be ignorant of the awe-inspiring effects of the Husaynī martyrdom in the Muslim World, especially in the Shī'ah World, throughout these nearly fourteen centuries.

Throughout the vast treasury of Islamic jurisprudence, the teachers of which are the lineage of the Prophet (S) as per the widely transmitted Hadīth al-Thaqalayn, there is no hadīth related from Sayyid al-Shuhadā' ('a).²¹⁷ Indeed, some scholars are quoted to have said that only one hadīth has been found from him.

This is the product of ten years of Sayyid al-Shuhadā's ('a) Imamate! This clearly indicates that the incrimination ignited during the twenty year reign of Mu'āwiyah, generated such a woeful situation for the Holy Prophet's (S) family to the extent that the people turned away from Sayyid al-Shuhadā' ('a).

---

²¹⁶ Sūrat al-Naml 27:14.

²¹⁷ The Shī'ahs cite narrations from Sayyid al-Shuhadā' ('a) in jurisprudential issues. However, they are narrations through other Imāms such as Imām al-Sādiq, Imām Mūsā ibn Ja'far, and Imām al-Ridā ('a). For instance: That which I refuted were narrations that people other than the Imāms cited, showing consultation of the people.

Now compare the benefits of the Imām's ('a) short life against the astonishing and enduring effects manifested in the Muslim World throughout the thirteen hundred years subsequent to his martyrdom, in order to understand the truth or untruth of the following disputation: why would the Imām ('a) divest the Muslim World of his existential blessings with his martyrdom?

In addition to what has already been said regarding this issue, if there must be a criticism, it cannot relate to Sayyid al-Shuhadā' ('a) but to divine decree and pose the question: why should God, the Exalted, from whom the world must take benefit, decree martyrdom causing his servant's blood to spill upon the earth?

Does this criticism—assuming that one does not understand or feel partial to the previous reply—have any response but to say that God, the Almighty, is absolutely Wise and performs nothing unwisely and without benefit?

Like His other decrees, the decree of the Imām's ('a) martyrdom is not without wisdom even assuming the case that we do not understand it and, even if we do direct this criticism towards the Imām ('a), this same answer is relevant because the Imāms ('a) are manifestations of God's Wisdom and they will never perform an unwise or useless deed.

Discourse Fourteen: The Purpose of Covenants

In nonreligious societies, especially so-called advanced civilized ones, society and social laws have no aim other than to further and better the enjoyment of material life. Therefore, there is no reason for them to bind themselves to anything save rules and regulations that can secure material aims. It is evident that in such environs, spirituality has no value except to the extent that it is in agreement with the materialistic values of the people.

For instance, truthfulness, humaneness, kindness, beneficence, valor, and other moral virtues are only considered useful and necessary when they further the realization of personal material interests.

However, if moral virtues are not compatible with material benefits, not only are they considered unnecessary, but it is believed to be necessary to act in opposition with those virtues.

Authenticity of Matter

It is for this reason that governments, ruling parties, and official congresses consider no duty for themselves other than protecting the interests of the society's material life. The covenants and treaties they make are in accordance to prevailing interests and instant benefits. Their value is determined by the international weight of the obligor and their power and dominance. Naturally, their continuation depends on the balance of powers.

However, if one side becomes more powerful, they invalidate the covenant using fabricated excuses and accusations. They resort to excuses to preserve the semblance of global laws, the annulment of which would jeopardize the life of the society or a portion of its vital interests; otherwise, there would be no problem with repudiation of any treaty without the least excuse.

Furthermore, lies, betrayal, and transgression against the rights of others are not an obstacle in measures taken to attain material gain. Such people do not consider morals and spirituality to have any authenticity; rather, they are tools they use to realize the aims of the society, i.e. enjoyment of material life.

With some study of global events, especially international events over the past century, the value of treaties and covenants, and the reason for their invalidation becomes clear, giving us substantial evidence for this claim.

Authenticity of Matter and Spirit

On the other hand, Islam neither considers material life to be the true life of humankind, nor does it consider enjoyment of its benefits to be true prosperity. It instead considers the true and authentic life of humans to be the sum of matter and spirit, and true happiness to be in things that entail the prosperity of both worlds.

> *An inevitable result of this view is that the laws of life should be based upon fitrah and genetic make-up and not upon going along with what people consider to be in their own interests. Another result is that Islam founds its invitation on adherence to Truth not following the desires and caprices of the majority, which are based upon inner feelings and emotions. The Glorious Qur'an states:*
>
> *"So set thy face toward the pure religion; it is in accordance with the nature [fitrah] of God upon which He has formed the nature of humankind. There is no alteration in the creation of God. This is the enduring (and true) religion; however, most humans do not know."*[218]

"It is He who sent His Messenger with guidance and the True Religion to make it supreme over all religions, though idolaters be averse."[219]

"We have sent them Truth..."[220]

"And if Truth had followed their caprices, the heavens and the earth and all in them would surely have been thrown into confusion and corruption..."[221]

This religion necessitates that true beliefs are observed and virtuous

---

[218] Sūrat al-Rūm 30:30.

[219] Sūrat al-Tawbah (or Barā'ah) 9:33.

[220] Sūrat al-Mu'minūn 23:90.

[221] Sūrat al-Mu'minūn 23:71.

morals and actions are heeded. Also, its teachings must neglect neither matter nor spirit. It should continually observe human virtues whether they are to the people's benefit or their apparent detriment, though it is certain that except for those who have deviated from the path of truth and righteousness no harm will come to the society.

It can be seen that the reason God, the Exalted, negated the treaties of idolaters was that they violated their vows. Even so, by His mercy He gave them four months reprieve. However, He commands those who kept to their covenant to persevere and be steadfast in their commitments.

> *"(These verses are a declaration of) estrangement from Allah and his Messenger toward those of the idolaters with whom you made covenant. Journey freely in the land for four months but know that you cannot disable Allah. Know that Allah debases the unbelievers... except those of the idolaters with whom you made covenant who then did not fail you in anything nor aided anyone against you. Fulfill your treaty with them to the end of their term. Verily Allah loves the righteous."*[222]

At the time, events had demeaned the idolaters and they had become humble before the magnificence of Islam. Even so, the Prophet asked them to cancel the covenant if they feared betrayal; however, he commanded them to publicly announce their choice. When asked why he commanded thus, he stated: God does not like betrayal.[223]

---

[222] Sūrat al-Tawbah (or Barā'ah) 9:1-2, 4.
[223] Extracted from the journal, "Kitāb-e Fasl".

Discourse Fifteen: Ijtihad and Taqlid According to the Shi'ah

Discourse Fifteen: Juristic Authority [Ijtihād] and Following [Taqlīd] according to the Shī'ah

The words ijtihād and taqlīd, with their opposite meanings (which we superficially know), are used extensively among Muslims. Of course, in view of the well-known Shī'ah law that one cannot initially follow a deceased authority—which is a Shī'ah juristic dogma whereby after the death of a mujtahid (an expounder of Islamic laws) his followers [muqallidīn] are obliged to follow a living one—these two words are used by Shī'ah Muslims more than by other Islamic sects.

In short, nowadays ijtihād and taqlīd are used to mean the qualities of having jurisprudential authority and of following a person with such authority, respectively. However, by referring to the history of the advent of Islam, we see that after the death of the Prophet (S) in the parlance of the sahābah and tābi'īn the word ijtihād was used to mean things other than the common meaning used today.

However, in light of the fact that in this paper I intend to talk about the currently established meanings of ijtihād and taqlīd and their religious roots, and due to the fact that determining their other meanings is historical in nature, I will refrain from discussing the latter.

The Religious Origins of Ijtihād and Taqlīd

In order to understand the comprehensive meaning of ijtihād and taqlīd and their religious origins, I must note several points:

First of all, in the opinion of the Shī'ahs, in addition to the fact that the pure religion of Islam consists of a series of primary teachings regarding the Origin [mabda'] and Resurrection [ma'ād] and other teachings regarding moral principles, it also possesses a string of rules and regulations regarding human actions that completely cover all aspects of human life in the society.

These laws obligate all responsible [mukallaf] persons—including the black, white, Arabs, non-Arabs, men, and women in all possible environments and conditions—to conform their personal and social behavior to said laws and to adhere to them, the entirety of which is called the sharī'ah.

Of course, no action can be collated to its respective law before the law is scientifically analyzed and understood. This is why acquiring knowledge of the scientific laws and secondary decrees of Islam is one of the duties of Muslims. This is both proven by intellectual reasoning and verified by statements from the Book [kitāb] and Tradition [sunnah].[224]

---

[224] The intellectual reason is that doubtless if a person does not know about something, doing it is beyond their ability and logically there is no duty in the absence of capacity. Hence, the commands and injunctions that confirm our religious responsibilities also confirm the necessity to learn about them. This matter is also substantiated by Qur'anic verses that rescind obligation from those who are incapable of performing them such as:

Secondly, in view of the fact that religious statements in the Book and Tradition are general and limited, and that there are an unlimited number of actions and events that make up problematic areas, in order to realize the details of religious decrees there is no way but ratiocination [istidlāl]. It is clear to us that no other way has been shown in religious statements.

Here it becomes evident that in order to discern religious responsibilities, we must tread the path followed by intellectuals of the society in extracting personal and social responsibilities from general, specific, and normal commandments. Stated concisely, a series of specific rules must be utilized in order to deduce canonical duties and precepts from religious statements.

"Allah does not charge a soul more than it can bear..." (Sūrat al-Baqarah 2:286)

"Except for the weak among men, women, and children who have been divested of their ability and cannot..." (Sūrat al- Nisā' 4:98)

"Surely, Allah will not wrong people in the slightest..." (Sūrat Yūnus 10:44)
And verses indicating that calling to account depends upon adequate notification of the individual such as:

"That the people might have no argument against Allah..." (Sūrat al-Nisā' 4:165)
There are also many narrations that acquit uninformed wrongdoers exempt of blame. These verses and narrations entail the requirement of learning one's duties. A famous saying of the Prophet (S) is that, "Seeking knowledge is an obligation for all Muslims." Furthermore, Shaykh Mufīd quotes the sixth Imām as saying, "God, the Exalted, will ask His servants on the Day of Judgment, 'Did you know?' If they answer, 'Yes', He will ask, 'Why did you not act according to what you knew?' On the other hand, if they answer, 'I did not know.' He will ask, 'Why did you not learn so you could act accordingly?' Thus, He condemns His servant and this is the meaning of 'hujjat al-bālighah' in the following verse:

"So for Allah is the conclusive argument..." (Sūrat al-An'ām 6:149)

One who researches narrations of the Imāms will observe many cases where they engage in debate with sahābah, other followers, or their opposers whereby they deduce canonical precepts from the Book of Allah and Traditions of the Prophet (S) in the standard way. This is the meaning of ijtihād used in modern speech.

Therefore, ijtihād can be defined as gathering precepts of the sharī'ah from religious statements through logical reasoning and a specific set of techniques—the formulae of religious jurisprudence.

Hence, one of the duties Islam charges upon the Muslim society is scientific determination of religious

precepts through ijtihād. Clearly, not all Muslims are able to take up this duty and only a select number can become specialists and carry out this charge—obtainment of Islamic precepts through study of religious statements utilizing logical reasoning and rules of inference.

The facts that not all people can employ ijtihād to discern precepts and that all people are obliged to learn religious precepts necessitate that Islam gives those who are not able to perform ijtihād another duty. That is, they receive religious precepts required by their circumstances from individuals proficient in ijtihād and deduction. This is the meaning of the frequently used term taqlīd.

The best reason justifying the precept of taqlīd regarding the uninformed is the ongoing practice among Muslims that has existed from the advent of Islam until today. Those who did not have the ability of ijtihād and were unable to directly use the deductive sciences to attain canonical precepts always referred to jurists and reliable scholars to learn religious issues relevant to their state of affairs.

Besides, there are proofs in the Book and Tradition that attest to the necessity of taqlīd by the uninformed such as Qur'anic verses that enjoin the unlearned to follow the knowledgeable and narrations that discuss taqlīd or encourage some disciples to proclaim religious decrees [fatwā] and similar statements that explicitly or implicitly speak about the issue of taqlīd.

Taqlīd Due to Inability or Lack of Opportunity to Specialize in Deduction

The foregoing discussion made clear the meaning of ijtihād and taqlīd and their religious origins. However, after a more circumspect and deep consideration, one will realize that these concepts possess roots even deeper. Following the path of ijtihād or taqlīd is in fact one of the most basic elements of life, so where a person knows he is unable to perform ijtihād, he has recourse to taqlīd.

Therefore, the dictates of ijtihād and taqlīd in Islam are guidance for the people towards the course demonstrated in the human fitrah.

In explanation, like other general types that exist in the world of creation, humankind has a purpose in accordance to its existential make-up and in line with this objective it is equipped with a specific set of abilities and mechanisms. Using these faculties, they endeavor to maintain their lives and attain their perfectionistic purpose.

The human struggle to achieve life aims is a voluntary activity emanating from human-specific thought. Humans understand the situation of the world, events they encounter, and the matter upon which they work. They weigh the good and evil, the benefit and harm, the dos and don'ts of the actions and endeavors from which they expect facility. After they discover an endeavor corresponding to their life aims and mark it "this must be done", they begin the act.

Through our God-given nature, humans grasp that until we understand the causes and factors or the prerequisites and effects of something, we will not judge it as real and also, until we reckon the factors and means or the effects and benefits of an act, we will not engage in that act.

We directly perceive within ourselves that every phenomenon and event in existence manifests in one of our senses.

We even seek the causes of the smallest sound we might hear. Whatever we intend to do, we first consider—at times comprehensively at others briefly—the reason behind our action, even if we are ignorant of the reason, we at least bear in mind the benefits of the act. Finally, as regards this intellectual discernment, we carry out a cognitive activity on causes and benefits. This mental activity or investigation is what is scientifically called deduction [istidlāl].

Hence, through our God-given nature and genetic actuality humans are deductive beings and naturally make use of deduction both in scientific theories and in practical applications.

It is a fact that the theoretical knowledge and scientific needs of humans are without bounds and no normal human individual can ever enumerate them all much less give them a comprehensive deductive treatment and independently reason about the truth or falseness and the good or evil in them.

Of course, this is one of the things that naturally draw human individuals to form civilized communities and distribute vital activities among members.

Appreciation of this truth (imperatively) compels each human to take up deduction and scientific discernment—i.e. ijtihād—in areas of life in which they possess a certain extent of skill and proficiency.

On the other hand, with regard to other aspects in which they are not skilled, they must follow trustworthy specialists in whom they have confidence and thus deem the expert's scientific determination as their own. In other words, they must conform their actions to the expert's view and in effect imitate them [taqlīd].

If we want to do something and do not know how, we consult an authority in that discipline. If we want to enter a profession, we ask how to do so from a professional in that field. If we want to learn a craft we become an apprentice of an experienced master craftsman. We seek cures from doctors and expect house plans from an architect. In essence, the structure of public education and instruction in human societies is based upon this fundamental principle.

It is concluded from the foregoing discussion that:

First, the issues of ijtihād and taqlīd constitute the most general, basic and vital issues of humankind. Every human entering the society has no alternative but to accept the approach of ijtihād and taqlīd.

Second, individuals perform ijtihād in only a small portion of their lives and progress in other spheres of existence—which cover the greater proportion of life—by means of taqlīd. Indeed, those who think they have never been subjected to taqlīd and never will are deluding themselves with a false and amusing notion.

Third, according to fitrah and common sense, taqlīd is necessary only in cases where a person is ignorant and is not able to judge and intellectually research the matter and where a competent authority—i.e. an expert that can be trusted—exists; otherwise, taqlīd is reproachable.

In further explanation of the first conclusion—that ijtihād and taqlīd are fitrī—I should say:

As the clear and frequent statements of the Book and Tradition show, Islam is the religion of fitrah (nature) that invites humanity towards a series of vital issues that are indeed also pointed out by the God-given human make-up and fitrah. In His heavenly book, the Exalted God declares:

> ***"So with moderation and resolve welcome and accept the religion that is congruous with the special human genesis. Because genesis is invariable—and stabilizes the religion based upon it. This is the religion that can govern the***

people and lead them to prosperity..."²²⁵

Considering that ijtihād and taqlīd are fundamental fitrī issues, the holy religion of Islam, which invites towards primeval fitrah, also invites towards these concepts.

The Opposition to Blind Imitation

In the end, I must point out that the taqlīd I am talking about is different from the taqlīd that implies blind imitation and mindless following, something that Islam opposes with all its might.

The Holy Qur'an describes this type of taqlīd as one of the basest and most censurable of human qualities and regards those who unconditionally and illogically employ taqlīd and follow their ancestors, great personages, or capricious persons to be like animals because they do not utilize their cogitative minds. In this case, their human quality, the fitrah of reason and curiosity, is ravaged.²²⁶ The following holy verses accentuate this point:

> *"And when it is said to them, 'Come towards what Allah has revealed and towards the Prophet.' They reply, 'Suffices us that which we discovered from our fathers.' Do they follow their fathers even though they knew naught and were not guided?"*²²⁷

> *"They reply, 'No, we will follow that which we discovered*

---

²²⁵ Sūrat al-Rūm 30:30.

²²⁶ Extracted from a discussion regarding religious authority [marja'iyyah] and the clergy [rawhāniyyah].

²²⁷ Sūrat al-Mā'idah 5:104.

from our fathers.' Do they follow their fathers even though they were void of knowledge and guidance? A person who invites these disbelievers is like a person who calls upon animals who perceive naught of the invitation save its sound. They have become deaf, dumb, and blind and thus do not understand nor think."[228]

---

[228] Sūrat al-Baqarah 2:170-171.

Discourse Sixteen: A Short Study of Christ and the Gospel

Even though Jews attach great importance to their national history and recording of events that occur throughout their lives, there is no mention of Jesus Jesus, the conditions of his birth and appearance as a prophet, his lifestyle, and the miracles God manifested through him. As to what caused this chronicle to be hidden from them or what caused them to hide it, is not clear.

Regarding the Jewish people, the Holy Qur'an declares:

> *"And that they uttered against Mary a tremendous calumny and that they said, 'We killed the Messiah, Jesus son of Mary, the prophet of Allah'..."*[229]

Was the evidence for this claim a story they cited without support of any historical book—just as other nations have many both true and

---

[229] Sūrat al-Nisā' 4:156-157.

mythical stories that are not considered creditable without correct and reliable evidence—or had they heard the name of Jesus and his birth and appearance from Christians then slandered Mary and claimed to have killed Jesus?

There is no way to arrive at a clear answer without resorting to the fact that the Noble Qur'an only explicitly attributes the claim of killing the Messiah to them. It also notes that they had doubts and disagreements among themselves in this regard.

On the other hand, what Christians believe about the Messiah, the Gospel, and the good news [bishārat] is based on the New Testament, that is Matthew, Mark, Luke, John, the Acts of Prophets, and other books such as Paul, Peter, Jacob, and Judas. The authority of all of these is based upon that of the Gospels therefore I will discuss the latter.

Writers of the Four Gospels

The gospel of Matthew is the oldest written; composed in 38 CE according to some. Others, however, maintain that it dates between 50 to 60 CE.[230] Even so, it was clearly written after the time of Jesus Jesus ('a). Researchers hold that it was originally written in Hebrew then translated into Greek and other languages. The original Hebrew text is not available and its translator and the quality of its translation are unknown.[231]

Mark, the author of another of the Gospels, was a student of Peter. He was not one of the Apostles himself. It is said that he wrote his gospel at the behest of his mentor.

He did not believe in the divinity of the Messiah. That is why some Christians say that he wrote his gospel for nomads and peas-

---

[230] Refer to "Qāmūs-e Kitāb-e Muqaddas" (Dictionary of the Holy Book).

[231] Refer to "Mīzān al-Haqq" (Criterion of Truth). "Qāmūs-e Kitāb-e Muqaddas" (Dictionary of the Holy Book) also hesitantly confesses to this.

ants introducing the Messiah as a prophet and conveyor of God's precepts.[232] Regardless, Mark's gospel was written in 61 CE.

Luke, who wrote yet another of the Gospels, was neither an apostle nor had he met the Messiah. Paul had converted him to Christianity. Paul was a zealous Jew who greatly harassed the followers of Jesus.

One day he suddenly claimed to have suffered an epileptic fit wherein he touched Jesus Jesus, who prohibited him against persecuting his followers. He converted to Jesus' faith and started to proselytize the gospel in the Messiah's name.

It was Paul that established the prevailing foundations of Christianity and based his teachings on the idea that faith in the Messiah alone without any good deeds is enough for the deliverance of humanity.

He also permitted eating dead meat and the meat of pigs! He also considered circumcision and many other precepts from the Torah to be forbidden. The gospel of Luke was written after the gospel of Mark and the death of Paul and Peter. Some emphasize that this gospel did not come as divine revelation and the words at the beginning of this book indicate this fact.

John, author of the fourth gospel, was according to some accounts the son of a fisherman, one of the twelve Apostles of the Messiah, and greatly loved by him.

It is said that because Sharintus, Ebisun, and their followers believed that Jesus was a creation of God and his existence did not precede that of his mother, the bishops of Asia and others went to John in 96 CE and asked him to write that which others had not written in their gospels. In other words, they asked him to explain the divinity of the

---

[232] In "Qāmūs-e Kitāb-e Muqaddas" (Dictionary of the Holy Book), it says (regard carefully):"It has been expressly cited of the ancients that Mark wrote his gospel in Rome and it was published after the death of Peter and Paul. However, this is not very credible because it appears that it was written for tribals and villagers not for city- dwellers especially inhabitants of Rome."

Messiah and he could not deny them their request.²³³

There is disagreement as to the date John's gospel was written; whether it was in 65, 96, or 98 CE. However, some profess that its author was not even John, the Apostle. Some of these believe it was written by a student of the Alexandrian School.²³⁴

Others however, believe that it and the other books of John were written by a Christian in the second century of the Common Era who attributed these books to John, the Apostle, to give them credibility. Still others maintain that the gospel of John originally had twenty chapters and after his death, the Church of Afās added the twenty-first chapter.

These are the conditions of the Four Gospels that go back to seven persons (Matthew, Mark, Luke, John, Peter, Paul, and Judas) and their ultimate credibility is based on the Four Gospels, ending in the gospel of Matthew, the oldest of the Gospels. As we previously mentioned, the original Gospels were originally written in Hebrew and are currently unavailable. It is not clear who translated them or whether the teachings of the original were based on the prophethood of Jesus or his divinity?!

The current bible states that among the Children of Israel a man named Jesus, son of Joseph the carpenter, appeared who invited the people to God. He held that he was the son of God and was created without having a human father and that his father had sent him to be crucified in reciprocation for the sins of the people.

He brought back the dead, cured congenital blindness and leprosy, and healed the mad by exorcizing the evil spirits within them.

---

²³³ Cited in "Qisas al-Anbīyā'" (Stories of the Prophets) from the book of Gorges Zadīn Futūhī Lubnānī.

²³⁴ Cited from "Catholic Herald"; this is also indicated in "Qāmūs-e Kitāb-e Muqaddas" (Dictionary of the Holy Book) under the heading Yūhannā (John).

Jesus had twelve students, one of which was Matthew. He gave them blessings and sent them to invite the people and promote Christianity...

This is a summary of the Christianity that has enveloped the East and West of the world. As you can see, its foundation is an isolated report from someone (refers to the translator of Matthew) who neither his name nor characteristics are known!

This astounding weakness in the origin of the story has caused some European writers to say that the Messiah is basically a mythical character created by religious revolutions in favor of or against the government of the time!

This is confirmed by another myth that is similar to it in every way: that of Krishna. The ancient idolaters of India considered him the son of God who descended from the divine realm to be hanged in this world and in this way sacrifice his life for the people and save them from their sins.

It has also caused another series of critics to believe that there were two people with the name Messiah with more than five centuries between them and that the reputed Christian era conforms to neither.

Rather, the first Messiah was born over two hundred years before the starting point of this era, lived around sixty years, and died without being crucified. On the other hand, the second Messiah was born after 290 CE, lived for nearly thirty-three years, and was crucified.

It should be noted that, in short, Christians do not deny that the starting point of the Christian era does not conform to the birth of Christ (refer to "Qāmūs-e Kitāb-e Muqaddas" (Dictionary of the Holy Book)).

In addition to what has been said, there are other dubious issues. For instance, in the first two centuries of the Common Era many gospels were written; reputedly over one hundred. The Four Gospels are among these. Later, the Church banned the other gospels and authorized only these Four Gospels which were in line with its teachings.

One of these abandoned gospels is the Gospel of Barnabas. A suspected copy of it was found several years ago and was translated to Arabic and then Farsi. That which has been written in this account about the story of Jesus ('a) is congruous with the Noble Qur'an.[235]

---

[235] Extracted from the yearbook, "Ma'ārif-e Ja'farī".

Discourse Seventeen: Adherence to Superstitions

"And when it is said to them, 'Follow that which Allah has sent down.' they reply, 'We will follow that which we discovered from our fathers.' Do they follow their fathers even though they were void of knowledge and guidance? The likeness of disbelievers (in hearing the truth) is the likeness of a person who is called upon but perceives naught save shouting and yelling. They are deaf, dumb, and blind and are void of reason."[236]

The beliefs of humans are of two types:
   Theoretical views and beliefs which without an intermediary are unrelated to action, such as mathematics and the supernatural.

Practical views and beliefs which are linked to action without the need for intermediaries, such as principles regarding proper behavior.

---
[236] Sūrat al-Baqarah 2:170-171.

The way to attain the first type is to follow knowledge and certainty which lead to proof or 'feeling'. Regarding the second, the means is to adhere to things that lead to a goodness, which either entails human prosperity or promotes it, and also to abstain from things that either lead to adversity or harm prosperity.

Belief in the truth of something that one has no knowledge of (in the first type) and also belief in something, the good or evil of which is indeterminate (in the second type) are called superstitious beliefs.

Indeed, humans are lead by their fitrah. Fitrah examines the causes of phenomena and encourages humans to follow the path leading to their true perfection. In accordance with this principle, humans do not humble themselves before a superstitious view that has been adopted through blindness and ignorance. It is the case though that feelings and emotions aroused by imagination are many and can cause a person to believe in superstitions. The majority of these feelings consist of fear and hope.

Imagination depicts mental forms linked with fear or hope. These feelings preserve their related forms and do not let them become concealed from the fearful or hopeful self.

For instance, if a person is stuck alone and friendless in the middle of an eerie wasteland on a gloomy night, unable to see, devoid of any refuge in which to calm their heart and become safe, bereft of a torch with which to discern danger from safety, imagination will enter the field and turn every shadow into a fearsome monster that intends to kill them or a ghost that is in no way real!

The imagined shadow moves, it comes and goes, it flies into the air and dives back down to the earth, metamorphosing into various shapes and figures. Whenever the person is afraid, the fantasy of that mysterious shadow is repeated. This state might be transferred to another person, creating within them a mood similar to the previous person's. It will gradually spread even though it is a superstition entirely unfounded in truth.

Is There Anything Beyond the Senses and Experience?

From the most ancient of times until today, humankind has been afflicted by superstitious beliefs. Some believe that superstitions are a quality of Easterners however this is not true. Even if Westerners are not more superstitious than Easterners, at least, they also have superstitious beliefs like the people of the East.

Scientists and scholars have continually used delicate stratagems to erase the vestiges of these superstitions integrated deep in the souls of the masses and awaken them and make them aware. However, this is a sickness that has exhausted its doctor.

Humans are not free of imitation in theoretical views and pure knowledge and also possess feelings and emotions. I am sorry to inform readers that until today scientists have been unsuccessful in remedying this illness.

Strangest of all is the view that modern civilized people and natural scientists have regarding this matter. They say that modern knowledge is based upon the senses and experience and refutes all else.

Civilization and advancement have based themselves upon evolution of the society: the society must attain perfection to the utmost extent possible and in every conceivable aspect. They have based their education on this premise.

This is a very strange statement which is itself adhering to superstitions! This is because natural sciences only speak of the features of nature and prove the existence of these features within natural fields. To state matters differently, materialistic sciences only unveil the secrets of matter; however, they cannot deny the supernatural.

Therefore, if someone comes to believe that something that cannot be experienced and sensed does not exist, their belief is without basis and the most obvious of superstitions. The same is true of civilization since its structure is based upon attaining the aforesaid perfection.

This perfection and progress towards social prosperity sometimes necessitates that some people be deprived of individual prosperity.

For example, in order to defend their country, law, or beliefs some people endure death and sacrifice and are thus divested of individual prosperity to preserve the society. No human endures these deprivations save in order to attain perfection and on the basis that they believe that these acts entail perfection. However, the truth is contrary to this.

These are not perfection but divestment and loss. Even if there are perfections here, they pertain to the society not the individual in the sense that the society is a society (without regard to individuals rather to the identity of the society which is an identity at variance with individual identity) whereas humans want the society not for its sake but for their own!

It is based on this premise that the leaders of these societies plan schemes regarding their people and inculcate in them that humans leave a lasting glorious name for themselves—in other words, they attain everlasting life. This is a superstition. After annihilation what life is there left? This is nothing but a designation. Do we have to unduly name it life?! It is an empty designation that has nothing behind its façade.

This statement is like saying that humans must endure the bitterness of law and have patience regarding privations keeping them from their heart's desires so that the society may persevere and that it may attain perfection in its perpetual life.

A person who says this believes that the perfection of the society is his own perfection. This is a superstitious statement since the perfection of the society is the perfection of individuals only when they coincide (not when the individual is completely annihilated). If this perfection does not concur with that of the individual and does not convey him to perfection, it is not the perfection of the individual.

If through oppression and persecution a person or nation is able to attain their every wish and desire without any power opposing them dominating the entire world, will they believe that the perfection of the society is their own preserving their glorious name?! Never! Powerful nations aim at exploiting the people of weak nations!

You will find no place but that they saunter there! There is nothing that they want that they will not strive to attain. There is no person or nation that they do not make their slave. Is this approach anything other than curing a chronic disease by destroying the patient?

The path set forth by the Glorious Qur'an in this matter is as follows:

In theoretical views it commands humans to follow that which God has revealed. No one has the right to say even one word without knowledge.

In practical aspects it commands that people seek out actions that are approved by God, the Exalted, and abide by Him. If the act conforms to one's heart's desires, it will entail prosperity of both this world and the next and if it necessitates privation from one's desires, the Almighty Lord will give a great reward:

> *"However, that which is with Allah is better and more enduring..."*[237]

Is Following Religion Imitation?

Materialists say that adhering to religion is imitation and science prohibits imitation. They also say that religion is superstition remaining from the second age of human life. They have divided human life into four ages:

---

[237] Sūrat al-Qisas 28:60.

The Age of Myths   The Age of Religion
The Age of Philosophy   The Age of Science

This statement is not based on science and is itself a superstitious view. The answer to the statement that following religion is imitation is that: religion is a series of teachings pertaining to the Origin [mabda'] and Resurrection [ma'ād] and a string of social, devotional, and behavioral laws that have all been received though divine revelation and prophets.

The truth of revelation and prophethood has been proved with logical rationales.

Reports imparted by a truthful person are true and following them is following knowledge. This is because our premise is that we have attained knowledge through logical rationale that the reporter is truthful. It is strange that the people who say this have no life standards or social methods of food, clothing, drink, marriage, dwelling, etc. except imitation and adherence to desires and caprices; blind imitation and following inconsistent standards.

It is interesting that they have created a different name for 'imitation'—adherence to that which the advanced world approves.

In this manner, the name of imitation has been wiped away but its practice has endured. The word imitation has become an alien and unfamiliar term but its essence is well-known. The motto that 'When in Rome, do as the Romans do' is considered a scientific one that has brought about the advancement of civilization but the following slogan is considered a religious imitation and a superstitious statement!

"Do not follow caprices and desires because they will debar

you from the path of Allah..."²³⁸

Hence, religion springs from the source of divine revelation and knowledge and is completely scientific. However, the conduct of the civilized world is exactly the opposite and entirely imitation. Their classification of the course of human life into four ages is repudiated by the history of religion and philosophy which has been available since the advent of Abraham's ('a) religion, after the era of the philosophies of India, Egypt, and Chaldea.

The religion of Jesus ('a) came after the philosophy of Greece. The religion of Muhammad (S), Islam, came after the philosophies of Greece and Alexandria. In short, the final climax of philosophy occurred before that of religion and I have mentioned before that the era of monotheistic religion has precedence over that of all other religions.

The classification of the Holy Qur'an regarding human history is as follows: The age of naivety

The age of unification of nations

The age of senses [hiss] and matter [māddah]²³⁹

---

[238] Sūrat Sād 38:26.

[239] Extracted from the newspaper, "Wazīfah", issue 127.

Discourse Eighteen: Are Dreams True?

The natural scientists of Europe do not believe that dreams can be true and do not consider their relationship with external events to have scientific weight barring a few psychologists that have done research on the matter and use dreams that uncover hidden truths or reports of future events which cannot be considered accidental as rationales against the opposition.

What does the Qur'an say?

In the Glorious Qur'an dreams of prophets and other people have been cited and substantiated. Among these are the dreams of Prophet Abraham ('a) regarding the sacrifice of Ishmael, of Prophet Joseph ('a) and his fellow prisoners of Egypt's sovereign, and of the Holy Prophet (S) regarding the conquest of Mecca. There is also evidence in narrations cited from the Holy Prophet (S) and Imāms ('a).

We have all either had dreams that indicated hidden matters, resolved scientific problems, or divulged future events ourselves or heard of them from others. These dreams, especially clear dreams that do not require interpretation, cannot be considered accidental and completely unrelated to the situation to which they conform.

Of course, it cannot be denied that various internal factors such as diseases, health conditions, fatigue, or a stuffed stomach, and also external ones such as heat, cold, etc. can affect the imagination which in turn affects dreams.

For instance, a person who was exposed to extreme heat or cold might dream of blazing fires or ice and snow; or a person who has an engorged stomach or indigestion might have disturbing or incoherent dreams.

A person's inner qualities and principles of behavior also have influences on dreams. As such, most dreams are the result of imaginations caused by external and internal factors and in truth indicate the effects of these factors. Natural scientists have mostly researched these factors whereby they conclude that dreams have no truth. However, just as we cannot deny the effect of these factors, we also cannot deny the verity of some dreams and their relationship with external affairs.

Is the Soul Linked to Dreams?

It is not possible to say that the soul of a person who dreams of the occurrence of a specific event at a specific time has connected to an event that has not yet come into being because existential association between an existent and non-existent is impossible.

Moreover, we cannot say regarding a person who dreams that a certain vessel is buried in a specific place containing a certain amount of gold and silver coins and after waking up goes there and recovers it that their soul has connected to that vessel because the contact of the soul with material things occurs through the senses and a vessel that is buried under the earth cannot be sensed. That is why it is said that the connection of the soul to these events and phenomena is through their causes.

By way of explanation, the world of existence incorporates three worlds:

The natural world ['ālam-e tabī'at] with which we are familiar;

The ideational world ['ālam-e mithāl]: the existential status of this world is above that of the natural world. Beings residing in this world are forms devoid of matter and they are causational in relation to material beings.

The intellectual world ['ālam-e 'aql]: This world is superior to the ideational world. It is where the truth of all beings exist free of both matter and form and are causational in relation to beings of the ideational world.

Because of its abstraction, the human soul is in the same class with supernatural phenomena. In sleep, a time when it is not engaged in sensory perception, it naturally returns to the world to which it belongs and apprehends truths from that world in accordance to its abilities.

The perfect soul, which possesses the faculty to perceive intellectual abstractions as such, apprehends causes as generalities. However, a soul that has not attained that level of perfection perceives general truths as discrete forms.

Just as we describe speed with a fast object and immensity with a mountain, a soul that has yet to attain intellectual abstraction, thus remaining in the ideational world, sometimes observes the causes of phenomena in the ideational world in its real form without alteration. These are the clear dreams that are usually seen by the people of truth and purity.

They sometimes perceive ideational beings in forms that they are familiar with, just as they see knowledge as light and ignorance as darkness. The mind might even transfer from one meaning to a contradicting one.

One such dream is cited as follows: a man went to Ibn Sīrīn, the famous interpreter of dreams, and said, "I dreamed that I held a seal with which I sealed the mouths and privates of the people." Ibn Sīrīn said, "You will become a caller of adhān [mu'adhdhin], the people will fast by your adhān, abstaining from eating and marital relations."

Clear and unclear dreams

In accordance to what has been said, dreams are of either two types: clear dreams which have not been altered by the dreaming soul and do not require interpretation, and unclear dreams in which the soul alters what it perceives and therefore require interpretation and restoration of the mental form to its true and primary status, such as interpreting light as knowledge and darkness as ignorance and bewilderment.

Non-vivid dreams are also divided into two categories: dreams with a coherent story and transitions and can easily be interpreted, such as the previous example, and dreams wherein the soul has made complex and vague alterations. Understanding the original observation of the soul in the latter case is difficult or even impossible for dream interpreters. Such dreams are termed muddled dreams [adghāth ahlām] and considered nonsensical and uninterpretable.

This was a summary of what scholars of the soul state about dreams that is also supported by the Noble Qur'an. For instance, the return of the soul to the supernatural realm in sleep can be understood from the following verses:

"It is He who takes your souls by night..."[240]

---

[240] Sūrat al-An'ām 6:60.

> *"Allah takes the souls when they die and also those that have not died He takes in their sleep; He keeps those whose deaths have been decreed and sends back the rest..."*[241]

The surface meaning of these verses is that the soul is taken from the body when sleeping losing its attachment to the five senses, and it returns to the Lord—a return similar to death.

There are also indications of the three types of dreams. For instance, the dreams of Prophet Abraham ('a) and the Holy Prophet (S) are of the first type, the dreams of Joseph's (S) fellow prisoners are of the second type, and it also speaks of complex and vague dreams where the Egyptian dream interpreters of considered the dream of the pharaoh as a muddled dream [adghāth ahlām].[242]

---

[241] Sūrat al-Zumar 39:42.

[242] Extracted from the journal, "Kitāb-e Fasl".

Discourse Nineteen: Miracles

²⁴³ The Holy Qur'an claims to be a miracle in many of its verses. This claim in fact is comprised of two claims.

That, essentially, miracles exist in the world; That the Qur'an is one of these miracles.

Obviously, if the second claim (that the Qur'an is a miracle) is proven, the first (that miracles exist in the world) will also be proven.

An important point in this discussion is that, basically, how can a miracle occur in the external world whereas they are contradictory to the laws of nature. A prevailing and constant law of nature is that every effect has a cause.

This is a certain natural law that can never be violated. How can a miracle occur in the external world while simultaneously not harming

---

²⁴³ This is a translation of a Farsi translation of an original Arabic text by 'Allāmah Tabātabā'ī. The Farsi translation and original glosses were done by Mr. Hujjatī Kirmānī.

the generality of this law, causing an exception in causality? Therefore, the Qur'an must reveal two things:

First, what is the essential truth of miracles and how it is possible for something to happen in the natural world against the laws of nature?

Second, miracles exist and the Qur'an is one of them.

Miracles according to the Qur'an

There is no doubt in the fact that the Qur'an testifies to the occurrence of miracles in the natural world. The miracles spoken of in the Qur'an do not necessitate the impossible which would negate an incontrovertible intellectual axiom.[244]

Some people who consider themselves scientists interpret the verses regarding miracles such that they conform to modern science. However, these endeavors are in vain and the belief is rejected. I will explain the Qur'an's definition of miracles in two parts:

Part one: the Qur'an Validates the General Law of Causality

Just as reason, scientific discussion, and logical judgments prove the existence of causes for natural events, the Qur'an also confirms the general law of causality and considers all natural phenomena to have causes.

In explanation, humans innately believe that every physical event

---

[244] Something that reason demonstrates as impossible will never come to pass. Doubtless two times two is equal to four and it is impossible for the solution to be five. A miracle is not to perform an impossible thing in the world. However, sometimes humans consider things that have never happened as impossible. For example, a thousand-headed person is not impossible; however, because it has never occurred we mistake it as an impossibility. A miracle is a phenomenon that defies normality but is not intellectually impossible in the strictest sense.

has a cause which brought about the event. Natural and other sciences also demonstrate events and their related phenomena as fitting causes distinct from them.[245]

What does cause mean? What I mean by cause is that wherever an event takes place there must be one or several things preceding it such that whenever those things transpire, another thing will surely come into being. This phenomenon that has come into existence is called an effect. This is understood though experience.

By way of example, experience shows us that whenever combustion occurs, there must be a cause anterior to it, such as a spark or friction, resulting in a flame. Through careful deliberation of the meaning of 'cause' it is clearly understood that two irrefutable qualities of 'causality' are 'generality' and 'inviolability'.[246]

In all the cases where the Qur'an speaks of life, death, livelihood, and generally, all events, both heavenly and mundane, it is totally clear that the Qur'an endorses this law. It should not be forgotten, however, that the Qur'an ultimately attributes all causes to God since they all eventually must end in a single central cause.

In short, the Qur'an asserts that the law of causality is authentic. This means that whenever a cause exists with the characteristics necessary for creating an effect, if there are no obstacles the effect will surely occur—by God's leave of course. On the other side of the coin, whenever an effect is found, perforce the existence of a cause is recognized.

---

[245] Because there must be affiliation between causes and effects, every effect is dependent upon a fitting cause and every cause entails a corresponding effect.

[246] The meaning of cause is that whenever it occurs, it must entail an effect. Thus, if the law of causality were violable, it would mean that we have found a case in which a cause exists without an effect whereas a cause that does not entail an effect is not a cause and naming it such is an error.

Part two: the Qur'an Verifies Miracles

The Qur'an informs of some events that are contradictory to the normal course of the natural world, which is based upon the system of causality. These events are the signs and miracles that the Qur'an ascribes to some great prophets, such as the miracles of Noah, Hūd, Sālih, Abraham, Lot, David, Solomon, Moses, Jesus ('a), and Muhammad (S).

These miracles are things that go against the prevailing routine of the natural world. However, it must be noted and carefully considered that even though these phenomena seem unfamiliar and highly unlikely[247] in relation to the normal way of the world, they are not essentially impossible and in no way warrant that two antitheses may co-occur or that one is not half of two.

These are things that the intellect deems as impossible and if a miracle were like this, no mind could accept it whereas we see that the minds of the people of many nations and religions have accepted these miracles without protest.

In addition, if one contemplates the matter, the essence of miracles is not completely unknown in the natural order of things. Every moment, the corporeal system of the world takes the life of the living and gives life to the dead; it changes one event into another and that into yet another; it alters one form into a different one and again into another; it transforms frailty into resilience and so on. The world system performs these transformations and alterations upon matter.

The difference between the manifest routines and miracles is that the normal causes we see everyday can only be effectuated under

---

[247] In the previous footnote, a simple example was given for better understanding of the matter. Bear in mind that things that have not occurred and are without precedence must not be considered impossible.

specific relations and temporal and spatial conditions. These relations and conditions necessitate that this effectuation be gradual.[248]

For instance, a cane may turn into a serpent or a decomposed and lifeless body may transform into a living human being. However, observation and experience shows that this alteration normally happens under specific temporal and spatial circumstances and causes.

As a result of these causes and conditions, matter transforms from one state into another until eventually it gains the form that we intend—such as a cane becoming a serpent or a dead corpse reconstructing and coming to life. Therefore, the normal material system is based upon graduation through specific conditions and relations.

However, the miracles the Qur'an speaks of did not occur in specific relations and temporal and spatial circumstances, rather they occurred under prevailing conditions or even without any causes and conditions at all or at the will of a certain individual![249]

Bear in mind that neither can simple sense and experience confirm these miracles nor can natural scientific theories corroborate them since natural sciences are on the same level as the manifest system of natural cause and effect; the same level that modern scientific experience and theories that explain material events are based on. Neither can normal and simple experience confirm miracles nor can the theoretical natural sciences. Even so, science cannot deny these phenomena either.

Science cannot conceal all those strange and miraculous per-

---

[248] Under the influence of specific relations and conditions, a seed that is planted in the earth grows a stalk and fruit. These conditions gradually produce their effect as opposed to a seed instantly becoming a grown plant with fruit.

[249] As you can see a cane can become a serpent and the dead may gain life in the natural world although in specific temporal and spatial conditions which may occur concurrently only after thousands of years.

formances of ascetics. Everyday people observe such events and newspapers, magazines, and journals record them. Such occurrences are so numerous that no sane person can doubt them. It is these wonders that have forced modern scientists—those who research spiritual effects—to consider them effects of an obscure type of electrical wave or magnetic field.

In short, the theory of electrical waves is that through strict self-discipline, humans gain the ability to exploit a mysterious type of waves. These waves are such that the will and intellect of the individual can take possession of them or accompany them. As a result of this appropriation and exploitation of these unknown waves, an ascetic can perform wondrous and extraordinary acts by expanding and compressing matter.

If this theory is comprehensive and free of exception, it entails another all-inclusive theory. This theory bases all the events that previous theories justified on a general and constant principle, i.e. force and movement, and relates all material events to a specific natural cause.[250]

This is what modern scientists say and in essence they are correct because it is meaningless to assume that a natural effect exists that does not have a natural cause. Bearing in mind that (in the natural world) the relationship between cause and effect must be natural, a natural effect must have a natural relationship with its natural cause.

To state matters differently, the coincidence of natural existents (i.e. natural causes) in specific proportions and relations brings about the existence of a new natural existent that is subsequent to its causes. This new being is related to its causes such that if the system governing

---

[250] The theory of mysterious waves regarding the miraculous deeds of ascetics can be summarized into these two words: force and movement. These two factors refer to a specific truth; movement is caused by force. In general, all material events are explained through this.

them was terminated then it would surely never have come into being.

In short, every natural effect requires a natural cause. However, we cannot insist that the natural causes are those that we think they should be. The ultimate natural cause may be something else—as shown in the wave theory posited by natural scientists.[251]

---

[251] Extracted from the journal, "Majmūʿah-ye Hikmat", issue 4.

Discourse Twenty: The Account of Shaqq Al-Qamar and the Evening Star

Is the miracle of "shaqq al-qamar" (halving of the moon) in agreement with the Qur'an and traditions [akhbār]? Can it be sanctioned by the laws of human logic and reason even though the size of the moon is in no way analogous to the size of the Holy Prophet's (S) hand—i.e. the container and the contained are entirely disproportionate?

The story of shaqq al-qamar is a trustworthy reality, the truth of which has been verified by the Qur'an and traditions. Even so, the narrations that cite this occurrence vary. Because each of these narrations is a "single tradition" [khabar-e wāhid]—they each have a single transmitter—and are thus undependable, we cannot rely on and discuss the qualities that are cited in each of them.

That which can be extracted from them all together is that the moon was split into two halves at the gesture of the Holy Prophet (S) and this is also what the Noble Qur'an indicates.

In the first verse of Sūrat al-Qamar, for which the Sūrat was named, the Qur'an states:

> *"The hour (of Judgment) drew close and the moon was cleft in two."*[252]

This is a miracle performed by the Holy Prophet (S) at the request of some who denied his prophethood
and wanted a miracle as proof. It is self-evident that after we accept the feasibility of miracles by the prophets we cannot deny a specific miracle performed by them especially after the Holy Qur'an—which is itself a miracle—verifies its occurrence.

Essentially, there are no rational explanations against miracles except mere unlikelihood. There may, of course, be causes for events beyond those we know of that can produce unusual events.

Response to the Critics of Shaqq Al-Qamar

Some critics say that the cleaving of the moon which is indicated in the Qur'anic verse is something that will occur on the Day of Resurrection when the natural world is destroyed and is not something that was done by the hand of the Holy Prophet (S).

The next verse negates this presumption. The Almighty Lord declares:

> *"And if they (the idolaters) see a sign (shaqq al-qamar) they say it is incessant sorcery."*[253]

It is clear that if the first verse signified the destruction on the Day of Resurrection, the disregard of the idolaters and attribution of this event to sorcery would be meaningless.

Other critics state that the verse indicates the severance of the moon

---

[252] Sūrat al-Qamar 54:1.

[253] Sūrat al-Qamar 54:2.

from the sun which is confirmed by modern science and that this is one of the miracles of the Qur'an that it made this known centuries before this theory was posited.

This view is philologically incorrect because when an object is detached from another in this manner the words ishtiqāq or infisāl are used not inshiqāq which means 'to be made into two halves'.

Still other detractors maintain that if such an event had transpired surely non-Islamic historians would have recorded it.

One should bear in mind that narrative history is always being written in accordance with the desires of contemporary powers and every story or event that contradicts the fancies of those powers will be hidden or completely forgotten. As we can see in ancient histories there is no trace of the stories of the great prophets such as Abraham, Moses, and Jesus ('a) whereas religiously speaking there is no doubt about the miracles performed by these prophets.

It was Abraham who did not burn in the fires of Nimrod, Moses who had the miracle of the cane, the shining hand, and many more, and Jesus who brought the dead to life. Finally, when the Islamic invitation of Prophet Muhammad (S) appeared, it was against the wishes of all world powers.

Besides, there are many hours of difference in the rising and setting of the moon between Mecca—where the shaqq al-qamar occurred—and Europe with all its historians. The celestial phenomenon that manifested for a short while in Mecca would not be seen from faraway western horizons such as Rome and Athens just as short-lived celestial events in such regions are not visible in the area of glorious Mecca.

Did the Evening Star Descend Upon the House of 'Alī ('a)?!

Does the story that the Evening Star descended upon the roof of Imām 'Alī ibn Abī Ṭālib's ('a) house have verified evidence?!

This story is cited in several narrations; however, they are neither widely transmitted [mutawātir] nor are their sources certain [qat'ī al-sudūr]. Hence, they are not scientifically reliable.[254]

---

[254] Extracted from "Sīmā-ye Islām".

Discourse Twenty-One: Clarity, Ambiguity, and Interpretation in the Qur'an

Discourse Twenty-One: Clarity, Ambiguity, and Interpretation in the Qur'an[255]

> *"It is He who sent down upon thee the Book wherein are clear verses that are the Mother of the Book and other verses that are ambiguous. Those in whose hearts is doubt and divergence follow the ambiguities in it seeking discord and to interpret them. However, no one knows their interpretation save Allah and those who are steadfast in*

---

[255] This is a translation of a Farsi translation of an original Arabic text by 'Allāmah Tabātabā'ī. The Farsi translation and original glosses were done by Mr. Hujjatī Kirmānī.

gaining knowledge. They say we believe in it, all is from our Lord. Yet none remember save those possessed of minds."[256]

The Meaning of These Words

Morphologically, the word muhkam (clear) comes from the root hakama which means an object that nothing can penetrate, take apart, and destroy. Thus, words such as ahkām, tahkīm, hūkm (meaning judgment), hikmah (meaning wisdom), and hikmah (meaning harnessing a horse) all have the meaning of firmness and solidity.

Mutashābih (ambiguous) means things that are similar to each other in some qualities and aspects. Ta'wīl (interpretation) means the referral and return of one thing to another.

The Terms Muhkam and Mutashābih According to the Qur'an

In some verses the whole Qur'an is identified as muhkam[257] and in others mutashābih[258]. Also, in verse seven of Surat Āl 'Imrān some of the Qur'an is considered muhkam and the rest mutashābih. This same verse describes muhkam verses as "umm al-kitāb" (Mother of the Book).

---

[256] Sūrat Āl 'Imrān 3:7.

[257] Sūrat Hūd 11:1."This is a Book whose verses have been established (for a specific intention) then when they are broken down they become detailed verses. It is a Book from the Wise and Aware."

[258] Sūrat al-Zumar 39:23."... a book whose verses are similar to each other and are repeated. By these verses the skin of those who fear their Lord trembles, then their skin and heart (their whole being) softens to the remembrance (and praise) of Allah. That is the guidance of Allah with which He guides who He will and whoever Allah leaves to stray will have no guidance."

It must be noted that the muhkam-ness or solidity of the entire Qur'an existed before the Book was revealed[259] and the mutashābih-ness or similarity of the entire Book means that all its verses have a single style—they all possess a pleasant order and solid form, describe truths in a uniform manner, and guide people towards Truth. Thus, here muhkam and mutashābih possess meanings different from what is usual in the whole of the Qur'an.

Considering that the prime meaning of umm is the source, referent, and refuge of objects, the term umm al-kitāb means that the referent (to understand) mutashābih verses are the muhkam ones. In this verse, muhkam and mutashābih are opposites. Then, the verse speaks of people whose hearts have been afflicted with doubt and deviation from Truth and follow mutashābih verses because they seek discord and 'interpretation'.

This shows that a mutashābih verse is one the meaning and intent of which cannot be understood by just listening to it; rather, there is doubt between various meanings until muhkam verses are referred to and its meaning is made clear. Hence, a mutashābih verse becomes muhkam by muhkam verses however a muhkam verse is muhkam in and of itself.

For instance, in verse five of Sūrat Tā Hā (20:5) it is stated:

"The Rahmān (Beneficent) is established upon the Throne."

A person who hears this verse will not understand it. However, if, for instance, they refer to verse eleven of Sūrat al-Shawrā' (42:11), they will realize that the meaning of establishment upon the Throne is that God is predominant over all of existence not that there is a place

---

[259] This is understood from verse one of Sūrat Hūd. Thus, its 'solidity' was elaborated and revealed gradually.

where He rests which would necessitate that He be material—which is impossible for God:

"There is nothing like Him..."

Another example can be found in Sūrat al-Qiyāmah (75:23):

"Looking towards their Lord."

And Sūrat al-An'ām (6:103):

"Eyes do not perceive Him and He perceives the eyes."

By referring the first verse to the second, we understand that the 'looking' indicated in the first verse is not physical.

This is also correct for abrogative [nāsikh] and abrogated [mansūkh] verses. When we refer the abrogated verse to the abrogative one we realize that the abrogated verse comprised a precept that was only applicable until the nāsikh was revealed.[260]

Mutashābih Verses Indicate a Specific Intent

A person who carefully studies the whole Qur'an will without doubt not even find one verse lacking signification and explanation.

There is no verse that does not indicate its signification. This

---

[260] Tabātabā'ī explained the meaning of muhkam and mutashābih in detail in his "Tafsīr al-Mīzān". Refer to "Tafsīr al- Mīzān" for more information.

signification may either be a single one that a person who is familiar with the discourse will understand or several which may be mistaken with each other. Even so, all these meanings together certainly cover a true and real meaning and intent, otherwise there would be no signification.

This true meaning is not a stranger to the obvious principles of the Qur'an such as existence of the Creator, monotheism, appointment of prophets, canonization of precepts, and so on. It is harmonious with these principles which necessitate and entail that specific meaning. Among all the possible significations, it clarifies a truth. Some verses elucidate others and some verses are the root and source of others.

An attentive person who examines the verse we are discussing (3:7) will have no doubt that muhkamāt are verses that comprise clear and certain Qur'anic principles and mutashābihāt are verses whose meanings are made clear using those principles.

Why are Some Verses Mutashābih?

Some might say: true, subsidiaries must be applied to principles and this is not specific to the Qur'an but this does not necessitate that the Qur'an has mutashābih.

In answer I must say that the reason for mutashābih in the Qur'an is twofold. There are two types of knowledge imparted in the Qur'an:

The first type consists of divine teachings that are beyond the domain of matter and the senses. However, normal intellects halt here and are in doubt as to whether the meaning is physical. For instance, in Sūrat al-Fajr (89:14, 22) it is stated:

"Verily your Lord lies in ambush."

"And your Lord came..."

These statements are fashioned for a mind that is familiar with tangibles, and the verses seem to signify physical properties. However, when we refer to related principles which repudiate matter and corporeality in such matters, the initial (physical) meaning is removed from the mind.

This pertains to all non-material and transcendent knowledge and it is not specific to the Holy Qur'an. This method is common in other divine books in teachings that have not been altered or distorted and also in theological discussions in philosophy. The Qur'an indicates this where it states:

> **"He sent down water from the sky that flowed in every channel to the extent of its capacity..."**[261]

> **"Verily We have made the Qur'an an Arabic book that you may understand and it is with Us in the Mother of the Book, high in dignity and correct in foundation."**[262]

As you can see these verses make it clear that the Qur'anic wisdom is highly exalted. Even so, every individual understands it differently and to a certain extent. Thus are the mutashābih verses of the Qur'an. The fault comes from the reader not the words of God.

The second type is comprised of matters related to social norms and subsidiary precepts. This type also encompasses abrogative [nāsikh] and abrogated [mansūkh] verses. These verses are abrogated because

---

[261] Sūrat al-Ra'd 13:17.

[262] Sūrat al-Zukhruf 43:3-4.

the reasons for their establishment were superseded. Also, the Qur'an has been revealed gradually.

These two issues, i.e. nāsikh and mansūkh, in the Qur'an and gradualness of the Qur'an's revelation lead to tashābuh (i.e. the property of being mutashābih) in the Qur'an. Nevertheless, this tashābuh is resolved by referring mutashābih verses to muhkam ones and mansūkh to nāsikh.

Following Mutashābih Verses

God states:

> *"Those in whose hearts is doubt and divergence follow the ambiguities in it..."*[263]

In explanation I must say that this verse divides the people into two groups according to their attitude towards the Qur'an. The first consists of deviants who seek sedition, to corrupt the people, to (re)interpret (the Qur'an), and follow mutashābih verses. The other group is composed of those with firm knowledge and steadfast hearts who apply muhkamāt in order to employ mutashābihāt.

This explanation makes it clear that by 'following mutashābih verses' practical adherence is meant not belief. It does not mean that believing in mutashābihāt is blameworthy, rather that it is wrong to exploit them in practice, seeking sedition and reinterpretation of verses. Clearly this culpability only arises if one follows mutashābih verses without referring them to muhkam ones.

If we refer mutashābihāt to muhkamāt and understand and conform

---

[263] Sūrat Āl 'Imrān 3:7.

to the signification of the mutashābih verses, we are in truth adhering to muhkam not mutashābih.

What is Ta'wīl (interpretation)?

Basically, the word ta'wīl means referral. Therefore, the ta'wīl of mutashābih is the reference of a mutashābih verse and the ta'wīl of the Qur'an is the main source of Qur'anic wisdom. In order to clarify this matter, we must first know that exegetes[264] have defined many meanings for the term ta'wīl, the most illustrious of which is: ta'wīl is a meaning that is contrary to the superficial meaning of the words.

This definition has become so established among recent exegetes that, even though the term ta'wīl primarily means referral, it has now come to mean 'that which is contrary to the appearance'. This meaning is not acceptable for the following reasons:

First, the usage of ta'wīl as 'against appearance' is something that emerged after the revelation of the Qur'an and there are no grounds for defining ta'wīl, which has been mentioned in the Qur'an sixteen times, as 'against appearance'. In fact, if one seriously contemplates the Qur'anic usage of this word, it will become clear that none of the meanings that exegetes have mentioned are completely accurate although a number of them are relatively correct.

Secondly, this definition of ta'wīl necessitates that there exist a series of meanings in the Qur'an that are in opposition to the appearance of the verses and because these appearances are against the muhkamāt of the Qur'an, they bring about subversion and deviation of the people.

---

[264] It must be noted that in the original Arabic text 'Allāmah Tabātabā'ī wrote the various meanings of ta'wīl and its difference with tafsīr (exegesis). However, for the sake of brevity, I (the original Arabic-Farsi translator) only included the most common definition and the 'Allāmah's discussion regarding it. I also altered the style to make it more understandable for the respected readership.

This would mean that there are contradictions among Qur'anic verses that cannot be resolved without stripping some verses of their formal meanings and restoring them to significations not understood by the general public.

If we maintain such a discrepancy in the Qur'an, the following argument would be invalid:

> *"Why do they not ponder upon the Qur'an? If it was from other than Allah surely they would find within it much discrepancy."*[265]

In order to fully understand this it must be noted that if the discrepancy between two verses is resolved by professedly 'ta'wīl-ing' one verse to another and saying that it has a meaning other than what it appears to mean, something known by no one but God (and those firm in knowledge), the verse with such a meaning will be completely invalid.

In explanation, we can also ta'wīl the statements of people in a similar manner, even ones that are surely lies. We could say that the apparent meaning is not meant rather the signification is the true meaning intended by the speaker, which others cannot understand!

In short, if we want to resolve discrepancies in the Qur'an in this manner, it is in opposition with what the previous verse (4:82) has declared. This verse clearly expresses that the Qur'an can be understood by the minds of the general public and they can discuss and contemplate it and there is no verse in the entire Qur'an whose intent is something contradictory to its Arabic wording or is some kind of riddle.

Even so, with our so-called ta'wīl we have forgotten these truths.

265

Essentially, we cannot say that words that we believe to be elevated above normal statements and contradictory views, beyond reproach, perfect in every way, are to be 'ta'wīl-ed' in the same manner that one could ta'wīl lies and nonsense.

Now I will first define ta'wīl in my own view and then bring various verses as proof in accordance with my exegetical style.

Ta'wīl is the real external truth upon which Qur'anic statements, including precepts, exhortations, and wisdom, are based. This truth exists in all Qur'anic verses whether muhkam or mutashābih. That verses have ta'wīl has nothing to do with them being mutashābih and their referral to muhkam.

> Ta'wīl is not specific to mutashābih verses. The whole Qur'an has ta'wīl, muhkam has ta'wīl, and mutashābih also has ta'wīl. Ta'wīl is something apart from textual concepts and meanings; therefore, words cannot impart it. It consists of exalted truths that words cannot contain. God has moderated these lofty truths into words so that they may become closer to something we are able to comprehend. These words are analogies used to explain things in a way we may better understand. The Qur'an states:
> **"By the Book that makes things clear, verily We have made the Qur'an an Arabic book that you may understand and it is with Us in the Mother of the Book, high in dignity and correct in foundation."**[266]

Bearing in mind the purport of this verse and similar verses that implicitly or explicitly express this meaning, it becomes clear that the Qur'an possesses a lofty status in the transcendent realm where it is beyond the understanding of the people; however, in order to make

---

[266] Sūrat al-Zukhruf 43:2-4.

it more accessible to human understanding it has been presented this way. That lofty reality that is beyond general understanding is called ta'wīl and it pertains to the whole Qur'an, whether muhkam or mutashābih.

Several Proofs from the Qur'an

1. Ta'wīl of the deeds of Khidr ('a): In the story of Moses ('a) and Khidr ('a) the word ta'wīl is used where Khidr tells Moses:

> *"I will soon inform you of the ta'wīl of that for which you could not bear patience."*[267]

And at the end of the narration he says:

> *"This is the ta'wīl of that for which you could not bear patience."*[268]

Now we will examine the account to understand the meaning of ta'wīl. Khidr ('a) did three things that according to Moses ('a) did not seem right and he protested:

> *"When they embarked upon the boat, he made a hole in*

---

[267] Sūrat al-Kahf 18:78.

[268]

it..."²⁶⁹

*"When they met a young man he slew him..."*²⁷⁰

*"When they came to the people of a town, they asked them for food but they refused them hospitality. They came to a wall that was close to falling down and he repaired it..."*²⁷¹

These were acts that Khidr ('a) performed and Moses ('a) protested each of them. That is to say, the semblance that Moses perceived for these deeds were as follows:

*"Did you make a hole in the boat to drown its passengers? Thou has indeed done a dreadful thing."*²⁷²

*"Have you killed an innocent person and that not for retaliation against a person slain? Thou has indeed done a horrible thing."*²⁷³

*"If you wanted, you could have taken payment for it."*²⁷⁴

Clearly Moses ('a) objects to the deeds of Khidr ('a) because they do not have appropriate outward appearances.

---

[269] Sūrat al-Kahf 18:71.
[270] Sūrat al-Kahf 18:74.
[271] Sūrat al-Kahf 18:77.
[272] Sūrat al-Kahf 18:71.
[273] Sūrat al-Kahf 18:74.
[274] Sūrat al-Kahf 18:77.

Now, let us examine the ta'wīl of Khidr ('a), that is, the true and good aspects and designations of these deeds:

> *"As for the boat, it belonged to some poor people who worked upon the sea. I intended to mar it because there was a king before them who seized every ship by force."*[275]
>
> *"As for the young man, his parents were people of faith. I feared that he would impose upon them rebellion and disbelief. Thus I intended that their Lord give to them in exchange a son better than him in purity and closer in affection."*[276]
>
> *"As for the wall, it belonged to two orphan boys in the city. Beneath the wall there was a treasure cache belonging to them and their father had been a righteous man. So your Lord intended that they become full adults and unearth their treasure as a blessing from your Lord."*[277]

After Khidr ('a) gave his answers for each of his deeds, he gave another comprehensive answer for all the criticisms of Moses ('a):

> *"And I did not do these things willfully..."*[278]

As my dear readers see, the meaning of ta'wīl in these verses is for everything to be referred to its own aspect and designation and to realize its true significance. For instance the word 'zadan' in Farsi

---

[275] Sūrat al-Kahf 18:79.

[276] Sūrat al-Kahf 18:80-81.

[277] Sūrat al-Kahf 18:82.

[278] Sūrat al-Kahf 18:82.

designates chastisement however 'rag zadan' signifies the aspect of medical treatment.

It is true that, lexically, the word ta'wīl means 'referral' and it includes all kinds of return and reference.

For instance, when we say 'John came' the point of reference of this sentence is that 'John' must have 'come' in the external world. However, the word ta'wīl is not idiomatically used in such cases; rather, it denotes the specific reference and return to true significance the like of which we saw in the verses regarding Moses ('a) and Khidr ('a).

1. Ta'wīl in the story of Joseph ('a): In the story of Joseph the word ta'wīl is repeatedly used. For instance, it is said:

> **"And he lifted his parents upon the throne and they fell down before him in prostration. And he said O father! This is the ta'wīl of my dream from before. Verily my Lord has made it true..."**[279]

The earlier dream of Joseph ('a) was as follows:

> **"O father! Verily I saw eleven stars and the sun and the moon. I saw them bowing down before me."**[280]

Also, it is used in the verses regarding the dream of the king where

---

[279] Sūrat Yūsuf 12:100.

[280] Sūrat Yūsuf 12:4.

the interpreters of dreams said that we do not know the ta'wīl of distorted dreams. Finally, Joseph's ('a) friend from prison went to him and heard the ta'wīl of the king's dream from him.[281] It is also used in the case of the dreams of Joseph's two prison companions who asked him to tell them the ta'wīl of their dreams[282] and also where the Qur'an speaks of ta'wīl-i ahādīth which was taught to Joseph ('a).[283]

In all these cases the word ta'wīl is used regarding events that are the reference and reality of the dream.

Dreams are aspects or examples of external truths and future events which are seen by a person who is asleep. In fact, that external truth is like the meaning, and the dream is like the form which clothes the meaning. In effect, ta'wīl is related to that which is 'ta'wīl-ed' (e.g. a dream that has an interpretation) in the same way that meaning is related to form or truth is related to metaphor.

With careful consideration it is evident that in both this story and the story of Moses ('a) and Khidr ('a) the meaning of ta'wīl is the same.

1. Ta'wīl in verses regarding the Resurrection: In some verses that discuss the Day of Resurrection, the term ta'wīl is seen. For instance, in the following verse and with reference to the next verse we know that the nature of seeing things on the Day of Resurrection is not related to the senses we use in this world; just as the occurrence of these phenomena and the system governing that Day are different from what we are used to in this world.

"Do they look to anything save its ta'wīl? The Day its ta'wīl

---

[281] Refer to verses 43-49 of Sūrat Yūsuf.

[282] Refer to verse 36 of Sūrat Yūsuf.

[283] Refer to verses 21 and 101 of Sūrat Yūsuf.

comes..."[284]

"Verily you were in ignorance of these (truths) but We took away the veil from before you so today your eyes are sharp."[285]

Of course this must be discussed in detail; however, here we merely intend to say that the notifications of the Qur'an and the statements of the prophets refer to significations that manifest on the Day of Judgment. However, this reference is not the same as the reference of prophesies of future events to that which will occur in the future.

To sum up the discussion, by preserving the lexical meaning of ta'wīl, i.e. referral, and careful consideration of verses containing this word, and also taking into account the truth that the Qur'an possesses a status above and beyond mere words and lexis before God, the Almighty, we clearly understand that ta'wīl of Qur'an is that lofty truth and hidden reality that is far from the grasp of general understanding. It is like a soul in regard to its body or the symbolized in relation to the symbol.

It is what God terms "Kitāb-i Hakīm" (Solid Book), meaning something that is the basis and reference of the wisdom and concepts in the Qur'an that has been revealed and made available to us. It is that which is neither from the class of words nor meanings; rather, it is something objective, real and external.[286]

---

[284] Sūrat al-A'rāf 7:53.

[285] Sūrat Qāf 50:22.

[286] Extracted from the annual, "Ma'ārif-e Ja'farī".

Epilogue: A Message to the Conference Held in Honor of Tustari

The following text is a message written for the conference held in Lucknow, India, in honor of the martyr 'Allāmah Qāḍī Nūr Allāh Tustarī (a.k.a. Shūshtarī), author of the famous book, "Ihqāq al-Haqq".

* * *

In the Name of Allah, the Beneficent, the Merciful

God, the Almighty—glorious is He—addresses His Noble Prophet (S) in the Holy Qur'an thus:

> *"(O Prophet!) Say (unto your nation), I do not ask of you a reward for this (invitation) but that some people find a*

way to their Lord."²⁸⁷

In accordance to this miraculous statement, the reward for the Holy Prophet's (S) twenty-three years of invitation is the pure religion of Islam that has opened a place for itself in the human society and has become established. Elsewhere, in the Qur'an, He declares:

*"(O Prophet!) Say (unto your nation), I do not ask of you a reward for this (invitation) save love for (my) Household (the Ahl al-Bayt)..."*²⁸⁸

By combining these two Qur'anic verses it is clear that the religion that the Exalted Lord wants of us and determines as the reward for the invaluable invitation of the Holy Prophet (S) is the religion that is fused with affection for his Ahl al-Bayt—specific members of his family.

The Holy Prophet (S) has explained the meaning of this fusion of the Ahl al-Bayt's affection in the two widely-transmitted hadīths of safīnah (ark) and thaqalayn (two precious things):

"The analogy of my Ahl al-Bayt is that of Noah's ark. Whosoever embarks upon it is saved and whosoever turns away from it is drowned."

"After I leave, I will leave among you two precious things: the Book of Allah and my Household, the Ahl al-Bayt. They will never be separated until they come to me (on the Day of Judgment) at the Pool [hawd]. As long as you cling fast to these two things you shall not be led astray."

---

²⁸⁷ Sūrat al-Furqān 25:57.

²⁸⁸ Sūrat al-Shawrā' 42:23.

In a clear expression the Noble Prophet (S) teaches that Muslims must set his Ahl al-Bayt as their leaders and acquire their religion from them. This is the creed of Shī'ah which today nearly one hundred million people of the world's population identify as their official religion.

The Shī'ah creed is that same pure religion that God, the Almighty, has made his Noble Prophet's reward and the fruit of his prophethood.

The Shī'ah creed is that same valuable religion whose continuity cost the pure blood of eleven Imāms—of the twelve leaders of the Infallible and Immaculate Ahl al-Bayt—foregoing which was the pure blood that spilled to the earth from the forehead and mouth of the Prophet in the battle of Uhud.

The Shī'ah creed is that same tormented religion that has, in the fourteen centuries ensuing the passing of the Holy Prophet (S), lost at the hands of its opposers tens of thousands or rather hundreds of thousands of its followers among which are many prodigies and scholars such as the First Martyr, Muhammad ibn Makkī, the Second Martyr, Zayn al-Dīn Ihsā'ī, and the martyr Qādī Nūr Allāh Tustarī who rests in this radiant and glorious grave.

By observing these works, we must remember the endeavors and sacrifices achieved by our forerunners in the way of God to preserve and vitalize this religion of Truth.

Thus, we must strive to preserve, safeguard, and spread the religion that embraces the Truth that came to us at the price of, first and foremost, the pure blood of our leaders from the Infallible Ahl al-Bayt ('a), the blood of our great intellectuals and academics, and finally, the blood of hundreds of thousands of martyrs who were our innocent fellow Muslims—we must withhold nothing of our lives and wealth to uphold this path.

"Slack not, nor sorrow for you are superior if you are truly believers."[289]

Muhammad Husayn Tabātabā'ī
Qum, Rajab 10, 1390 AH[290]

---

[289] Sūrat Āl 'Imrān 3:139.

[290] Extracted from the annual "Ma'ārif-e Ja'farī".

www.ingramcontent.com/pod-product-compliance
Lightning Source LLC
Chambersburg PA
CBHW021438070526
44577CB00002B/210